Education in Human Values for Human Excellence

Education in Human Values for Human Excellence

Edited by:

Dr. Yoginder Verma

KANISHKA PUBLISHERS, DISTRIBUTORS
NEW DELHI-110 002

KANISHKA PUBLISHERS, DISTRIBUTORS
4697/5-21A, Ansari Road, Daryaganj,
New Delhi-110 002
Phones : 2327 0497, 2328 8285
Fax : 011-2328 8285
E-mail : kanishka_publishing@yahoo.co.in

Education in Human Values for Human Excellence

First Published 2007

ISBN 81-7391-901-1

PRINTED IN INDIA

Published by Madan Sachdeva for Kanishka Publishers, Distributors, 4697/5-21A, Ansari Road, Daryaganj, New Delhi-110 002; Typeset by Sunshine Graphics, Delhi, and Printed at Nice Printing Press, Delhi.

Foreword

At the commencement of the new millennium, we find ourselves at a crucial point in the long and tortuous history of the human race on Planet Earth. The last century was extraordinary and had witnessed unparalleled progress but also unimaginable destruction. We live in a shrinking world in which the malign heritage of conflict and competition will have to give way to a new culture of convergence and cooperation. Scientific and technological ingenuity has given us the capacity to overcome all those challenges, but what is missing is the wisdom and compassion to apply them creatively. Knowledge is expanding but wisdom languishes. The astounding communications technology, which today encircles the globe, seldom uses its tremendous potential to spread global values and foster a more caring, compassionate consciousness. It is essential that the spiritual dimension be given central importance in our new educational thinking. The need to effect fundamental changes in our educational system without further loss of time has become paramount. Since the present century will provide unprecedented means for communication and for the circulation and storage of information, it will impose on education new demands. This is the age of Science. Natural Sciences have placed in our hands a dangerous instrument. Social Sciences will place in our hands a second instrument as dangerous as the first. Men who are learned in Social Sciences have used the technique of propaganda for correcting human nature by pandering to its material and emotional greed. In such a complex situation, we cannot rest content with an educational system which is confined to academic achievement. It has to promote simultaneously human virtues. The more human values are cherished; the better will be the growth of society, the nation and the world. We in this country have a plural society which means there are a variety of religions, languages and regions. There has to be a constant endeavour to identify generally acceptable values and promote them. So far as the individual values are concerned they may vary from society to society, religion to religion. But some values like Truth, Right Conduct, Peace, Love and Non-violence should be free from controversy.

Speaking on the role of the Educational System in building the right values, Bhagavan Sri Sathya Sai Baba observed, as early as 25 years ago, that human values are the need of the hour – not only in educational institutions but in every walk of life and throughout the world. Human values- *Sathya, Dharma, Shanti, Prema* and *Ahimsa* cannot be promoted merely by repeating the words. It is only through action that the change will take place. There is an organic link between the human values and the human personality. Mental happiness comes from Peace, Peace comes from Love, Love is linked with Non-violence, Non-violence is the outcome of Righteous Conduct and Righteous Conduct without Truth cannot be thought of.

The four pillars of education now widely publicized after De Lors Commission report – learning to know, learning to do, learning to live together, and learning to Be, echo the Indian philosophy of *Jnana Yoga, Karma Yoga*, Saha *Yoga [sahana Bhavatu, sahanau Bhunaktu]* and *Atmanaam Riddhi* are the four pillars of Indian life; in the international context, they are now seen as the four pillars of education. There are two important aspects which would need to be addressed by the Educational System. The first is the global development in communication technology which today encircles the globe seldom uses its tremendous potential to spread global values. The second dimension relates to probity in public life in India. It is a disturbing thought, but there is little doubt that we are living dangerously. Under constant pressure of materialism clothed in the language of development, the fundamental issue of recreating the society with right values needs to be addressed immediately.

My background is civil service. I had the opportunity of observing the functioning of the governmental machinery for over forty years from the grassroots to the policy making levels. As Education Secretary to the Government of India, and later as the Central Vigilance Commissioner, I had occasion to see how much the power of the government had come to be misused for personal benefit. It was clear to me that, if the distortions had to be set right, it should come through the right type of education which, in our tradition, is man-making and character building and transforming the students into caring, sharing and responsible citizens. My good fortune in working as the Vice Chancellor of the Sri Sathya Sai Institute of Higher Learning for well over six years has given me the hope and the conviction that such a type of education is not just at the level of an ideal, but is entirely practicable. The Sri Sathya Sai system of Integral Education, which is operational in the Sri Sathya Sai Educational Institutins, is an outstanding example of education as a total, joyous and transformational experience.

In the subcontinent, we experience the dilemma caused by a nation of gigantic proportions suffering the hangover of centuries of turbulence and colonial rule. We in India have no comparative advantage in becoming a world leader in materialism, but we have a great opportunity to become the world leader in integrating science and spirituality. Our universities should spearhead a movement in this direction and foster a humanistic rather than a materialistic pattern of development.

I congratulate Prof Yoginder Verma for bringing together the views of eminent academics and practitioners with varied experiences on the vital issue of education in human values. Prof. Verma has been able to draw on his personal experience as Director of Academic Staff College and also as Professor of Management in providing a conceptual framework and practical insights. I am confident that Prof. Verma's work will be an extremely useful addition to the literature on the subject.

Prasnathinilayam, S.V.Giri (I.A.S. Rtd)
Andhra Pradesh-515 134

reflection, rethinking, and action. Let the whole humanity think of education which produces world citizens, who share similar concerns and value system. 'Living together' is possible when human beings perceive their interests, desires and emotions being honoured by others. Sensitisation to others' welfare will make the man conscious of his responsibility toward others.

It is largely being realized that education rooted in human values can only produce complete man. Human values are within an individual and are present naturally along with one's blood. It is not knowledge but practice which reflects human values. If there is unity of word, thought and deed, there will be beauty in character.

While talking about imparting value-oriented education, we have to be cautious of certain hard realities of our country. India is a multi-lingual, multi-religious and multi-cultural society. Majority of its population follows: Hindu religion, Buddhism, Jainism and Sikhism originated in this country. Christianity from the West and Zoroastrianism from West Asia have found wider acceptance on this land. India is the second largest Muslim country in the world. Indians have tolerance and appreciation for all the religions. There are six different ethnic groups—Negrito, Austrics, Mongoloids, Dravidians, Western Brachy-Cephals and Nordic Aryans. Today, we have more than 1600 langauages used as the mother tongue. Indeed, our country is a synthesis of very diversity of the world. It is this synthesis, which is subsumed in what we generally understood as the composite culture of India. Ancient wisdom, *vaasudhaiv kutumvakam*, makes India truly a versatile land for the growth of human values movement.

Education has increasingly become a mere instrument of filling minds with certain information regarding science, technology, materials, places, people, planets, etc. This is much beyond the true meaning of education. The purpose of true education is to make a complete man, who is fully developed in terms of five facets of human existence namely—the physical, intellectual, emotional, psychic and spiritual aspects. As stated earlier, various Committees and Commissions set-up at the international and national levels, such as Radhakrishnan Commission (1948), Kothari Commission (1966), International Commission on Education (1972 and 1996), National Policy on Education (1986, 1992), etc., have endorsed the development of human personality through strengthening the moral

Preface

Today, the whole world is passing through an unprecedented crisis of search for peaceful and happy living. Despite affluence of various kinds, man is perplexed about from where to get love, inspiration and trust. Selfishness seems to have entered in thoughts, words and deeds. It is evident from the rising incidents of corruption, violence, rapes, exploitation and cheating. The rising generation has unsafe future. The present generation is starved of peace and contentment, which can be shared with the future generation. We are ignorant about the true meaning of life. Innovations in technology and science have brought revolution almost in all walks of life. Huge array of luxuries and material prosperity is of no avail when one is not getting eternal and perennial flow of peace and bliss. Over-fed stomach and over informed head have produced not only incurable and fatal diseases but have also polluted the mind with the "deadly sins" of envy, hatred, jealousy, violence, corruption, etc.

Over the previous decades, selfishness has become the watchword of human endeavour. Diversity in terms of desires, patterns of living, socio-economic status, achievement orientation, development perspectives, etc., has emerged the root cause of conflicts and dissensions rather than a source of fostering human values of harmony, peace and co-existence, resulting in the blossoming of human excellence. It is because of the neglect of human values that diversity has assumed horrendous dimensions leading to terrorism, favouritism, nepotism and other evils making human life miserable.

It is only the education which can lay down the foundation for the future of our imagination. The 'future of education' and 'education of the future' are interlinked; like the 'future of man' and 'man of the future'. The destiny of nation is, and should be, decided in the classrooms. And it has to be realized by the students, parents, teachers, administrators and policy makers at all levels throughout the world-sooner—the better; now or never. This is the time for fiber in education. Moreover, there is an ever-increasing concern the world over for the revival of human values in every walk of life. Yet unfortunately, the gulf between precept and practice continues to persist.

In India, it is through the unswerving and unrelenting efforts of eminent personalities, such as Sri Aurobindo, Rabinder Nath Tagore, J. Krishna Murthy and Swami Dayanand that a modicum of value education has survived. In modern times, there is some hope as personalities like Sri Sathya Sai Baba (the Chancellor, Sri Sathya Sai Institute of Higher Learning, a deemed university, Prasanthi Nilayam, India), are venturing to realize the dream that there is only one religion: the religion of love; there is only one language: the language of the heart; and there is only one caste: the caste of humanity.

At different international and national fora, a need for synthesis between moral and ethical values and the scientific and technological innovations is being largely felt. The *Vedic Rishis* in India and Socrates and Plato in Greece laid a great emphasis on right kind of education. The freedom fighters like Mahatma Gandhi, Pt. Balgangadhar Tilak, Madanmohan Malviya and Dadabhai Naoroji pleaded with the British Government for the introduction of value education in Indian schools. They emphasized that the role of education is to realise the emancipation of Indian masses. After the emergence of Mahatma Gandhi on the political scene around 1915, a number of educationists came out in support of value education. Dr. Annie Besant, Dr. Bhagwan Das, Rabindra Nath Tagore and Sarojni Naidu strongly advocated for the development of value based education.

Wardha Education Conference (1937) resolved that the values that are common to all religions should be taught to all children. Radhakrishnan Commission (1948) recommended that "The fundamental principles of our constitution call for spiritual training. There is no State religion. The State must not be partial to any one religion. All the different forms are given equal place, provided they do not lead to corrupt practices. Each person is at liberty to approach the unseen as it suits his capacity and inclination. To be secular is not to be religiously illiterate. It is to be deeply spiritual and not narrowly religious." It further advocated that Indian education, in order to be purposeful, must link itself with the *Vedic* tradition of human values. Mudaliar Commission (1952-53) in its Report recommended that moral instruction through inspiring talks given by persons of excellence will help to drive home the lessons of morality. A Committee on Religious and Moral Instructions (1960) under the Chairmanship of Sri Prakash made very forceful recommendations about how to introduce moral education into Indian education system from the elementary to the highest levels.

Kothari Commission Report (1964-66), known as Bible of Education, highlighted the importance of values in the development of the country. It suggested, "A serious defect in the school curriculum is the absence of provision for education in social, moral and spiritual vales. In the life of majority of Indians, religion is great motivating force and is intimately bound up with the formation of character and inculcation of ethical values. A national system of education that is related to the life, needs and aspirations of the people cannot afford to ignore these very useful forces. We recommend, therefore, that conscious and organised attempts be made for imparting education in social, moral and spiritual values with the help, wherever possible, of the ethical teachings of great religions."

National Policy on Education (1986) stresses the acculturating role of education and totally endorses the programme of value-oriented education. In pursuance of this, Ministry of Human Resource Development, Government of India and different national level organisations such as UGC, NCERT, All India Council of Technical Education, National Institute of Educational Planning and Administration (NIEPA), Academic Staff Colleges etc., have initiated a number of programmes for incorporating value-orientation in educational process. What is required today is practice what we preach. A strong commitment and faith in ourselves can help us to implement different programmes of value education at formal and non-formal level.

NCERT has established a National Resource Centre on Value Education (NRCVE), which is an outcome of strategic planning to realize the objectives of value-based education at school stage in the country. The NRCVE has adopted a multi-pronged strategy and planned a number of programmes. The main activities of the Centre are: *(a)* starting networking with the pioneering institutions and NGOs within the country and abroad working in the area of value education; *(b)* preparation of annotated bibliography on value education and making it available all over the country; *(c)* setting-up of reference library related to values, values in education, Indian concept of values, cultural values, character education, ideologies of national heroes, self-discipline, etc., with provision for continuous enrichment; *(d)* giving due place to the teachings of Sri Sathya Sai Baba, and the philosophy and ideology of Chinmaya Mission, Ramakrishna Mission, Brahma Kumaries, Sadhu Vaswani Missiom, Bahai, etc.; *(e)* acquiring literature for children, some of the which relates to teaching of values through religious texts and picture stories; and *(f)* reaching out to the beneficiaries through journal of value education and lecture series on value education.

During the Tenth Plan, the UGC plans to promote value education and human rights and duties education in universities and colleges. Realizing that there is erosion of human values and desecration of moral landscape and also that disproportionate and excessive emphasis on the rights of citizens, as against duties has ignored the fact duty is inalienable mandatory part and source of right, value education should be made an integral part of various regular courses and programmes. It can also be incorporated as foundation course at the undergraduate level.

This volume is a collection of 33 essays contributed by educationists, religious thinkers, educational administrators and social scientists. These articles include scholarly and philosophical ideas about education in human values for achieving human excellence. The thoughts expressed in these writings will help the readers to understand the fundamentals which are the roots of various dimensions of human values. The solution to human problems at global level lies in value based living and that is possible only if a person becomes true human being. It is education that develops the humanness in a person. Besides formal education, the role of parents, teachers and societal environment is of paramount significance in helping the child to develop human values, the source of which lies within a person.

All the papers included in this volume have been grouped under five sections. In the *first section*, articles by Swami Atmapriyanada, Rekha Jhanji, B.H. Briz Kishore, Anurag Gangal and Renu Gangal, Bhoomittra Dev, Mohd. Akhtar Siddiqui deal with the Philosophical Foundations of Human Values. The authors in their essays have attempted to unravel the true meaning of values by their scholarly analysis and simple presentation. The *second section* includes essays pertaining to human values, society and diversity. Pooja and Sangeeta, Ashwani Rana, S.L. Sharma, Suraj Pathak and D. R. Vij have attempted critical analysis of the crisis prevalent in contemporary society. They have also unearthed the Relevance of Human Values in the Present Context. They advocate that the solution lies in imparting education in human values. According to them, human values act as binding force amidst diversity of various kinds.

Third section presents Techniques and Approaches to Value Education. The articles by Anuradha Agnihotri, Sucheta, Kirandeep Singh, S. Abdul Kareem, Kulwant Singh Pathania, P.L. Gupta, Anant Ram Thakur and Yadavendra Kumar Sharma contain discussion on approaches, methods and techniques for inculcation of values. In addition to certain identified techniques of value education, in some essays the importance of parents, teachers and the environment has been considered significant in value education.

The articles by Ramachandra Janti, A.S. Sethi, Kalplata Pandey, Madhu Kapani and Yoginder Verma included in the *fourth section* present the concept, process and importance of teacher education in the inculcation of human values. *Fifth section* contains essays regarding the application of values in different fields and also the teaching of values in different subjects. The contributors in this section include K. Aiyadurai, Y.P. Sharma, Neeta Khanna, Mehraj Uddin, J. Shashidara Prasad, K. Anil Kumar, Shashi Verma, Kiran Rekha and N. Sivakumar and U.S. Rao.

I am highly grateful to all those philosophers, thinkers, scientists and the leaders in different fields who inspired me to think about compiling a volume on education in human values for human excellence. I am thankful to Ford Foundation for sponsoring Campus Diversity Initiative Project under which a number of activities including workshops and seminars were conducted. It was realized that diversity of various types is good for delightful living but that is possible only with strong human value system. My interaction with Sri Sathya Sai System of Education has inspired me lot. All the authors deserve my heartfelt gratitude. My thanks are due to my colleagues and family members.

Yoginder Verma

Contents

List of Contributors

A.S. Sethi, Former Chairman, Department of Psychology, H.P. University, Shimla.

Anant Ram Thakur, Lecturer, Government Polytechnic College, Gagret, District Una, Himachal Pradesh.

Anuradha Agnihotri, Lecturer, Dev Samaj College of Education, Chandigarh.

Anurag Gangal, Reader, Department of Political Science, Jammu University, Jammu.

Ashwani Rana, Lecturer, Department of English, ICDEOL, H.P. University, Shimla.

B.H. Briz-Kishore, F.I.E. Chairman, National Council of Rural Institutes, Government of India, Shakar Bhavan, Hyderabad, India.

Bhoomittra Dev, Former Vice-Chancellor, Gorakhpur University, Gorakhpur and Rohilkhand University, Bareilly.

D.R. Vij, 36, Tagore Park, Jalandhar, Punjab.

J. Shashidhara, Vice-Chancellor, University of Mysore, Mysore, Karnataka.

K. Aiyadurai, Lecturer Aru-Anandar College, Karumathur, Tamil Nadu.

K. Anil Kumar, Department of Chemistry, Sri Sathya Sai Institute of Higher Learning, Prasanthi Nilayam, Andhra Pradesh.

Kalplata Pandey, Reader in Education, M.G. Kashi Vidyapith, Varanasi.

Kiran Rekha, Deputy Director, Academic Staff College, H.P. University, Shimla.

Kirandeep Singh, Lecturer, Department of Education, Punjab University, Chandigarh.

Kulwant S. Pathania, Deputy Director, Academic Staff College, Himachal Pradesh University, Shimla.

Madhu Kapani, Reader, Faculty of Education, Sri Sathya Sai Institute of Higher Learning, Anantpur, A.P.

Mehraj Uddin, Registrar, University of Kashmir, Sri Nagar, J&K.

Mohd. Akhtar Siddiqui, Director, UGC—Academic Staff College, Jamia Millia Islamia, New Delhi.

N. Siva Kumar, Department of Commerce, Sri Sathya Sai Institute of Higher Learning, Brindavan Campus, Kadugodi, Bangalore, Karnataka.

Neeta Khanna, Lecturer, St. Bede's College, Shimla.

P.L. Gupta, Reader, Department of Education, ICDEOL, H.P. University, Shimla.

Pooja, **Lecturer,** Home Science College, Chandigarh.

Ramachandra Jantli Principal, University College of Education, Dharwad, Karnataka.

Rekha Jhanji, Professor, Department of Philosophy, Punjab University, Chandigarh.

Renu Gangal, Senior Lecturer, Atman College of Education, Jammu.

S. Abdul Kareem, Principal, Anjuman-e-Islam's Nehru Arts, Science and Commerce College, Hubli, Karnataka.

S. L. Sharma, Director (Academic), Institute of Correctional Administration, Sector 26,Chandigarh and Former Dean, Social Sciences, Punjab University, Chandigarh.

Sangeeta, Lecturer in Special Education, Department of Education, Kurukshetra University, Kurukshetra, Haryana.

Shashi Verma, Reader, Institute of Management Studies, H.P. University, Shimla.

Sucheta, Deputy Director, Academic Staff College, Kurukshetra University, Kurukshetra.

Suraj Pathak, Former Principal, MLSM College, Sundernagar, H.P.

Swami Atmapriyananda, Vice Chancellor, Ramakrishna Mission Vivekananda Educational and Research Institute (Deemed University), Belur Math, Hawarah, West Bengal.

U. S. Rao, Dean, School of Business Management, Accounting and Finance, Sri Sathya Sai Institute of Higher Learning, Prasanthi Nilayam, Andhra Pradesh.

Y.P. Sharma, Chairman, Department of Physical Education, H.P. University, Shimla.

Yadvendra Kumar Sharma, Chairman, Department of Education, H.P. University, Shimla.

Yoginder Verma, Director-Professor, Academic Staff College, H.P. University, Shimla.

PART–I
PHILOSOPHICAL FOUNDATIONS OF HUMAN VALUES

1

Value of Education vis-à-vis Value Education: Swami Vivekananda's Fundamental Thoughts on Education and Their Practical Application in the Present-day Context

Swami Atmapriyanada

Education in the modern context has come to be dominated by information. What with an explosion of enormous and mind-boggling variety of information, the one main concern of the human brain has become the avaricious accumulation, systematic storage and rapid retrieval of mountain loads of information. To this end, man has invented super giant computers with monstrous memory storage and retrieval mechanism. How cleverly one can manipulate the huge amount of information one has accumulated forms a major component of modern education, which has become insensitive to cultivation of higher emotions, richer perceptions and deeper sense of values. Education has thus been reduced to a systematic drill by which the human brain is trained to cleverly perform certain tasks at a maddening pace and with staggering skill.

The so-called modern civilization might assign great value to this type of education, but whom does it really serve? Does it really enrich the person, the human being who works himself or herself to death to acquire such an education? Isn't this human being, with thoughts and feelings, love and hate, sensitivity and fear, hope and anxiety, and a host of other psychological emotions to grapple with, the very centre of all this educational exercise? Isn't the human being, the one who acquires education in the first place, of the greatest value?

Value education is that education which inculcates in the educated person the profound sense of the person's own value, an unshakable conviction that, in reality, it is the Higher Self of a person that is the very source of all values. A super computer may perform its assigned task at mind-boggling speed. But after all, it is the mind of a human being that has created this super giant in the first place. Roger Penrose's prologue in his masterpiece Emperor's New Mind and Narada-Sanatkumara dialogue in *Chhandogya Upanishad* comes to mind in this context. Narada assigned such great value to his vast learning—immense and vast in its sweep and variety. *Sanatkumara* then showed Narada how valueless all his learning was unless he knew and realized the Self in whom all learning, all knowledge, and all wisdom actually inhered. Sanatkumara then taught Narada Self-Knowledge, *Atma-vidya* as the greatest of *vidyas*. This supreme science of the Self, *Atma-vidya*, is the same as *Brahma-vidya*, which has been spoken of in the Upanishads as *sarva-vidya-pratishtha*—the very basis, the substratum of all knowledge. The Self, the Atman, then, is the greatest value and the ultimate source of all values. Modern science and technology, in their mad pursuit of the outer, are increasingly getting knocks on their head by the demons of their own creation—demons boomeranging with alarming speed. Throttled by the Frankensteins of their own production, they are thus turning a full circle towards the science of the inner Self.

What Swami Vivekananda predicted more than hundred years ago appears to be fast becoming realizable: "Science and religion will meet and shake hands. Poetry and philosophy will become friends. This will be the religion of the future, and if we can work it out, we may be sure that it will be for all times and peoples." This realization of the Self, the Atman, as the Ultimate Source of values will engender a totally new weltanschauung and revolutionize all sciences including social sciences. Swami Vivekananda's fundamental thoughts on education and their practical application in the present-day context thus assume increasing relevance for the resuscitation of the basic human values in education.

Value of Education *vs.* Value Education

Let us begin with three beautiful stories. One is from Sri Ramakrishna's Gospel, the second from *Chhandogya Upanishad* and the third from Roger Penrose's Emperor's New Mind.

Parable in Sri Ramakrishna's Gospel

A highly educated Pundit was travelling in a boat. He was parading his knowledge before the fellow travelers, who were looking on with wonder. The 'uneducated' helmsman was one of the admirers. The Pundit would question him now and then: 'Hey, have you studied the philosophy of the Sankhya?' The helmsman would say in dismay: 'No, Sir, I know nothing of philosophy.' 'Ah', the Pundit would say, 'you have wasted a quarter of your life, poor fellow.' Again he would ask: 'Do you know anything about yoga?' 'O no, Sir' would be the reply, to which the Pundit would say with a chuckle: 'Half of your life is gone—useless and without value'. 'What about some Vedanta, man?' would be the next question. And the gentle boatman would say: 'I have no idea at all, Sir'. 'Well, three-fourths of your life has already gone a waste. What value does life have without the knowledge of Vedanta, eh?' Just at that time there was a storm. The gale wind began to rock the boat violently. Everybody including the Pundit began to panic. The helmsman asked the Pundit anxiously: 'Sir, can you swim?' 'No' replied the scholar. The ignoramus of a helmsman quipped gently: 'Sir, now that the boat is about to capsize, your whole life is gone! I may not know Sankhya, Yoga or Vedanta, but I know how to swim!' The message coming from this simple story is powerfully telling: what is the value of our knowledge, our education, our scholarship, if it cannot help us swim across the current of life, to face and conquer the gales and storms that should inevitably come to everyone in the course of life? Shankara's famous hymn, with the burden: *tatah kim, tatah him, tatah him, tatah him* (meaning 'what of that, what avails it, so what, what thence') comes to mind in this context. What is the value of all our 'boast of heraldry and pomp of power', our knowledge and education, if they fail us when we need them most—in the hours of crises? We pride ourselves as being highly 'educated', but drown helplessly, 'unwept, unhonoured and unsung' in the currents and cross-currents, in the whirlpools and eddies of life. What is the value of that education that cannot provide us with the strength to encounter and withstand a thunderstorm in the course of our life?

Narada—Sanatkumara Dialogue in the Chhandogya Upanishad

Narada, the highly educated scholar, goes to Sanatkumara, illumined sage, to unburden the agony of his soul. (Refer *Chhandogya Upanishad*, Chapter VII, Section 1). Narada is restless, he does not have peace of mind, and he feels unfulfilled and lost. He approaches Sanatkumara and humbly requests to be taught. Sanatkumara replies: 'First tell me in detail all that you have studied so far. I would then be able to teach you further.' Narada then gives a huge list of things he has already mastered. He then adds in humble desperation: "Sir, with all this knowledge that I have acquired, I feel I have merely become learned in plenty of words and formulae; I have not known the Self, the Atman that is the Source of all knowledge. I have heard from men of wisdom like you that he who realizes the Self overcomes sorrow. I am deeply afflicted with sorrow. Venerable Sir, kindly be gracious enough to help me cross over to the other shore of the ocean of misery." The compassionate guru, Sanatkumara, then utters a powerful one-liner: 'Whatever you have studied is only a name'. One is reminded of Sri Ramakrishna's telling example: the almanac predicts that there shall be so much rainfall. But then squeeze the book and you will not get a single drop! This Upanishadic story once again emphasizes the same truth—of what value is our education if it cannot take us beyond sorrow, beyond the anguish and the ennui of the soul eating into our very vitals? Herein lies the urgency of that education, of that knowledge, that would help us discover the real value of all that we study and perceive.

Roger Penrose's Prologue in his Book Emperor's New Mind

The greatest super computer in the world is being inaugurated—a machine that could handle several billion calculations in a microsecond. Pose any problem, and it would not even be a split of a nanosecond before the answer is flashed on the screen. Among the audience are scientists, mathematicians, engineers, bureaucrats, political heavyweights and of course, the inventor of this super-intelligence. The President of the country is getting ready to inaugurate. The inaugural ceremony consists in asking the first question of this super machine and the prerogative should naturally go to the honourable members of the audience. "Who will put the first question?" the inaugurator quips. All the wisemen of science and engineering among the audience look at one another in dismay. Who would be so foolish as to expose one's ignorance before this mighty giant, this near-omniscience never before known to humankind? The silence was broken by a shrieking voice of a little boy. "May I put the first question, sir?" asked the boy. "O come on" said the inaugurator, hardly hiding his smile at the innocence of this foolish little boy. The boy smartly asked: "What does it feel to be a computer?" The super computer began to respond. Its lights—red, yellow and orange—began to blink and wink. Seconds passed, minutes passed and it was more than an hour. The computer went on and on with its elaborate calculations and finally the answer flashed on the screen: "I don't know". The entire audience burst into laughter, giggling and chuckling at the plight of this super-intelligence unable to answer a simple question. Penrose was arguing against the blind ally of algorithmic thinking by the human brain. He was building up a case against the so-called Artificial Intelligence (AI) and against the so-called strong AI protoganists. The man-vs.-machine conflict as exemplified the Kasparov-vs.-Deep Blue fight for superiority is a wonderful modern re-enactment of the Puranic Bhasmasura story—one who endows the *asura* with superior power is himself threatened to be destroyed at the hands of this power!

Human civilization is desperately struggling to create super machines at whose hands it threatens to get vanquished and ultimately annihilated.

Character—the Sum and Substance of Value Education

We celebrated the golden jubilee of our independence some years ago. But whether we have been able to free ourselves from the psychology of dependence is as many years is a question, whose answer, alas, is no. 'What is lacking? O! what is lacking?' is one question that is a subject of perennial discussion everywhere, and by everybody—from the Parliament to the market-place, by the country's top leaders down to the man in the street. We seem to be advancing in all spheres. Then why are we in this appalling state of affairs? What is lacking in us? The answer is quite simple: 'character'. Character appears a rather simplistic virtue. Of course, it is really a very simple virtue. Indeed, all great truths are simple because simplicity is the hallmark of greatness. But then, simplicity seems to be the most difficult thing to acquire, much less to practise. It appears simple because it is not so much acquired as it is discovered in the core of one's being. It is our very essence, as fundamental to us as our very existence. There are two simple characteristics of a person who is endowed with impeccable character. Both of them owe their origin to Sri Ramakrishna's sayings: "Keep your speech and mind in unison" (in Bengali he would say, *man much ek karo*). This is in fact an echo of the Vedic mantra: *vang me mani pratisthita; mano me vachi pratishthitam*). "Do not allow perjury in the sacred shrine of your heart" (in original Bengali: *bhaver ghare churi karo na*). These two together would mean: (1) Speak what you deeply think and feel to be true; and do what you actually speak. (2) Allow no deception in your thought, word and action. In modern language, be absolutely transparent. The illustration of *sphatika*, the beautiful, transparent substance, is well known in our scriptures to describe the mind of a person who has been established in this virtue. Character building is the aim and end of all education, according to Swami Vivekananda. His educational vision needs to be re-emphasized and re-focussed, if our present-day educational system is to survive the shock of collapse into mediocrity. Swami Vivekananda's fundamental thoughts on education, with hints on their practice and application are given below. These form the core of the philosophy of Ramakrishna Mission's educational institutions, which have been created to experiment with and actualize Vivekananda's thoughts.

Swami Vivekananda's Fundamental Thoughts on Education Including their Practice and Application

(The words under quotation marks are Swami Vivekananda's original words, while the rest is a paraphrase of his ideas.) Education is not mere accumulation of information. "We must have life-building, man-making, character-making assimilation of ideas. If you have assimilated five ideas and made them your life and character, you have more education than any man who has got by heart a whole library." "Education is the manifestation of the perfection already in man." It is the manifestation of the potential perfection, the infinite possibilities of the human soul, for which the teacher and the environment act merely as catalysts. "Vedanta says that within man is all knowledge and it requires only an awakening, and that much is the work of a teacher. You cannot teach a child any more than you can grow a plant." "Mere book learning won't do. We want that education by which character is formed, strength of mind is increased, the intellect is expanded, and by which one can stand on one's own feet." "The training by which the current and expression of will are brought under control and become fruitful is called education." "We have but one method of acquiring knowledge and that method is what is called concentration. There is no limit to the power of the human mind. The more concentrated it is, the more power is brought to bear on one point; that is the secret. This, the power of concentration, is the only key to the treasure house of knowledge. To me the very essence of education is the concentration of mind, not the collecting of facts." "Along with the development of concentration we must develop the power of detachment. We must learn not only to attach the mind to one thing exclusively, but also to detach it at a moment's notice and place it upon something else. This is a systematic development of the mind."

Students should be taught the glorious spiritual and cultural heritage of our country. "We must have a hold on the spiritual and secular education of the nation. We must have the whole education of our country, spiritual and secular, in our hands, and it must be on national lines, through national methods, as far as practical." The personal life of the teacher is one of the most powerful influences on the student. "One should live from his very boyhood with one whose character is like a blazing fire, and should have before him a living example of the highest teaching. In our country, the imparting of knowledge has always been through men of renunciation. The charge of imparting knowledge should again fall upon the shoulders of *tyagis*." Indian spiritual idealism must be combined with Western science and technology to tackle comprehensively the problems of life. "What we need is to study, independent of foreign control, different branches of knowledge that are our own, and with it the English language and Western science; we need technical education and all else which may develop industries, so that men, instead of seeking for service, may earn enough to provide for themselves." Education should be productive of human good. Every educated man and woman should strive for the uplift of the masses. "The greatest national sin is the neglect of the masses. ... They pay for our education; we must work for them." "So long as the millions live in hunger and ignorance, I hold every man a traitor, who, having been educated at their expense, pays not the least heed to them." True religion or spirituality should be the prime motive force in the process of education. "I look upon religion as the innermost core of education." "We are the children of the Almighty, we are sparks of the infinite, divine fire. ... teach this life-saving, great, ennobling, grand doctrine to your children, even from their very birth." "True education is gained by constant living in communion with Nature." "The true teacher is he who can immediately come down to the level of the student, and transfer his soul to the student's soul and see through his eyes and understand through his mind. Such a teacher can really teach and none else. The conditions necessary for the taught are purity, a real thirst for knowledge, and perseverance. Purity in thought, speech and act is absolutely necessary." (for more thoughts on education, please see Appendices I and II.)

Value Education in Ramakrishna Mission's Educational Institutions

Some of the practices successfully adopted in Ramakrishna Mission's educational institutions to actualize the above educational thoughts of Swami Vivekananda are briefly mentioned below seriatim:

- That the aim of education is not mere book learning or accumulation of vast amounts of information, is impressed upon the students from the very start of the courses. They are shown the ills of having cartloads of information without seriously assimilating any of them through such simple methods as framing questions that need penetrative thinking rather than mere cramming of information.

- They are taught the lives of great men and women with outstanding character energy, those who reshaped the history and destiny of humankind, although not 'educated' in the sense of passing examinations or securing degrees. The idea that passion for knowledge, undivided focus on an idea and assimilation of the ideas being taught are the prerequisites of education, and are being inculcated in the students through the study of lives of great scientists and men of letters like Srinivasa Ramanujan, Marie Curie, Rabindra Nath Tagore etc.

- Eminent persons in various fields of science, arts and social sciences interact periodically with the students to inspire them with the educational ideals.

- By teaching them the Vedantic doctrine of the infinite power and glory residing in the Self, the Atman, which is the innermost core of one's being, the students are taught self-esteem, self-reverence and self-confidence. Independent thinking, rather than much dependence on outside resources, is encouraged.

- Free discussions, debates and expression of views through various fora bring out the inner potentiality of the student.
- An atmosphere of freedom together with strict discipline is sought to be maintained. Expansion of intellect and increase of mental strength come through a wide range of interactions and through wide reading about various peoples, their cultures and civilizations.
- Practical fieldwork and falling back upon one's own inner resources in trying situations are the means for developing a strong mind and a powerful will. The students are always taught to think positive, elevating thoughts and not be carried away by all the negative projections especially by the media.
- To help the students to bring under control the current and expression of their will, small practices like fasting on fixed days, denying simple necessities which they are used to, keeping night vigil on some special occasions in order to overcome sleep etc., are taught. Vow of silence (*mouna-vrata*) for some fixed period is also a great help in the exercise of speech control. The secret is to make them get a taste of self-conquest and self-mastery.
- Teaching the students some practices in order to help them develop concentration through: *(i)* observance of strict *brahmacharya* while one is a student (antevasin) *(ii)* keen observation of one's own mental gyrations and extrovert tendencies with a view to calming the mental waves *(iii)* constant *vichara* (discrimination) about their inner thinking and outer activities.
- To test out their level of concentration in practical life, some simple exercises may be given, like quoting from memory certain elevating passages after reading them only a few times, quick responses to questions on topics that they might have studied only a few times before.

- Further, telling them some inspiring anecdotes from the lives of great men, not only from the spiritual field (like Swami Vivekananda and Shankaracharya's phenomenal memory—they were called *srutidharas*), but also from the so-called secular field like Napolean etc., is a great help. To develop detachment, encourage the students to give up certain common things which they are used to. Ask them to restrain for some fixed period from communicating, either verbally or in writing, with people dear to them.
- Encourage them to give away some of their possessions that they hold very dear, like a pen, a shirt, books etc. The glory and power of our hoary spiritual heritage should be taught to the students through regular classes, dramas, film/video shows, exhibitions etc.
- They should be encouraged to commit to memory some of the immortal verses from the Gita, the Upanishads, Mahabharata, the teachings of great saints etc. A sense of pride in our rich heritage and ancient wisdom should be inculcated in the students by showing them how these principles and truths are in perfect accord with modern science and by exposing them to the statements of scientists like Eddington, Einstein etc. Besides, they should also be encouraged to study books showing the parallels between Vedanta and modern science.

Unless the teachers show a sense of dedication, self-sacrifice, deep love for their pupils, lack of greed etc., mere talk will never influence the students. A suitable congenial atmosphere should be created and proper teachers should be recruited for this to be possible. If at least some of the teachers are men of blazing character, they would help to mould the lives of students in a big way. Swami Vivekananda wrote to one of his disciples: "Can you become an Occidental of occidentals in your spirit of equality, freedom, working energy, and at the same time a Hindu to the very backbone in religious culture and instincts? This is to be done and we will do it." By this Swamiji meant that we should combine the best elements of the Occident and the Orient, West and the East, Western scientific temper and Eastern inward contemplation. Then alone could we make men of all-round character, calm, contemplative, *satvik* in their outlook, pious, noble, forbearing and peaceful, and at the same time, persevering, tenacious in approach, bold, daring, aggressively good (in contrast to being passively good), efficient, hard-working, intensely practical and endowed with scientific, rational outlook.

Our students should be trained in such a manner that they would delve deep into their inner consciousness at the time of prayer and meditation, and work like lions with girded loins in the field of action. They should be made to be proficient in both English and Sanskrit. Such proficiency would open the doors of both the modern and ancient worlds, making for a wonderful combination. At the same time, they should have technical skill and proficiency. To make the students feel for their unfortunate and underprivileged brethren, they should be made to work in the slum areas, in villages, mixing freely with the rural people, with the uneducated men and women there and try to help them in all possible ways. Regular free coaching classes of slum children etc., could be easily arranged. Unfortunately, in this land of religion and spirituality, the words 'religion' and 'God' are becoming taboos. If the Vedantic religion and philosophy could be revived and taught in modern language, this taboo could be easily removed. Vedanta teaches the two important doctrines of *(i)* divinity of all beings—the same Infinite Self or Atman resides in everyone, and *(ii)* oneness of existence (or solidarity of the universe). Vedantic religion, therefore, is free from all dogma, creed, narrow bigotry and any specific religious doctrine. It is scientific, rational, and elevating, for it tells everyone, from the lowest worm to the highest angel that he is a Divine Being, though encased in a limited body and a conditioned mind. This brings hope and develops a positive outlook in the life of a student. Swami Vivekananda believed and taught that Vedanta would be the future religion of thinking, rational humanity. The more these broad, life-giving principles of Vedanta are taught to students, the more would they become strong, positive, elevated in thinking and powerful in their inner convictions.

Unfortunately, our present system of education has taken the students and teachers far away from Nature. Study of Nature, what to speak of communion, has become a rarity. The result is there for all to see. There is an alarming lack of Nature-awareness. Environmentalists, all the world over are deeply concerned about this trend and are trying to reverse it by developing environmental awareness. The simplest way of doing this is to go back to our ancient method of encouraging the students to 'commune' with Nature, observe, watch, appreciate and get absorbed in the beauty of flowers and plants, animals and insects, rivers and ponds, stars and planets, the sun and the moon. A sense of wonder, a feeling of awe at the majesty and beauty of Nature, a profound emotion of gratitude for all the rich wealth of resources that Nature is giving us unasked and in boundless abandon—these higher sentiments are among the greatest assets of an educated person. The pre-requisites and the qualifications necessary for both the teacher and the taught have been beautifully spelt out in our ancient scriptures and re-emphasized in modern times by prophets and saints like Sri Ramakrishna and Swami Vivekananda. An awareness of these will engender in both the teacher and the student a genuine striving to acquire and achieve these qualities and endow them with mutual respect. Just as the disciple should have *shraddha* in the guru, the guru too should have *shraddha* and love for the disciple. Such an atmosphere of mutual shraddha, love and respect would be the most harmonious for the cultivation of knowledge and wisdom. Only then the Vedic prayer: *tejasvinavadhitamastu, ma vidvishavahai,* (may our learning be illuminative and powerful; may there be no disharmony between us) would become meaningful. *Om Shantih, Shantih, Shantih!* (Om Peace, peace, peace.)!

Appendix–I

EDUCATION AS HARMONY OR SYNTHESIS OF YOGAS

(*Yoga Samanvaya*)

Swami Vivekananda's concept of a truly 'educated' person—in fact, his view of a *complete* human being—is one who has successfully harmonized or synthesized the four yogas: *jnana, bhakti, karma* and *dhyana.* These four yogas correspond respectively to the faculties of thinking, feeling, willing and passionate, one-pointed focussing of all energies. Swamiji, therefore, spoke of the combination of the three Hs: head, heart and hand, with the capacity for one-pointed focussing interpenetrating all the three. He emphasized that intense feeling was the first step, deep thinking about the plan of action the second step and the perseverance, indomitable courage, iron will to translate the plan into reality the third step. We could do no better than to quote Swami Vivekananda's own words, spoken at his famous lecture *My Plan of Campaign* delivered at Madras after his triumphal return from the West:

> "Three things are necessary for great achievements. First, feel from the heart. What is in the intellect or reason? It goes a few steps and there it stops. But through the heart comes inspiration. Love opens the most impossible gates; love is the gate to all the secrets of the universe. Feel, therefore, my would-be reformers, my would-be patriots! Do you feel? Do you feel that millions and millions of the descendants of gods and of sages have become next-door neighbours to brutes? Do you feel that millions are starving today and millions have been starving for ages? Do you feel that ignorance has come over the land as a dark cloud? Does it make you restless? Does it make you sleepless? Has it gone into your blood, coursing through your veins, becoming consonant with your heartbeats? Has it made you almost mad? Are your seized with that one idea of misery of ruin, and have you forgotten all about your name, your fame, your wives, your children, your property, even your own bodies? Have you done that? That is the first step to become a patriot, the very first step.
>
> "...You may feel, then; but instead of spending your energies in frothy talk, have you found any way out, any practical solution, some help instead of condemnation, some sweet words to soothe their miseries, to bring them out of this living death? Yet, that is not all. Have you got the will to surmount

mountain-high obstructions? If the whole world stands against you sword in hand, would you still dare to do what you think is right? If your wives and children are against you, if all your money goes, your name dies, your wealth vanishes, would you still stick to it? Would you still pursue it and go on steadily towards your own goal? As the great Kind Bhartrihari says, "Let the sages blame or let them praise; let the goddess of fortune come or let her go wherever she likes; let death come today, or let it come in hundreds of years; he indeed is the steady man who does not move one inch from the way of truth." Have you got that steadfastness? If you have these three things, each one of you will work miracles. You need not write in the newspapers, you need not go about lecturing; your very face will shine. If you live in a cave, your thoughts will permeate even through the rock walls, will go on vibrating all over the world for hundreds of years, maybe, until they will fasten on to some brain and work out there. Such is the power of thought, of sincerity, and of purity of purpose."

Appendix–II

ALBERT EINSTEIN'S CONCEPT OF A 'HARMONIOUSLY DEVELOPED PERSONALITY' AS ECHOING SWAMI VIVEKANANDA'S AND SISTER NIVEDITA'S IDEA OF A COMPLETE, 'WHOLE PERSONALITY'

Swami Vivekananda's idea of harmony or synthesis of yogas could be seen reflected in Sri Aurobindo's *Integral Yoga*. Such a complete person, fully developed in all the faculties, is Swamiji's conception of a *full man* (*purna manush*). Only such a person would Swamiji call a truly "educated person." It is interesting to see how Albert Einstein, one of the greatest men of the last millennium, echoes the same views as Swamiji and Aurobindo, when he talks of acquiring "a harmoniously developed personality." We quote below a beautiful passage from Einstein's writing on education:

"I want to oppose the idea that school has to teach directly that special knowledge and those accomplishments which man has to use later directly in life. The demands of life are much too manifold to let such a specialized training in school appear possible. Apart from that, it seems to me, moreover, objectionable to treat the individual like a dead tool. The school always has as its aim that the young man leaves it as a harmonious personality, not as a specialist. ... It is not enough to teach man a specialty. Through it he may become a kind of useful machine, but not a harmoniously developed personality. It is essential that the student acquires an understanding of and a lively feeling for values. He must acquire a vivid sense of the beautiful and of the morally good. Otherwise, he with his specialized knowledge more closely resembles a well-trained dog than a harmoniously developed person."

Compare the above statement of Einstein with Swami Vivekananda's powerful words:

"Is that education which is slowly making man a machine? It is more blessed, in my opinion, even to go wrong impelled by one's free will and intelligence than to be good as an automaton. ... The education that does not help the common mass of people to equip themselves for the struggle for life, which does not bring about strength of character, a spirit of philanthropy, and the courage of a lion - is it worth the name?"

Sister Nivedita's telling words on the development of whole personality—harmoniously integrate personality—is worth quoting in this connection:

"Our conception of education must have a soul. It must form a unity. It must take note of the child as a whole, as heart as well as mind, will as well as mind and heart. Unless we train the *feelings* and the *choice*, man is not educated. He is only decked out in certain intellectual tricks that he has learnt to perform. By those tricks he can earn his bread. He cannot appeal to the heart, or give life. He is not a man at all; he is a clever ape. Learning, in order to appear clever, or learning, in order to earn a livelihood—not in order to become a man, to develop one's own manhood and manliness— means running into this danger. Therefore, in every piece of information that is imparted to a child, we must convey an appeal to the heart. ... There is one way, and one way only. It, throughout the early years of education, to remember that there is nothing so important as the training of the *feelings*. To feel nobly, and to choose loftily and honestly, is a thousand-fold more important to the development of faculty than any other single aspect of the educational process."

2

Good Life in *Mahabharata: Purusarthas* Revisited in the Light of Narrative Ethics

Rekha Jhanji

Whenever there is crisis of values, we need to look into our cultural resources because that helps us in firmly grounding ourselves and dealing with the situation. However, not everything from the past is to be uncritically accepted, but the exercise of delving into the past does definitely provide us with a perspective to view the present. This paper is an exercise in that direction. The focus is on *Mahabharata* and the objective is to dig out from it an exemplar for living life. The *Mahabharata* (as it is available to us today) is a voluminous text running into one million *slokas*. It has several levels of discourse, which ranges from a pure narrative of the story of the Great War to an exposition of complex cosmological and ethical theories. The canvas of the text is so large that it is claimed that whatever is there in the world of experience is found here, and whatever is not here cannot be found anywhere else.

For the purpose of the present discussion, it will be useful to limit the scope of our inquiry to the problem of *purusarthas* because that provides the foundation for moral life. We will carry out a two–pronged approach to the understanding of *purusarthas*: *(a)* we will see how *purusarthas* get crystallized through the narrative structure of the text and *(b)* We will view the *purusarthas* through the eyes of the different protagonists. This would be followed by a comparative evaluation of the *purusarthas* in terms of their relevance to life.

In the world of *Mahabharata, purusarthas* play a seminal role in defining the purpose of human existence. However, since it is an epic and not a philosophical text, resolution of philosophical issues is attempted not through pure conceptual analysis but also through parables and allegories. In matters of existence when abstract discussions reach an impasse, a simple story, a parable or an allegory helps to provide a breakthrough. Perhaps that is why many of our ancient philosophers, the world over, took recourse to parables and allegories to explain problems. Our ancestors, the ancient Indians, were quite aware of the power of images and they often used them to educate the young. *Hitopadesa, Pancatantra* and *Jataka* tales are amongst the numerous examples of such stories.

This can hardly be contested that despite the great technological revolution, last half a century has evidenced a moral and spiritual decline. Despite regaining political freedom we have lost touch with our spiritual values. We are gradually losing are moorings and seem to find little to hold on during critical phases of our lives. Notwithstanding all the changes that have come about in the material conditions of human life during the past century, the essentials of human life have not become different. So long as the scepter of death remains and the fear of the unknown looms in our psyche, the human condition remains the same in its essentials.

Turning to the solutions our ancestors offered to life's problem may help us to see our life from a vantage point, which we may have dismissed out of hand as archaic. This paper is not an attempt to reverse the sequence of time and re-establish our past ways of life. The idea is to integrate the past into our present with a view to make our life qualitatively better. The degradation of our moral environment has one major reason—the loss of a holistic vision of life. We have stopped looking at our life as a totality and thus seek short-term gains that may often entail long-term losses. The solution to this crisis lies in tempering our present approach with the wisdom of our ancient sages.

In any culture, the idea of good life is related to the concept of happiness or fulfillment it nurtures. A particular way of life is good if it is conducive to happiness or what the Greeks called *eudaimonia*. In classical Indian thought the primary source for the exploration into the modes of fulfillment is the concept of *purusarthas*. Taken together the *purusarthas* provide for the different kinds of needs that human beings experience in life. *Kama* refers to desires and sexuality, *artha* to the accumulation and acquisition of wealth, *dharma* to ethical conduct and one's place in society and *moksa* to liberation. Together, the four *purusarthas* can account for our entire quest for meaning in life. They harmonize and balance the different pursuits of existence with a view to paving the way for the final end of life. Mortality and finitude being the inherent condition of all living beings, no final goals of existence can be conceived without coming to terms with this condition. The narrative structure of the *Mahabharata* itself bears this out—although originally it was a story of victory, the narrative does not end after the victory of the Pandavas. It ends with the principal protagonists reaching heaven and merging in their originating deities after their heavenward journey. Thus, the author wants to make it clear that victories and defeats are all transitory because everything in the mundane word is governed by time *(kala)*. One's essential nature is timeless, consequently all temporal existence must strive for the final timelessness. The dichotomy of time and timelessness is the basis for the distinction between *Trivarga* and *moksa*. While *Trivarga—dharma, artha* and *kama*—is motivated by abhyudaya (worldly well being) *moksa* is motivated by the need to go beyond worldly gains and losses because it is nisreyas.

However, when one is immersed in worldly life, one has to strive for worldly gains according to one's station and stage (*varnasrama*) in life. Despite being aware of the ultimate purpose of life in terms of liberation, the Pandavas strive for regaining their kingdom, which they finally abandon and hand over to their grandson to leave for the Himalayas. The narrative gives a clear message for the phasing of *purusarthas*. It sees the purpose of human life in terms of liberation, which comes by gradually detaching oneself from all that one, holds dear—wealth, power and even human relationships. The whole thrust of the text is towards balancing the different dimensions of human life with a view to liberate oneself from all impediments. Each aspect of life is significant at a particular period of one's life. What one values in youth, one does not value in the same intensity in old age. If one can understand the constant change that life enforces, one does not cling to anything. Thus there is a time for the pursuit of *dharma*, *artha* and *kama*, a time for the pursuit of *moksa*. However, in a deeper sense, all the four *purusarthas* are interconnected. *Dharma* cannot be practised without *artha* and *kama* and all the three must lead to *moksa*. For each one of them is an integral part of this holistic vision of human life.

In the *Vanaparva* there are interesting dialogues between Yudhisthira and his four brothers regarding *Trivarga* and *moksa*.

Thinking of the inevitable massacre of millions of innocent people, Yudhisthira did not feel enthused to fight the war because he thought it too dear a price to pay for a kingdom. Each one of his brothers reminded him that since he was a *KSATRIYA*, he could not live by alms and the only course of action left to him to live a dignified life was to fight for his rights. The outcome of the war was of no concern, if they win they get the kingdom and if they lose they go to heaven.

There is a very interesting statement made by Bhima on the *purusarthas*, this occurs in the *Vanaparva*. This more or less sums up the position of a worldly person pursuing *Trivarga*. Bhima says to Yudhisthira:

O! Sir, virtue is sometimes (the indirect cause of) the weakness of men. *Dharma* and *Artha* forsake such men, as pain and pleasure forsake a dead man.

He who practises virtue only for the sake of virtue always suffers afflictions. He can never be called a wiseman. He cannot know the real purpose of virtue, as a blind man is incapable of seeing the light of the sun.

He, again who pursues *Artha* (profit or wealth) too much without pursuing *Dharma* (virtue) and *Kama* (pleasure) deserves to be censured and killed by all creatures.

He who always pursues *Kama* without pursuing *Dharma* and *Artha* loses his friends and also loses virtue and profit.

It is for this, those that are wise always pursue both virtue and profit for the union of virtue and profit is the essential requisite for pleasure, as wood is of fire. (*Vanaparva*, Ch. 33, Slokas 22-23, 25-26, 28)

The principal reason for this prudential statement on the part of Bhima is to persuade Yudhisthira not to abandon the idea of war.

In the *Santiparva* there is another dialogue in which each of the Pandavas expresses his views on the comparative value of *purusarthas* to Yudhisthira it concludes with Yudhisthira's own view on the subject. Arjuna and the twins give precedence to *artha* because they hold that without it neither *kama* nor *dharma* is possible. Bhima gives precedence to *kama* because he contends that if one has no desires, one neither feels like earning money nor practising *dharma*. Yudhisthira concludes this dialogue by declaring the superiority of the pursuit of *moksa*, for it frees one from the sorrows of this world.

The dominant message of the text seems in favour of Yudhisthira's view and the means to the end of *moksa* is *dharma*. Vidura further sums up the hierarchy of *Trivarga* by placing *kama* at the lowest rung, *artha* after it and *dharma* at the highest. In fact *Dharma* is the bridge that connects the worldly values like *kama* and *artha* to *moksa*. *Dharma* has several levels—in its mundane form it refers to duties related to varnasarma but on a deeper universal level it refers to the virtues that make human life livable. In one of the dialogues between Bhisma and Yudhisthira the former lists *Sadacara*, *Smrtis* and Vedas as the three main guides to the path of *dharma*. The primary source of light that illuminates all these three is the search for truth, Bhisma refers to it as a universally accepted and eternal duty. He declares:

Truth is always a duty with the good. Indeed, Truth is eternal duty. One should respectfully bow to Truth. Truth is the greatest refuge (of all).

You should hear also as to how truth may be won. Truth, O! Bharata, as it exists in the entire world, is of thirteen sorts.

The various forms of truth are impartiality, self-control, forgiveness, modesty, endurance, goodness, renunciation, meditation, dignity fortitude, compassion and abstention from inquiry. These, great king, are the thirteen forms of truth.

Truth is immutable, eternal and unchangeable. It may be won through practices, which do not oppose any of the other virtues. It may also be won through Yoga. (*Santiparva*, Ch. 161, Sloka 7-10)

It is interesting to note here that Bhisma clearly states that truth cannot be practised in isolation; it has to go in harmony with other virtues. If one does not cultivate impartiality self-control, forgiveness, modesty compassion, non-violence, meditation goodness, renunciation, fortitude, endurance and dignity, one cannot pursue Truth Corresponding to a cultivation of the above virtues, he also holds it necessary to avoid the following thirteen vices: anger, desire, sorrow, loss of judgment, inclination, to injure others, jealousy, malice pride, envy, slander, incapacity to see the good of others, unkindness and fear.

Yudhisthira refers to the problems associated with interpreting the *Smrtis* and the Vedas because their language is not transparent.

The actions of the righteous (*Sadacara*) are gauged in terms of *dharma* and *dharma* is defined in terms of the actions of the righteous—this lands one in a circular definition.

Bhisma dispels Yudhisthira's doubts by referring to a dialogue between Jajali and Tuladhara Vaisya. Tuladhara vaisya is recognized as an embodiment of virtue for he is said to be the genuine practitioner of *dharma*. Jajali was an ascetic and was very proud of having done a lot of penance, but he was told by an unseen voice that he is not equal to Tuladhara vaisya in spiritual merit and righteousness Jajali was very virtuous since he was an ascetic, when he was asked to take lessons in *dharma* from a vaisya he was filled with anger but he decided to go and meet him. On meeting him, Tuladhara said to Jajali:

O! Jajali, I know with all its mysteries morality, which is eternal. It is nothing else but that ancient morality which everybody knows, and which consists of universal friendliness, and beneficence to all creatures. (*Santiparva*, Ch. 262, Sloka 5)

He said to Jajali that all creature were his friends, he neither hated nor was particularly attached to anyone. He neither praised, nor blamed anyone. He lived in harmony with all living beings.

The ultimate test of following *dharma* for Tuladhara is fearlessness. For a true follower of *dharma* there is no fear of any living being and neither is he a threat to anyone because he has complete trust and love for all beings.

Thus, the practice of *dharma* makes one completely at peace with oneself and full of compassion for all living beings. It is this that we all are seeking in our lives. The pursuit of wealth and sensuous pleasure is actually geared to the search for this inner joy, which every human being is in looking for. The practice of *dharma* puts us in harmony with all living beings and thus makes our life worth living. And this is what good life stands for.

I will conclude by quoting the following verse attributed to Bhisma in the *Svargarohanaparva*.

Thousands of mothers, and fathers and hundreds of sons and wives arise in the world and depart from it. Others will arise and similarly go away.

There are thousands of occasions for joy and hundreds of occasions for fear. These affect only him who is ignorant but never him who is wise.

With uplifted arms I am crying aloud but nobody hears me. From virtue originates profit and pleasure.

For the sake of neither pleasure, nor of fear, nor of cupidity should anyone renounce virtue. Virtue is eternal. Pleasure and pain are not eternal. Jiva is eternal. The cause, however, of Jiva being covered with a body is not. (*Svargarohanaparva*, Chapter V, Slokas 60-63)

REFERENCE

I have quoted from the Sanskrit text of the *Mahabharata* of the Gita Press Gorakhpur edition of 2045. For the English translation, I have used M.N. Dutt's English version of the *Mahabharata* Parimal Publication, Delhi, 1988.

3

Human Values for Human Excellence

B.H. Briz-Kishore

Formulation

It is universally recognized that the changes in education and the changes in all walks of life that did not occur over several millennia have taken place in a few decades, nay, a few years. The changes are narrowing down the boundaries of space and time and are making the whole world a micro village. The spectacular achievements of man, ranging from unraveling the secrets of genes to propelling the spacecraft to cross the solar system boundaries, are bewildering. However, we are witnessing the shivering of the entire globe due to fear from the arsenals of nuclear weapons and terrorism. We are also witnessing simultaneously in helpless condition, famine, drought and floods on one side and over- exploitation of human kind and the consequential human tensions on the other.

In this context, the education system, which was originally aimed at improving the quality of human life as well as bringing about social harmony, appears to be losing track of its original objectives. Resultantly the education is becoming a subject matter of debate and criticism. It is making us address a series of pointed questions, like whether the modern education system has correctly diagnosed the fundamental problems plaguing the human world; whether priorities of the contents in the education need to be reassessed; whether the special stress on the Science and Technology is desirable in view of the defects and side effects which are felt all around; or whether there is something else which is wanting and require to be incorporated in the education system.

A detailed scrutiny of the education reforms over the past few decades reveals that the system by allowing and encouraging excessive stress advancement of material contents and ignoring the human values has resulted in 'power centered' and 'money power centered' human society.

This has resulted in drawing a sharp line between knowledge force on one side, and army force, money force and labour (work) force on the other and making the knowledge subservient to the other three. In most of the countries, these four forces were treated separately and were given preferential treatment of one over the other, at different time spells, widening the diversity.

The excessive dumping of data and (mis)information into the brains of billions of children is resulting in the distortion of knowledge base system. The money power systems like USA, UK and France are known for their hesitation to bridge the gaps between the developed and developing countries. The Russian experiment in the previous century was an illustration of labour (work) force, which ultimately collapsed.

The surprising aspect in the entire episode of human suffering is that the same problems are manifesting repeatedly in many a different form. The roots of the problems and the solutions lie, neither in the systems nor in the instruments of the institutions, but in the human nature and the very mind itself. It is interesting to find that the problems are known to everybody and the solutions are equally known to all. Hence unified effort is not beyond our reach to arrest the malaise and offer solutions because of the availability of strong infrastructural facilities and resources, devoted, sincere and visionary personnel and the vast reservoir of knowledge accumulated by the human race over ages. To our surprise, India had offered a solution in the hoary past.

Human Nature

The greatness of Indian approach lies in the total understanding of human nature and 'human in nature'. The quality formation of an individual is a long drawn process, contributed by the family, society and external and extraneous ambience. The individual is comprised of two distinct aspects, 'I' and 'Mine'. The 'Mine' always refers to 'I'. He has three different qualities, i.e., *Sattva* (Passive), *Rajas* (Dynamic) and *Tamas* (repulsive), as illustrated in Fig.1. It can also be seen from the presentation that the individual is involved with three states of consciousness, i.e., awakened state, dream state and deep sleep state. Because of subtle functioning of the above factors, the individual is involved in action, reaction, emotion and repulsion, in his dealings. This in turn creates a barrier whereby the individual is severely limited by forgetfulness and lack of wisdom. Only when the barrier is removed, the individual realises the supreme knowledge, i.e., the pure and fourth state of consciousness (*Sat + Chit + Ananda*), which is his own Self.

For a happy life of the individual and for harmonious co-existence in a society, it is essential that good qualities of the human beings continuously prevail. In ancient Indian system, there was a special effort for encouragement of the good qualities i.e., values through the education system itself. Our scriptures have listed several great values like truthfulness, righteous behaviour, treating people with human dignity, being compassionate towards all beings, abhorrence of theft, sacrifice of all kinds, and so on. In fact the *Bhagavadgita* enumerates 26 qualities for a person to become a total personality (Table1). These were termed as the gems of values one has to possess either by birth, or learn from teachers, or acquire by practice.

The values mentioned in *Gita* are briefly summarised in the great statement *Isha Upanishad:* (त्यक्तेन भुञ्जीथाः) viz., first sacrifice and then enjoy. Of course, this is in direct contrast of the modern way of living, i.e, enjoy without bothering for others.

Samskaras in Terms of Values

The method adopted by our *Rishis* for strengthening the values was through the process of developing the *Samskaras* in every individual and in the society as a whole. This process was given the highest priority, and place of importance in every walk of life in the Indian system.

The process of inducting Samskaras in the individual starts right from the event of the conception and birth onwards. They were called *Shodasa Samskaras*. While fifteen of them are to be performed through different stages of human life, including *Brahmacharya, Grihastha, Vanaprastha* and *Sannyasa*, i.e., student phase, family holdership, forest life and renunciation, the sixteenth one is to be performed after demise.

During the Student phase, a boy has to live with his teacher in *Gurukul* system, conduct his behaviour as per the dictums of his teacher and learn the subjects like *Vedas, Shastras, Puranas, Itihasas, Smritis* and *Dharmasastras* along with their commentaries. This is an important stage when the boy learns several virtues like controlling of senses and also some *Samskaras* necessary for his future life. In the next phase, that is family holdership, he has to lead his life as per the guidelines given and take care of the society. During the third stage, i.e., *Vanaprastha*, the person has to slowly withdraw from the active life of society, settle for a forest life and practise the process of introspection. As a *Sannyasin* the individual has to dissolve his identity and prepare himself for oneness with the supreme self. These stages are helpful for accomplishing *Dharma, Artha, Kama* and *Moksha* (virtuous living, material gains, desire and liberation). The teaching of *Samskara* was imparted through various sources. While the Vedas conduct themselves from a state of authority, and insist on a long list of human values, the P*uranas* and the *Itihasas* convey the human values in a friendly way and the *Kavyas* treat the subject in a manner similar to that of a spouse.

For elaborating the details with illustrations, our *Rishis composed* literature like *Ramayana* and *Mahabharata*. We also have books like *Panchatantra* with several stories of fiction but conveying the *Samskaras*/values to be acquired through the stories of *Mitralabha* and *Mitrabheda*. The purpose of various books, teachers, and programmes was mainly the promotion of the values of an individual for the good of the self and for the good of the society simultaneously.

Senses—Diversity-Levels of Consciousness

The genesis of knowledge is from a set of five senses—sight, hearing, touch, taste and smell. They have a tendency to create distraction and illusion through their interrelated objects and become the sources of diversity. The lure for satiating the senses is noted as the fundamental reason for various actions and reactions, which in turn make the individual undergo varied experiences of suffering. For the same reason, our Indian system has made a series of *samskaras* mandatory, for controlling the causes of diversity.

It is well known that every living being has four levels of consciousness. With the first level of consciousness, the individual with his physical body, also called *Sthula sarira*, involves in actions and reactions and experiences sorrow and happiness. He maintains relations with all his fellow beings in nature. Our *Rishis* noticed that some *samskaras* are to be given at this level.

With the second level of consciousness, a person goes into dream state of sleep, where he enjoys both happiness and sorrow under the influence of mind. This state is called *Sukshma Sarira*. It was realized by our ancestors that the whole internal world and the external problems are nothing but various manifestations of the mind itself. Hence, they thought it necessary to introduce some *Samskaras* for the mind also.

The third state of human consciousness is felt at *Sushupti*, viz., deep sleep, where we experience an undisturbed level of happiness coupled with ignorance. This state is called *Karana sarira*, which retains all the impressions of the mind and body in a seed form, only for remanifestation at appropriate time. To see that only good comes out from the individuals basically, our *Rishis* discovered certain mechanisms in the form of *Samskaras*, even for this stage also.

The great contribution of the Indian system lies in realisation of a fourth level of consciousness for selective souls, wherein the trinity, viz., the aspirer, aspiration and the process of the aspiration converge into one, which experiences oneness with cosmic infinite energy, merges in supreme happiness and results in bliss. It was also noticed that even if one individual reaches the fourth state of consciousness out of billions of people, he will be able to lead and guide the society for its harmonious functioning.

The serious attempt made by the seekers of true knowledge in ancient times was illustrated in the following words. Saunaka, well known as a great householder, having approached Angirasa, duly asked:

"कस्मिन्नु भगवो विज्ञाते सर्वमिदं विज्ञातं भवतीति।"

"O! adorable Sir, (which is that thing) which having been known, all this becomes known?" In reply, Angirasa stated briefly, "Self knowledge, which is the supreme one!"

Attainment of Human Excellence Amidst Diversity—Past to Present

Diversity is basically a natural and universal phenomenon existing from the beginning. Yet, it is proved that the human excellence is achieved by the individuals by excelling in human quality. The classical examples from great epics demonstrate how the individuals can create history by their outstanding adherence to one or the other value.

As illustrations, Kautilya during the Greek period, Rana Pratap and Shivaji during the Moghul period, Mahatma Gandhi during the British period excelled themselves with their distinct adoption of human values. Even the great *Kavya* of *Ramayana* defines the qualities of an ideal personality. While responding to the query of Sage Valmiki (Table 2), Sage Narada responds with a list of ideal values. He further describes excellence through illustrious statements as given in Table 3.

Therefore, the heterogeneity in complex nature can be evened out by exhibiting one great quality that makes human as humane, which alone is the highest value. That great value is scripturally defined as *Dharma*.

In the present scenario, the micro-globe, with all its vision and ambition to reach out and explore the entire planetary system/galaxy, with borders being no longer the boundaries, is experiencing all varieties of turmoil. It is resulting in unrest and retrograde movement in the path of human race.

So, the need of the hour is to revive the core of all achievements of the human society, i.e., the VALUE and pledge ourselves on this great auspicious occasion of the great International union today.

"विद्ययाऽमृतश्नुते ।"

True Education Bestows Eternal Bliss!

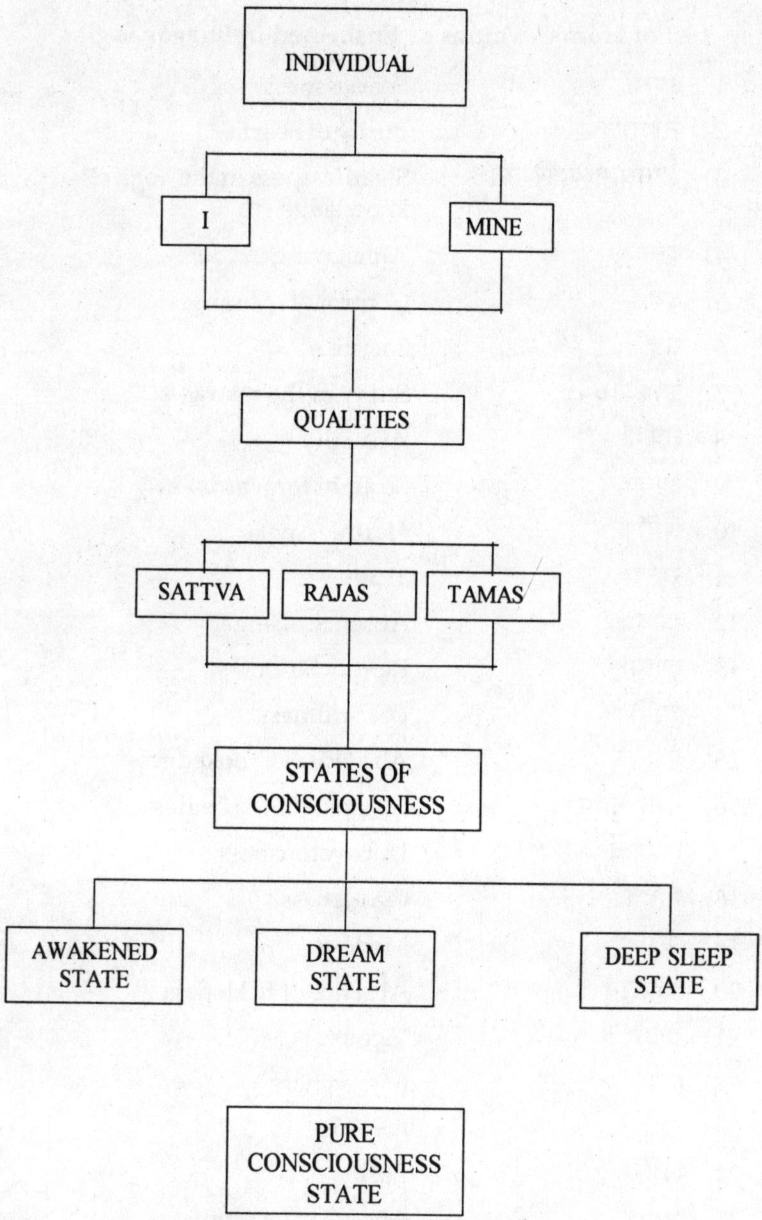

Figure 1: Representation of the Individual, Qualities and Levels of Consciousness

Table–1
List of Human Values as Enshrined in Bhagavadgita

1.	अभयं	:	Fearlessness
2.	सत्तसंशुद्धिः	:	Purity of heart
3.	ज्ञानयोगव्यवस्थितिः	:	Steadfastness in the Yoga of knowledge
4.	दानं	:	Almsgiving
5.	दमः	:	Control of the senses
6.	यज्ञः	:	Sacrifice
7.	स्वाध्यायः	:	Study of the sastras
8.	तपः	:	Austerity
9.	आर्जवम्	:	Straight for wardness
10.	अहिंसा	:	Harmlessness
11.	सत्यः	:	Truth
12.	क्रोधः	:	Absence of anger
13.	त्यागः	:	Renunciation
14.	शांतिः	:	Peacefulness
15.	पैशुनम्	:	Absence of Crookedness
16.	दया भूतेषु	:	Compassion to beings
17.	लोलुत्वं	:	Uncovetousness
18.	मार्दवं	:	Gentleness
19.	ह्रीः	:	Modesty
20.	चापलम्	:	Absence of fickleness
21.	तेजः	:	Vigour
22.	क्षमा	:	Forgiveness
23.	धृतिः	:	Fortitude
24.	शौचं	:	Purity
25.	अद्रोहः	:	Absence of hatred
26.	नातिमानिता	:	Absence of Pride

Table–2

Virtues for Total Personality from Valmiki Ramayana

1.	गुणवान्	:	Person possessing virtues
2.	वीर्यवान्	:	Person possessing prowess
3.	धर्मज्ञः	:	Person knowing Dharma
4.	कृतज्ञः	:	Person heaving gratitude
5.	सत्यवाक्यः	:	Person committed to speaking Truth
6.	छढव्रतः	:	Person with strong commitment
7.	चारित्रेण युक्तः	:	Person with good conduct
8.	सर्वभूतेषु हितः	:	Person compassionate towards all beings
9.	विद्धान्	:	Scholar
10.	समर्थः	:	Capable person
11.	एकप्रियदर्शनः	:	Person who is ever pleasant
12.	आत्मवान्	:	Person with knowledge of Self
13.	जितक्रोधः	:	Person who conquered anger
14.	द्युतिमान्	:	Person possessing splendour
15.	अनसूयकः	:	Person without jealousy

Table–3

Standards of Human Execellence from Valmiki Ramayana

1.	गाम्भीये समुद्रः	:	Like an Ocean in profundity
2.	धैर्येण हिमवान्	:	Like Himalyas in firmness
3.	वीर्ये विणुना सदृशः	:	Like Vishnu in valour
4.	सोमवत् प्रियदर्शनः	:	Like Moon in Pleasantness
5.	क्रोधे कालाग्रिसदृशः	:	Like Deadly fire in anger
6.	क्षमया पृथिवीत्तमः	:	Like Earth in partience
7.	त्यागे धनदेन समः	:	Like Kubera in charity
8.	सत्ये अपरः धर्मः	:	Like Dharma in truth

4

Value Education for Human Excellence

Bhoomittra Dev

We are living an age of guided missiles and misguided men. Our malleable conscience has created moral wastelands.

"Ehle khirad ne ye din dikhaye,

Ghat gaye insane badh gaye saye."

In the lines of Dinkar:

"Jhar gayee punch hemant jhare,

Pashuta ka jharna baki hai,

Upar-upar tan sanwar chukka,

Man abhi sanwarna baki hai."

Nature prefers diversity. Each person is like a unique genomic letter, kind of whom never existed in the past, can no where else be seen at present in the world, and shall, barring cloning, never visit the planet again. This has led to amazing levels of functional indeterminacy of human brain.

"Ekoham dwitiyonasti, na bhuto na bhavishyati."

It is our congenital right that "the letter" is read early and fully.

Left half of our brain is more concerned with reason and logic, while the right dominates in emotion, arts and music etc. Principle of "use or fuse" guides its development. When we take adequate care of both the parts, uniqueness unfolds fully. Both I.Q and E.Q. develop. Such a holistic and harmonized development is the result of the finest education in human values. It is a pity that many of us die much before realizing our full potential. When we integrate our thought, speech and action; live our true nature (*Sahaj*), inward flowering may ensue. Such a glorious "return to our ownself" (*Swaroop*) further improves our quality of life.

"Vidyaya, Vapusha, Vaaca, Vastrena Vinayaan cha."

We then epitomize—*"A Atma deepo bhav"*, *"Amritasya putrah"*—Children of immortality; and represent "Satyam, Shivam, Sundaram." We may also realize: *"Zindagi asl hai, khwab hai aur tarzae ada bhi."*

Excellence and simplicity often go together. With an open mind, noble thoughts are welcomed from all over the world. At such a peak level of human evolution, we epitomize the sanctified fire, fuel and the invocator—three in one. Levels of instinct, intelligence and intuition are crossed. We stand on the twilight zone of the known and the unknown. A tiny intuitive speak may widen our mental horizon, and the resulting break-through transgresses time. Such an excellent state of mind is attained when the doer merges with his aim. When somebody asked Picasso how he could, while painting, stand for so long without twitching an extraneous muscle, he told that he had left his body outside the chamber just as a Muslim leaves his shoes outside a mosque.

There are a few most essential human values, we need to acquire in the modern world today. First and the foremost is to uphold human dignity itself. While Gandhi distinguished between need and greed, he used what was unable because he wanted to salute the man who had spent a part of his life in producing it. Secondly, while he sang *"... Jane peer parai re"*, he valued human sensitivity.

We are living in an "ICE-age"—age of information, communication and entertainment. Information is power. Faster the information flow, lesser the poverty. In the past, necessity was the mother of invention. With the paradigm shift, invention has now become the mother of necessity. With "death of distance", geography is history. Strong mind-benders have unleashed war for mindscape. World war has changed into word war. An anecdote from Israel explains the change. A physicist under spell had become a frog. He could again become a human if a beautiful girl kissed him. The frog spoke of the curse when two girls passed by. One of the girls picked it up and put it in her purse. Her friend asked her, "Won't you kiss him?" She replied, "No, I would not kiss it, because a speaking frog is more precious than a physicist." In order to curb such a high tide of insensitivity, there is a crying need for human values today.

Faith has been eroded. Divisiveness is on the rise. We have to learn the art of conflict resolution to reduce attrition. Shall we realize that mud thrown is ground lost. Excellence can be achieved by cooperation only.

We should not be anthropocentric. Planet earth is on lease-hold, and not free-hold. Let us remember Voltaire, who said: "The bee was superior to human beings because one of their secretions is useful. Nothing that a human secretes is useful." We should extend the innate right of uniqueness to the biome also. Reckless industrialization brings in conformity. We produce fumes of progress, and effluents of affluence. Global influenza has to be controlled. When the environment deteriorates, the best flowers of our culture and civilization wilt and wither first. We should allow mother nature to choose her own dress more often, as in an Ashram, with its variety of foliage, flowers, fruits and seeds, with rainbow colours, shape, size and fragrance. We should cultivate the art of appreciation of earth's beauty and strive to leave the world better than we found it.

Early, we should learn to maintain eco-balance between getting and giving. Ego lives by getting and forgetting, while love lives by giving and forgiving. This alone can maintain the Niagara of happiness.

"Jeevane yavadadanam syatpradanam tatodhikam,

Ityesha prathasmakam bhagbvan paripuryatam."

"Pashbaddhah sada jivah

Pashmuktah sada shivah."

May I quote the words from your own emblem: *Shastre Shaastre cha Kaushalam.* This alone can form a valuable trilogy of education in human values for human excellence amidst diversity.

5

Relevance of Gandhian Values in the Twenty-First Century

Anurag Gangal and Renu Gangal

"Gandhi has a holistic vision or a way to world peace. He does not go into piecemeal solutions to diverse challenges of human life. It is contrary to Gandhi's world view to discuss various mundane issues in isolation either in terms of their economic, political, social, and educational thrust or in terms of their different levels." For instance, India and the world are facing a gargantuan threat to world peace in the menace of widespread terrorism. The terrorist outfits use modern armaments for intimidation and planned decimation. They get these arms through global mafia and channels of smuggling. This is again the result of international corruption, poverty, misuse of modern technology, growing unemployment, increasing exploitation and multiplying conflicts among nations. This scenario is causing inherent internal upheavals within the governing systems of national geographical boundaries. This causal systematic churning of issues specially involves concomitant dangerous facades of illiteracy, degenerating values and recurring social, political, economic and familial scandals. In the ultimate analysis, every predicament and crisis ends up with the need for revitalization of the individual and rejuvenation of deteriorating human values today. Therefore, Mahatma Gandhi's approach is primarily centred on the individual within the given holistic mould of a man's life.

"That is why Gandhi does not commit the logical error of advocating resolution of conflicts through war and force. Instead, he goes to the root of the problem and starts from the regeneration of the individual. With individual at the center, Gandhi has written voluminously on the relevance of the value of non-violence in the present-day world replete with war, violence and conflicts." For him, fundamental vows or values of *Sathya* (truth), *Ahimsa* (non-violence) and *Brahmcharya* (self-control) postulate the two remaining values of *Asteya* (non-stealing) and *Aparigraha* (non-possession) also. Gandhi's *nagnum opus*, in this regard, is his *Hind Swaraj or Indian Home Rule* written in 1908 and published in 1909. His *An Autobiography or the Story of My Experiments with Truth* is yet another bold and literary work on the making of India's Father of the Nation, published in 1927. In this *Autobiography*, among a number of other values utterly necessary for human life, he begins with the notion of self-assessment. He says, "In judging myself I shall try to be as harsh as truth, as I want others also be. Measuring myself by that standard I must exclaim with Surdas:

"Where is there a wretch

So wicked and loathsome as I?

I have forsaken my Maker,

So faithless have I been."

This type of harsh and truthful self-judgment is required for an individual to be really sincere and faithful to his or her Maker. One may wonder whether such attitude will be compatible with the modern trends of consumerism and blatant self-aggrandizement or personal highly projective advertisement at every stage of growth and development of a human personality. 'Self-projection-and-other-person's-effacement' is the essence of modernity today. Where do we go from this 'self-projection and other's-depression approach' of modern life style? Is there any possibility of bridging this apparent gap between Gandhiji's "practical idealism" and ultra-modernism? Why is it imperative to fill such a breach today? What are the other relevant Gandhian values today? Indeed, vows or values of Mahatma Gandhi are needed ever more in the present age where they appear to be depleting fast. However, within the holistic approach of Gandhi, values cannot be inculcated just by teaching or regular sermons. Instead, a man of conviction must put these values or humanity and peace into practice. Only then others will follow suit over a period of time.

Modern technology through the world of advertising has changed the erstwhile ancient and medieval values of individual's growth and development into high degree of self-centred approach to life. Technology works for the masses for it brings mass-profits through mass-production. Mass-media becomes the true source of mass-consumption in a modern democratic rule of masses! An individual has to become utterly selfish without even an iota of inherent benevolent-selfishness in the race for mutual cut-throat technological competition. This facelessness of the individual is leading to numerous sociological, psychological and economic disorders. One example can be easily seen in modern television and internet. They have brought the world and its continents into a "global village" network. Yet the television viewers and internautians are not able to give their quality time to their families because they prefer to remain glued to "idiot box" and internet "chat". Most of the television serials, programmes and even news dissemination projections also freely highlight the promiscuous, violent and socially harmful perspectives of modern life. The thinking of the vast masses and their behaviour are thus getting affected both knowingly and unknowingly. An individual and the understanding from individual to individual both are withering away under the surging ahead of modern technological ways of life.

"Modern technology has its positive dimensions too. Even Gandhi is not opposed to this present-day technology provided it does not displace human labour. Instead, it must streamline human effort and help individuals creatively." The exploitative and violent parameters of modern technology must be done away with.

For Gandhi, Truth must prevail. Truth has no fear. Truth can never be devoid of life. At times, Truth may appear to be harsh for a while. Truth never exploits. It is never violent and destructive. Truth never harms our fellow human beings. Truth is God and vice versa. It is then obvious what Truth is.

Gandhi's two volumes of *Nonviolence in Peace and War* published in 1948 and Gopinath Dhawan's *The Political Philosophy of Mahatma Gandhi* published in 1957 clearly indicate a Gandhian model for practically realizing a preferred and ideally peaceful society of nations. Gandhi has written about innate cooperativeness of human nature and behaviour. He regards individual and his behaviour as the mainspring of all social reforms. Having a look at quite a few of Gandhian pointers may be of great interest for us here. His approach has mostly been very flexible in matters of details through quite unyielding in essentials of life. Among essentials of this framework fall the following major points:

- Priority to labour intensive technology.
- "Eat thy bread by the sweat of thy brow."
- Truth is always relative, never absolute.
- No massive automation at the cost of individual's creativity, fundamental initiative and dynamism.
- Begin nearer home first.
- One step is enough at a time.
- From individual to global.
- No exploitation of any sort.
- Socio-political and economic order primarily based on cooperation or the cooperating instinct of the individual.
- Voluntary poverty.
- No involuntary poverty.
- Truth is Love/God.
- Nonviolence is a way of life.
- Essentially nonviolent defence of nation is possible.

The above mentioned "practical-idealism" and the following purview are the real basis of this research paper.

- From specific to general.
- Emphasis on life-size experimental dynamism to philosophy.
- Live theory-building.
- Setting examples through ever ongoing experiments in self-assessment and improvement.
- Value oriented objectivity derived from "practical-idealism."
- Dedication to socio-political and economic cause of individual's self-sufficiency, happiness and meaningful identity.
- What matters is the actual issue, problem and dilemma faced by individuals performing different tasks and roles.

- The nature of means.
- The nature of an end or aim.

"Beware the fury of the patient man," John Dryden had warned three hundred years ago. Unfortunately, the ruling authorities and modern global populace appear to have excellent reason to ignore that piece of ancient wisdom. Politics, in essence, means ecological settings of man and society and even much beyond. Any imbalance and ignorance is a very serious threat to a normal and peaceful system of values. As such, along with the current frenzy of information explosion and craze and fashion for the latest, more important is to go for knowledge and wisdom that may rest in virtues and values. Otherwise social cohesion and emotional balance is a consistent human impossibility.

Mahatma Gandhi, however, is more in favour of delving deep into the realities of life. He does not support the present-day university system of higher learning. This is his position. For him, simple and an activist approach to life leads to real depths of knowledge. Life must not depend so much—as it is today—upon acquisitive instincts but on self-restraint, Aristotelian mean/balance and widespread normalcy in socio-political life emanating from the individual. Such ideas for the followers of Gandhi are known as the Gandhian view of life.

When similar ideas are extended by others without reference to Gandhi then they are generally not called Gandhian. Hence, for ulterior reasons—if we do away with Gandhi in the absence of larger belief in non-violence, truth, non-stealing, non-possession and *Brahmcharya*, etc., even then the following main concerns and development paradoxes are likely to dominate human minds throughout the twenty-first century:

(i) limits to growth.

(ii) impact of information technology upon man.

(iii) over-production of conventional/other weapons.

(iv) over-exploitation of natural/other resources and ever widening consumerism.

(v) professionalisation of conventional and nuclear terrorism and similar acts.

6

Values of Peace and Justice in Islam

Mohd. Akhtar Siddiqui

Dr. Karan Singh, the renowned Indian scholar, in the capacity of a member of the International Commission on Education for the 21st Century, made a very significant statement in 1997. He said, "As we move through the last decade of this extraordinary century, which has witnessed unparalleled destruction and unimagined progress, the cruelest mass killings in the human history and the most amazing breakthrough in human welfare, the advent of weapons of unprecedented lethality and creative probing into outer space, we find ourselves at a crucial point in the long and tortuous history of the human race on Planet Earth. It is now quite clear that humanity is in the throes of a transition to a global society. We live in a shrinking world in which the malign heritage of conflict and competition will have to make way for a new culture of convergence and cooperation." The picture painted by Dr. Singh of enormous achievements of the human kind with a heavy shadow of violence, hatred, wars destruction and poverty across the globe seems to have got further blurred right in the beginning of the 21st century and has posed more serious challenge before the saner sections of the human race to ponder over the ways to save the human society from plunging into still darker times of mass destruction and human sufferings and ushering it into an era of peace, harmony and cooperation. We need to create without any further delay an atmosphere of tolerance of cultural differences and pluralism which is an essential precondition of social cohesion, peaceful co-existence and conflict resolution by negotiation, and ultimately, of world peace. Then alone the emerging new global culture of convergence and cooperation will be able to sustain in its right earnest. This obviously demands among many things, creation of a deeper understanding among different communities of the world having their allegiance to different faiths which will depend upon a clearer perception of each others cultural practices and a mutual respect and forbearance of the others ways of life.

One of the objectives of the present deliberations is that we rise from here more enlightened about the human, moral and spiritual values coming from any source, and with a greater sense of commitment to their inculcation and practice for the good of the human society. Keeping this object in view I have chosen to place before the readers the views held by Islam, one of the major religions of the world, about the values of tolerance, understanding of other's faiths, non-violence, justice and peaceful coexistence of different communities so as to help you understand and appreciate that these values are prominently and categorically ingrained in the philosophy of Islam and that Islam is essentially a religion of peace, justice and equality and that its followers are duty bound to abide by these values of their faith in their day-to-day life. I sincerely believe that this attempt will also help dispel any misconception and misunderstanding about this religion and about its believers which might have developed due to some painful events that took place in the world in the recent past and the way these were put before the world community, and thus pave the way for creating an atmosphere of trust and cohesion among various sections of society.

Islam is one of the great religions of the world, which is followed by about one billion people inhabiting this beautiful planet. It accords a fairly high ranking to peace and justice in the hierarchy of its values. Quran the holy book of Islam states "Believers! Be upholders of justice, and bearers of witness to truth for the sake of Allah, even though it may either be against yourselves or against your parents and kinsmen, or rich or poor; for Allah is more concerned with their well-being than you are. Do not, then, follow your own desires lest you keep away from justice. If you twist and turn away from (the truth), know that Allah is well aware of all that you do." (*Al Quran*, Chapter 4: 135). As is evident from the above pronouncement, Islam unflinchingly asks its followers to abide by the values of justice and truth in whatever situation or social relationships they are involved without any discrimination or bias that may creep in their minds due to their emotional association with those who are not on the path of justice and truth or for fear that speaking truth may apparently jeopardize their interest or welfare. The believer in Islam is required to do justice even if it goes against the dearest of all, his parents.

The Holy Quran begins with those words in which the Almighty God introduces Himself with the eternal qualities of mercy and beneficence for all the creatures on earth including the most respected, the human beings, and He bestows upon the mankind his love and all basic sources of sustenance of life without any discrimination of faith or sect or colour. One fails to understand how this benevolent sustainer of life for all can afford to see his followers in Islam or even others to hold hatred, discrimination, injustice or perjury against any human being. Islam does not assign superiority to its followers over others just because they are born in Muslim families, have acquired Muslim names and witnessed the Kalma-e-Shahada and does not guarantee their success in this world and in the world hereafter for these reasons alone rather, for it every thing depends on following the Islamic ethics by them in their lives. Spelling out the basis of success its holy book of rules enjoins that those who are afraid of appearing before their God on the day of judgment and who refrain themselves from following a wishful and unprincipled life not breaking the principles of justice and obedience to the Almighty will be rewarded with a place in paradise on the day of judgment. Thus those who might hail from a Muslim family but digress from the path of obedience, justice and compassion will not enjoy the grace of Almighty. What Islam expects of its followers in their individual and collective life and which it reckons as the moot principle of harmonious living with other fellow beings on earth is clearly described in Chapter 103 of Al Asr of the Holy Quran which reads as "the time bears testimony to the fact that man is certainly at loss except those who believe and perform noble deeds and keep reminding and advising each other of truth and justice and of observance of tolerance." The command on the one hand demands of each individual believer in Islam to engage himself/herself in noble deeds of help, cooperation, sympathy, justice, charity, etc., towards others with adherence to the principle of forbearance and tolerance and on the other also to motivate others sensibly and politely to follow this noble course of life thus creating a positive environment for peace and harmony in the society.

For creating conditions of peace in a society while on the one hand it is required that all members of the society enjoy equality in all kinds of socio-economic opportunities available in there, their aspirations are allowed to be fulfilled equitably without discrimination and the people are left free to choose right course of action for their personal, social and economic lives and follow cultural practices as liked by them so far these do not strain the fabric of national and social cohesion and the minimum level of morality. This also demands that the religious faith, moral and spiritual values and, social practices, held sacrosanct and dear by one group should not be trusted upon other groups or individuals forcing them to follow their line of thinking and thus taking away their own freedom of judgment about their ways of life. Islam is categorical in declaring that for people to have faith in a particular way of living, worshiping, etc., there is absolutely no compulsion. In Chapter 2:256 of the Holy Quran God pronounced that "there is no compulsion in the matters of religion" i.e., no one can be forced to follow the path of Islam or cannot be subjected to any discrimination for this purpose. It rather expects of its followers to always keep in mind the sensitivities and sensibilities of others in this regard and in case they present the Islamic morals to them it should be through their good behaviour and model of a pious life. Addressing the Holy Prophet in this regard God commands O! Prophet, invite people towards the path of Allah with wisdom and excellent advice and discuss it with people through a method which is best suited (Chapter 16: 125 of Holy Quran). At another place Quran has questioned the use of any dogmatic, repressive and unpleasant approach used by its followers while presenting its philosophy and principles to others and has prohibited Muslims from following such an approach in their preaching and has expressed in absolutely clear terms that all people have a right to live in peace with whatever beliefs and faiths they follow (Chapter 10: 99 of Holy Quran). In fact, in one of the culminating chapters of the divine book (Chapter 109) the principle of peaceful co-existence of different communities pursuing different faiths has clearly been specified when it is mentioned that "Say: unbelievers, I do not worship what you worship, nor do you worship what I worship. I shall never worship what you worship nor will you ever worship what I worship. You have your own religion, and I have mine." This has to be observed without any ill will or acrimony towards each other's faith and its followers and people of all hues and ideologies should be allowed to live together freely and harmoniously in the same society. Sternly prohibiting them from any such objectionable behaviour that may hurt sentiments of other communities it asks the Muslims "do not revile (the gods) which they invoke besides Allah" (Chapter 6: 108) Islam makes it incumbent upon all Muslims to involve themselves in noble deeds without observing any prejudice based on faith, caste, etc., as this kind of prejudice and discrimination gives birth to social discord and human frustration leading to subversion of conditions for peaceful co-existence in the society.

One of the essential conditions for peace in the society is that life and property of all members are respected and safeguarded from any violence, excesses and plunder. Subscribing fully to this condition Islam has declared violence of man against man and plunder as one of the worst kind of his deeds as may be seen from the pronouncement made in Chapter 5:32 of the Holy Book which reads as "Whoever killed a human being except as a punishment for murder or for plunder on earth, should be looked upon as though he had killed all mankind; and that whoever saved a human life should be regarded as though he had saved the entire humankind." In the light of this strong admonition it is unfounded to believe that Islam permits its followers to indulge in violence, terrorism or injury against innocent human beings. One wonders why many people including those expressing their allegiance to this great religion have not been able to appreciate this crucial command, which pleads for non-violence and harmonious co-existence of all sections of a society. Even in the face of wrongs done by others Islam always prefers pardon and forgiveness to revenge which alone it believes can help strengthen the bond of love and shun hatred and violent interfaces among the members of a society and create favourable climate for their peaceful co-existence. It educates its followers to adopt the path of kindness and conciliation in order to frustrate enmity created for whatever reasons. While emphasizing the need and importance of mutual understanding and friendship and the worth of self-restraint and kindness the Holy Quran reveals that "O' Prophet! You dispel evil with such good deed which is the best and soon you will find that one who was your adversary has become your staunch friend" (Al Quran Chapter 34). It further stimulates Muslims through the commands contained in Chapter 13 to follow the path of compassion and kindness towards perpetrators of atrocities on them.

It enjoins "forgive them and ignore their misdeeds for Allah likes those who follow the course of kindness." This advice came to Muslims during the times when the non-believers were at war with believers and believers would have been justified in taking revenge of the atrocities inflicted upon them by the enemies. Yet, in an effort to save people from the serious and prolonged ill effects of the chain of actions and reactions between two groups of human beings and thus buying a more valuable phenomenon of lasting peace and social cohesion in a multicultural and religiously divergent milieu it encouraged Muslims to tolerate and pardon and avoid the course of collision even though they had to bear some loss and suffering as inflicted upon them by their opponents. It rather exhorted them to come forward to oblige the perpetrators and soften their hearts and attitudes through good deeds. The Holy Prophet and his companions ensured the implementation of these noble ideals and history stands witness that they were able to construct a civil society, which enjoyed equality, justice, peace and liberty as its cornerstones. In a recent summit of World Muslim Leaders held in Jakarta (21-23 December, 2001) on the theme of Islam and a Future World of Peace the delegates reaffirmed that Islam is a religion of peace and justice. From its core values emanates respect for life and human dignity, which affects all ideals and actions that determine the Islamic way of life. These ideals guide the day-to-day life of the Muslim and that "Prophet Mohammad (PBUH) was sent as mercy for all mankind and his message of Islam and its teachings aim to produce peace and prosperity, promote love, compassion and forgiveness and create a humane society."

However, over the centuries one finds that the believers in Islam themselves, for varied reasons, have gradually lost sight of these cardinal principles given to them by their own religion for building a peaceful civil society. Very few of them realize the need for learning and imbibing the humane code of life enshrined in the Holy Quran and in the traditions of the Holy Prophet. As a result they grow up as little informed members of the community who often remain trapped in obscurantism and are always prone to all kinds of misguidance at the hands of vested interests. There is therefore a strong need for Muslims themselves to rediscover Islamic charter of life presented to them and to the entire humankind. Of course, other sections of the society also need to contribute equally in creating an atmosphere of understanding, mutual trust, justice and sustainable peace. Cultivating hatred and discord based on fanciful interpretation and misleading notions about a particular faith serves absolutely no purpose in the direction of building peace and harmony in the society. In this regard the aforementioned World Summit of Muslims rightly emphasized that "Muslim leaders and scholars are responsible for, and have a moral obligation to teach and promote knowledge about the fundamental ethics of Islam, thus providing the foundation for peace and peaceful co-existence and harmony in the world."

REFERENCES

1. Baghpati, Matin Tariq, *Islam and Rawadari,* New Delhi, Markazi Maktaba-Islami, 1997.
2. Ghauri, Umar Hayat Khan, *Doubts in Non Muslim Minds and Our Stand,* New Delhi, *Markazi Maktaba-e. Islami, 2000.*
3. Khan, M.W., *Indian Muslims : The Need for a Positive Outlook* , New Delhi, Al Risala Books, 1994.
4. Khan, M.W., *Islam: Creator of the Modern Age,* New Delhi, Islamic Centre, 1995.
5. Shaheed, Syed Qutub, *World Peace and Islam,* New Delhi, Markazi Maktaba-e-Islami, 1980.
6. Tajarwi, Mufti Mohd Mushtaq, *Terrorism and Islamic Teaching,* New Delhi, Markazi Maktaba Islami, 2001.

PART–II
HUMAN VALUES, SOCIETY AND DIVERSITY

7

Relevance of Value Education in the Present-Day World

Pooja and Sangeeta

With fast spreading consumerism, socio-cultural priorities have undergone a sea-change. Today, material gains draw our attention more than moral and ethical values. Professional education and training might have led our children high in the corporate sector but it is doubtful whether it has helped them become good, honest, responsible and dependable human beings. The closer a student is to the cent per cent point, the greater is the respect he or she will command. But has any body ever paused to think that the reams of printed matter between the covers of voluminous texts that a boy or girl crams to score hardly ever educate him or her in the absolute sense of term? They rarely polish one's finer skills. They seldom mould one into caring and sensitive human beings.

Education in schools and colleges has become a matter of routine. Education has lost its purpose and direction and hence its value. Educators, government, management and teachers do not know where the education is drifting. Education is considered as a means to keep children away from house. There is a big talk about falling standards of education. Nothing seems to be done to remedy the situation. School and colleges education is moving like a rudderless ship on troubled waters.

Anyone who has knowledge of 3 Rs. is a self proclaimed tutor. The world today is poised between EQ and IQ. The young people are bewildered a lot. The school teacher is looking for her results and the parents their. Education literally means to train mentally or morally or provide systematic instruction. Our great educationists since the time of *Ramayana* and *Mahabharata*, such as Vashishtha and Dronacharya and many more, down the ages besides honing the skills of their wards, made them good and complete human beings.

Attitudes Towards Value Education

Parents and teachers, in fact society at large, have always been concerned about morality and value education. Yet the question arises at once whether education should include any element or part that can be called specifically moral. Some people maintain that the education of children should involve no moral lessons or exercise, or no inculcation of moral rules or ideas, no use of moral praise or blame, no kind of moral language, argument or exhortation–only love and sincerity. This is rather drastic and paradoxical position that value education should include no value education – may, however, be an overly extreme reaction to an older, more traditional concept of moral education.

The rules or values of morality and a disposition to live by them should be inculcated in the individual, not through the means of law but through the means of education. These education values mean not only an appeal to reason but indoctrination in the forms of habituation, punishment and reward, praise and blame.

Programme of Value Education

The best programme of value education may take either of two forms. In both forms, moral discourse would appear throughout and education programme would fall roughly into two parts.

One is indoctrination or the use of examples, habituation, suggestion, exhortation, propaganda and sanctions like blame and punishment in such a way as to inculcate certain rules or virtues and with the purpose of ensuring behaviour that confirms with these rules, not of preparing the way for reflection and spiritual freedom. The other way is more properly education and should not be thought of as indoctrination. It involves the use only of these non-rational methods such as to keep moral education open and non-directive except wherein so far as an appeal to reason can be made. Fortunately, however, there is another alternative which takes a middle course between the two extremes. The best form of value education would not be wholly permissive, since during the early stage it would seek to teach certain rules, virtues, principles or ideals is unavoidable, it seems logical that it be done in terms of conscious formulated goals of moral development. As it stands that liberal teachers do not want to indoctrinate children with their own private moral values. Since the classroom social situation requires moralizing by the teacher, he ordinarily tends to limit his moralizing by the teacher, he ordinarily tends to limit his moralizing by focussing upon the necessities of classroom management, that is upon the immediate and relatively trivial types of behaviour that are disrupting to him or to the other children.

Movements of Value Education

Values Clarification

Values clarification—as a movement originated in mid-1960s and since that time has become widespread. The role of the school and the teacher is to help the child clarify his or her own values. The actual means by which values clarification is conducted are quite varied. In effect, values clarification is done through a series of classroom games and exercises that differ in time of requirements, complexity and subject-matter, so that teachers of children at all age levels and in all subject-matters can engage in values clarification. The purpose of value clarification is to give students an opportunity to grapple with issues of personnel reference, to discover or clarify what he or she believes or values. Through the activities, students bring their values to the surface to be seen both by themselves and their fellow students. The role of teachers in values clarification is to introduce the exercise and facilitate the students' clarification process. In recent years, value clarification has been criticized for forcing children to discover their values for themselves, thus playing down the rights and responsibilities of parents and others in society to more directly pass on their values to the young. However, value clarification has been seen as a possible helpful contributor to moral education, rather than a method that can stand well on its own.

Cognitive Developmental/Moral Education

Since the late 1960s, Lawrence Kohlberg and a group of his colleagues have been attempting to apply the cognitive developmental theory to educational programmes by developing ways for teachers to assist young people toward higher stages of moral thinking.

The key to the cognitive development approach is to confront children with ethical dilemmas to both stimulate and challenge their thinking. The challenge to a person's normal way of moral thinking brings about intellectual disequilibrium that causes the student to become dissatisfied with his or her current way of thinking and to search for a more complete and what turns out to be a higher form of moral thinking.

Value Analysis

It is third movement within moral education. Essentially, proponents of this view urge that the schools teach a process of moral reasoning, and way to analyse value positions and come to some defensible conclusion. To do this, students are taught the skills of ethical thinking in the same general way they are taught certain scientific methodology or the skills of mathematical problems-solving. The essence of this movement is well captured by Pascal's remark that the most moral thing a person can do is to think clearly.

Advocates of the value analysis approach believe that students should be able, for instance, to provide reasons why stealing should not be permitted. They should be able to deal rationally with questions such as "is capital punishment ever justified?" There are a number of value analysis approaches available and all represent a systematic and structured way to attack an ethical problem. This approach has its origins in two areas. First it can be traced to philosophical ethics, the study of moral reasoning. The value analysis movement is really taking the subject-matter that is part of university level education and revising it so that it is suitable to be taught to high school and elementary students.

Set of Values Approach

The fourth approach is different from the previous three. It is not confined to a particular methodology or set of procedures. On the other hand, aims at impulsing the school experience of the students with particular values that have been consciously chosen by adult community. Among them might be love of learning, respect for hard work and achievement, respect for property and settling differences in a non-violent manner and certain personable habits, such as courage, kindness and self-respect. The rôle of the school is to advocate the values and make them part of the life of the student, e.g., a value such as courage and settling disputes in a non-violent way would be exhibited in the literature and history encountered by students and teachers would help students to see their importance.

The set-of-values approach is a conscious attempt by the adult community to transmit its values to the young. In traditional societies, it is not a serious problem. However, modern, pluralistic societies have difficulty in transmitting a core of common values and a particular moral view.

Occasionally, there are some who say that teaching values have no place in public schools for fear that the schools will be found guilty of indoctrinating or inculcating values that are offensive to certain minorities or individuals. However, there are those who consider this objection questionable on several grounds. For one thing, schools of necessity teach and affect a child's sense of values and morality. Second, any government is clearly dependent on a set of values for its survival.

Holistic Approach of Educational System

Real education has to draw out the best from the boys and girls to be educated. This can never be done by packing ill assorted and unwanted information upon the students. Even though Mahatma Gandhi's thought dates back to 1933, its relevance strikes a cord with our present educational system, which demands *'revival'* and *'restructuring'*. Torn apart, the child today knows not to do. Teachers are required to build child's EQ. Make him a person of the environment with good values. The way, the world is today may not be possible to simplify but teaching the young people to rationalize and accept will make them happy and self-satisfied. Teachers within the hours allotted to learn to them, should love the students, inculcate those life-long values and be knowledgeable people themselves.

A spirit of give and take, which a youngster normally picks up on the sports ground, is missing today. Intellectual training may be one part of education. The other part must seek to enlighten an impressionable mind on the enduring values of life, without which no child can really attain humanity.

The aim of education is to identify the important moral and spiritual values which characterize successful living, to realize their importance to satisfy personal, family and community living. Education must cover a broad spectrum of value education correlated with science and technology contributing to spiritual, psychological and social development. Education must integrate modern scientific knowledge with the cultural and spiritual traditions of the past. The need for education is to address the perennial concerns of value orientation. Foundation courses in value education can be supplemented with interdisciplinary subjects, to equip the present generation to meet the future challenges more spiritually.

The curriculum must teach sense of loyalty towards community, school, family, town and country. It should develop peace, co-operation, friendship, tolerance in the world. A proper understanding and appreciation of different parts of India and the binding force between them helps in developing humanistic values among students. In curriculum subjects must incorporate the contents which develop social, moral and human values. Different activities like National Social Service, Scouting and Gliding, N.C.C., etc., help to develop character. Physical education subject, curricular activities and work experience are also helpful.

The teacher may use many methods to bring about aims of moral education. Co-operation and team work is learned inside and outside the classroom and less formally in sports and other activities involving team work. However, while the schools around the world have varying emphases and approaches, they share a common aim: the creation of an ideal person, an individual whose character reflects the major values and methods of responding to ethic issues of their particular social system. In times like these when strife, hatred and prejudices are so common—parents, teachers and society at large are the only hope of a society desperately dreaming of a sunnier morrow. We are to make our children and their future as beautiful as a sunrise on the sea shore. The need of the hour is to call upon the schools/society for evolving a system of education by which not only half baked literates are produced but truly refined and cultured people are produced who can make the world a better place to live in.

8

Understanding Human Values in Times of Cultural Conflicts

Ashwani Rana

> "Since the world in on a delusional course, we must
> Adopt a delusional stand point towards the world."
>
> —*Jean Baudrillard*

PART—I

It all began with Adam and Eve falling out of God's grace. Tasting the fruit of knowledge forbidden to man was a significant milestone in the history of humankind. Mankind has never been able to turn away from the temptation of the forbidden. Literary history has been a witness to conflicts of mankind—it is a record of man's frustrations with the 'givenness'. Absence has ever since intrigued man's imagination. Learning lured man to seek the forbidden. And so was born consciousness out of learning. Man became addicted to exploring the forbidden, the absence. This absence not only occupied his imagination but also manipulated all his activities from outside, as it were. Consciousness originated out of knowledge, out of learning. Adam and Eve after tasting the fruit of knowledge become self-conscious, shame-faced realizing that they were naked and therefore the birth of first 'notion' that they had to hide their nakedness. And it led to the birth of many more notions. The most important outcome of Adam-and-Eve episode was the birth of consciousness and the lure of the forbidden. Human beings were to dangle in between hereafter.

Evolving with itself a pattern of notions, a set of ideas or a value system, society was to run its course maintaining decorum. So were discovered methods of punishment to those who did not fall in line with social norms. Crime belonged to sphere of the state or the social sphere and sin to the higher realm, which belonged to the sphere of religion. It was mainly religion that not only dictated social norms but also became the custodian of value-system, which was to threaten man not to trespass into the garden of the forbidden. A Marxist definition of religion given by Christopher Caudwell in his book Further Studies in a Dying Culture would read thus: "Religion exists as a sum of human beliefs and actions, of beliefs held by real individuals acting in a real society." (*The Breath of Discontent*, 16).

Phrases like 'real society' hint at the sociological view of religion and suggest the existence of the Pope, the priest, a ritual or a bourgeois culture. This definition if stretched to Indian context suggests the existence of Brahmin culture that enunciated religious beliefs to its people. Marxists suggested a view of society in which religion, a sum of human beliefs and actions provided man with opium such that who tasted of it could sleep in ignorance of their oppression. It is relevant to point out here that Martin Luther (1483-1546) had proposed a new religion during European Renaissance—a break away from the institutionalism of the Roman Catholic Church. He proposed to have a direct transaction with God removing Church, priest, or sacrament. His attempt, too, can be seen as ousting the social denominators who for him were more in the nature of oppressors.

PART—II

Literature has ever since occupied artist's imagination to represent marginalized voice in doubts, a voice questioning. Rooted in a particular space and time it addressed issues, which troubled the individual. In English Literature of the 16th Century Christopher Marlowe's "Doctor Faustus" was not only a milestone in establishing norms of English Drama to come, but took up the issue of an educated mind lured by the forbidden:

> "These metaphysics of magicians,
> And necromantic books are heavenly;
> Lines, circles, scenes, letters and characters;
> Ay, these are those that Faustus most desires.
> O, what a world of profit and delight.

Of power, of honour, of omnipotence
Is promised to the studious artisan!"
(*Doctor Faustus,* Act I Scene I)

The experience of the forbidden for man was liberating, it fulfilled his desire for freedom. D.H. Lawrence in his *Preface to Dostevesky's 'The Grand Inquisitor'* echoes similar thoughts when he says, " But today, the most passionate believers in Christ believe that all you have to do is to struggle to give earthly bread (good house, good, sanitation, etc.) to the poor, and that is in itself heavenly bread. But it isn't. Especially for the poor, it isn't. It is for them the loss of heavenly bread. And the poor are the vast majority. Poor things, how everybody hates them today! For benevolence is a form of hate" *(Dostoevsky, 94)*. A little further he says, "... that most men cannot choose between good and evil, because it is so extremely difficult to know which is which, especially in crucial cases... So let the specially gifted few make the decision between good and evil, and establish the life-values against the money-values. And let the many accept the decision, with gratitude, and bow down to the few, in the hierarchy" (*ibid*, 97).

One can find evidence of similar predicament in many other works in which man/mass must submit however unwillingly to the only choice of some kind that would control his/their lure of the forbidden. Faust-myth became a motif for most of the literary texts to come. The discovery of the 'unconscious' made it known that the forbidden lay at the heart of man, that Adam and Eve's venture into the Garden of Eden was but a misadventure similar to Faust. It was an allegory of man burdened with lure of freedom. Such texts, however, had to exist in the periphery and not find a place in the canon of Great Literature.

The dismissal of the fantastic to the margins of literary culture is in itself an ideologically significant gesture, one which is not dissimilar to culture's silencing of unreason. As an 'art' of unreason, and of desire, fantasy has persistently been silenced, or re-written, in transcendental rather than transgressive terms. Its threatened undoing, disssolution, of dominant structures, has been remade, or recovered into moral allegory and magical romance. As Foucault writes of unreason, "Any transgression in life becomes a social crime, condemned and punished... imprisoned in a moral world [for offending] bourgeois society." From rational 'monological' world, otherness cannot be known or represented except as foreign, irrational, 'mad' and 'bad'.

(*Afterword: The Unseen of Culture,* Rosemary Jackson, 173)

The 'benevolence' of the 'specially gifted' has always silenced the voices of unreason. The fantastic must stay in lunatic asylum therefore Faust-myth should remain a play understood as a moral allegory.

A very interesting example is found in Shakespeare's *The Tempest* in which Prospero who represents dominant ideology tries to humanize Caliban by instilling in him values of reason, chastity, and self-control. Also noteworthy are Miranda's efforts to teach Caliban language:

Miranda: Abhorred slave,
Which any print of goodness will not take,
Being capable of all ill! I pitied thee,
Took pains to make thee speak, taught thee each hour

One thing or other…

Caliban:
You taught me language, and my profit on't
Is, I know how to curse. The red plague rid you
For learning me your language!

(Act I Scene I)

Miranda's speech contains elements of benevolence, which according to Lawrence is a form of hate; her pity suggests this. Also the speech between Miranda and Caliban represents existence of hierarchy—Miranda occupies a better social position while Caliban occupies a lower social position as that of the downtrodden savage. Caliban on his part calls language 'your language'—a dominating discourse, which is tyrannical to him. Prospero has not only cheated on Caliban by snatching away his island but Miranda is keen to colonize Caliban's discourse. Caliban's status is now that of an object. He identifies the root cause of his oppressive state in Prospero's books:

"First to possess his books, for without them
He's but a sot, as I am, nor hath not

One spirit to command. They all do hate him
As rootedly as I, Burn but his books."

(Act III Scene II)

Caliban knows that Prospero's power lies in his books. And to end this social hierarchy between them Prospero's books will have to be burnt. Caliban sees "books" (learning) as a kind cultural invasion—a culture gnawing to subsume the culture of the marginalized and make it part of their own.

William Blake (1757-1827) known as a precursor to the Romantic Movement, like Caliban, had revolted against 'humanization' of social subjects. In Songs of Innocence (1989) Blake was to suggest a life sans learning or in other words sans consciousness of life. Dostoevsky, too, in his notebooks enunciates similar idea. He says, "Strictly speaking: the less a man is conscious, the more fully he lives and feels life... He loses the ability to live proportionally as he accumulates consciousness" (*The Unpublished Dostoevsky,* Vol-I, 100). What gains primacy in Innocence is life itself whereas in Songs of Experience (1794) he talked about the damage done by dread-god Urizen. Urizen stands for Reason, arch-tyrant who propagates a religion of prohibitions. His representatives on the earth are the priests, kings, parents, nurses, school-teachers—people in position of some authority. One finds evidence of discontent in the voice of a boy in *The Chimney-sweeper*:

"And because I am happy, and dance and sing,
They think they have done me no injury,
And are gone to praise God and his Priest and King,
Who make up a Heaven of our misery."

One can see from the discussion above as to how the question of human values has been addressed by these texts and authors in different times. Faust-myth propagated the idea of a venture into the realm of the fantastic, a threat to the existing value-system, therefore it was read as a moral allegory as it challenged the dominant structures of society. It happens in *The Tempest* when Miranda tries to induce consciousness into Caliban, teaches him language to curb his savage instincts. Miranda's charity, which is based on pity or benevolence, creates "otherness" and oppresses Caliban. And one can deduce how finally "life" challenges laws of governance.

PART—III

Gary Saul Morson in his essay, *Bakhtin, Genres and Temporality* says that according to Bakhtin, "People do not develop the way a seed grows into a plant, their choices at every moment reshape them bit by tiny bit. Identity is ongoing project that is never complete. The same is true of social development. Societies are characterized by anachronism. The sort of actions or values present in one period may be implausible or impossible in another" (*New Literary History*, 1991,22: 183). It would be difficult to evolve a value-system that could satisfy all the human subjects. Such a value-system will always be monologic. It undertakes the impossible task of governing the destinies of people, quite like a monologic novelist who tries to guide his/her characters to a particular fate. A monologic value-system creates hierarchy, a pattern of high and low or in the other words an imposition of one's will on another. This world-view creates 'otherness', a world in which the other loses its place as a subject and becomes an object. Construction of such a monologic value-system is akin to patriarchy. Patriarchy at the level of family signifies relationships dictated by power at play with authority vested in the figure called the father. Patriarchy also finds its representation at the level of society, which is normally dictated to follow a pattern of dos and don'ts. It would be pertinent here to remember Blake's revolt against monologic value-system. Monologic value-system by its very nature is a closed system. It sees development of man as 'a seed grows into a plant'—a linear approach to the development of man. Monologic value-system makes truth claims whereas truth cannot be owned.

Bakhtin was to develop a polyphonic world-view in his famous book, *Problems of Dostoevsky's Poetics*. It is in this book that he spoke about his polyphonic world—view. Speaking about characters in Dostoevsky's fiction he says:

> Dostoevsky, like Goethe's Prometheus, creates not voiceless slaves (as does Zeus) but free people, capable of standing alongside their creator, capable of not agreeing with him and even of rebelling against him.
>
> A plurality of independent and unmerged voices and consciousnesses, a genuine polyphony of fully valid voices is in fact the chief characteristic of Dostoevsky's novel. (*Problems of Dostevsky's Poetics*, 6)

This world-view not only applies to fictional characters but also visualizes a world in which there is no hierarchy between the master and the servant. The social subjects have the right to independent free voices and truth can be discovered only during a dialogic interaction between two voices lies the truth. This model is based on the method of Socratic dialogue. Bakhtin observes that, "Truth is not born nor is it to be found inside the head of an individual person, it is born, between people collectively searching for truth, in the process of their dialogic interaction" *(qtd. in Mikhail Bakhtin-Creation of a Prosaics, 60)*. So as not to make it appear like a utopian world-view Bakhtin introduces his concept of the carnival. Carnival or popular festivity is a time during which people get together, and are free to speak against the authority. Carnival gives the space to subvert the official norms, and other societal conventions. Bakhtinian world-view cannot conceive a self which is isolated, instead proposes that one can arrive at one's self only through a dialogic interaction with the "other".

What decides a person's action is the situation, the event, or the context. A person cannot be removed out of his event. In fact, it is only the event that reveals a person. Lawrence in his essay "Why the novel matters" says that, "Nothing is important but life. And for myself, I can absolutely see life nowhere but in the living" *(20th Century Literary Criticism—A Reader, 133)*.

Yeats' line, how can one know the dancer from the dance, also echoes similar opinion. It is the event that gives a person the space in which a person enacts himself. Dostoevsky in his notebooks was to write, "General principles exist only in heads, while in life there are only particular events" *(The Unpublished Dostoevsky,* Vol. II, 32*)*. As stated earlier a person's development is not linear like the growth of a seed to a plant. Life contains only 'particular events' and a person is colored by the events in which he participates. The language he speaks, his gestures, his mannerism, his clothes, his value-system, is determined by his context. Caliban can speak in no other language than the language he speaks. His speech, his manners and his value-system spring from his context. Any value system imposed by Prospero is a cultural invasion to him and has political overtones. It would be appropriate to deduce that our values are determined by our contexts and not vice-versa.

Value-system in Indian context is a problematic. It would be difficult to arrive at any kind of value-system, which could be acceptable to all. Multi-culturalism will certainly pose difficulties if one is to address the issue of human values in Indian context. To presume (even innocently) that human-values are universal and can transcend barriers of cultures, languages, castes, etc., would be a reductionist (or political) view of the problem. Can one arrive at secular human-values that would not threaten status quo of the minorities in India. If beef-eating is permissible in Christian culture, it is a sin in Hindu culture. In South-India it is perfectly normal to marry one's sister's daughter whereas in North it might seem incest. Could one create a distinction between habits, customs, rituals, and human-values? Do human-values exist "out there" as absolutes, beyond "lived life"? Do these two examples suggest only different habits and have no bearing on human-values as upheld by different cultures?

It is interesting to speak about how media has represented society since the late 70s and how there has been a shift in its representation in the 90s. Cinema of the late 70s and even 80s was built around motifs like— a boy, who in most cases belonged to the lower rungs of society would fall in love with a rich girl, girl not necessarily belonging to the same religion as that of the boy's. They would face opposition from their parents and would resort to eloping. Also in vogue was the angry young man who represented revolt against the elite. In most of the cases this angry young man was a trade unionist or a leader of the slum dwellers who would fight for justice. With the onset of technology in 90s, liberalization of economy, our country saw rapid growth in communication technology and of course, a new culture of the consumerists. Fiats and Ambassadors were replaced by H yundai and Ford, Crown and Texla were replaced by Thompson and Sony, and even the foodstuffs were to be imported. And it is in such an ambiance that cinema established a new motif—*Dil Wale Dulhania Le Jayenge* represented a boy who would refuse to elope and would require consent and blessings of the girl's parents. Until very recently *Kabhi Khushi Kabhi Gam*—'It's all about loving your parents', re-established more or less the same theme of love and blessings of parents. Television on the other hand took to making serials like, *Kasauti Zindgi ki, Kyunki Saas bhi kabhi Bahu thi, Kahani Ghar Ghar Ki* and the like. These serials not only chose to represent very rich families but propagated idea of joint family, patriarchy, religion

(Hinduism), ideal daughter-in-law represented by Tulsi, Parwati etc. Neelu Kang in her article "Glorifying retrogressive patterns" observes that, "The argument is that these representations glorify patriarchal values and women's victimization. They reinforce and perpetuate stereotypes and gender roles"*(The Tribune,* April 7, 2002*)*. Media has been so successful in achieving its purpose that surveys in leading weeklies showed girls and boys wanting their marriage arranged rather than opting for love marriages. There was also an increase in channels like 'Sanskar', 'Aastha' etc., which took to propagating Hindu way of life.

Is it not an apparent contradiction to find that while the liberal economy of the country has created a wider gulf between the haves and have-nots, and has challenged the traditional mindset, and despite all these developments we see a parallel thrust on the revival of traditional value-system. This leads one to questions like—Who is capable enough to speak about value-system? Why are they propagating it?—{Is Balaji Telefilms making serials only for earning money? Are these serials above ideological suggestions?}. Is it not appropriate to think that the State has the power to influence people through its structures of governance? Who owns and governs the media, and therefore, is media above bias?

The only approach in understanding human values is to maintain difference with other cultures and never try to identify or fuse with them. In her article, Caryl Emerson says that "Before anything can be loved, boundaries must be confirmed and respected *(Keeping the self intact during the culture wars... 112)*. Unity and wholes should not be understood as 'homogenization', 'completedness', or 'fusion' because to Bakhtin wholeness is not achieved "when all parts of something are the same, but rather when each disparate part of that thing has been made indispensable to it and fits together with every other part in a unique, unrepeatable way" (*ibid*,116). One has to learn to respect boundaries and this should form the basis of evolving a methodology in education in human values. Remember Robert Frost telling, "Good fences make good neighbours." This paper is not an attempt at quashing the significance of human-values. The issues and questions raised in this paper need to be debated and need to be first of all given the status of issues and questions by the intellectual community. It is only after the intellectuals shed their biases and reservations that one can arrive at the real discussion of such a serious issue like human-values.

WORKS CITED

Bakhtin, Mikhail, *Problems of Dostoevesky's Poetics*. Ed. and trans. Caryl Emerson. Manchester : Manchester UP, 1984.

Blake, Williams, *Songs of Innocence and of Experience*. Ed. A.M. Wilkinson. Delhi: Oxford, 1981.

Caudwell, Christopher, "The Breath of Discontent". *Further—Studies in a Dying Culture.* Ed. Edgell Rickword. New Delhi : Commonwealth Publishers, 1991.

Emerson, Caryl, "Keeping the Self Intact During the Culture Wars : A Centennial Essay for Mikhail Bakhtin. "*New Literary History 27.1* (1996): 107-126.

Jackson, Rosemary, "Afterword : The Unseen of Culture". *Fantasy—The Literature of Subversion.* London : Routledge, 1998.

Lawrence, D.H, "Preface to Dostoevsky's 'The Grand Inquisitor'". *Dostoevsky* Ed. Rene Wellek. Englewood Cliff, N.J. : Prentice Hall Inc., 1962, 90-97.

Lawrence. D.H, "Why the novel matters". *20th Century Literary Criticism.* Ed. David Lodge, London : Longman, 1981.

Marlowe, Christopher, "Doctor Faustus". Ed. C. Bhaskara Menon. Madras : Macmillan India Ltd. 1985.

Morson, Gary Saul, "Bakhtin, Genres and Temporality". *New Literary History* 22 (1991), 1071-1092.

Morson, G.S. and Caryl Emerson, *Mikhail Bakhtin—Creation of a Prosaics.* California: Stanford UP, 1990.

Shakespeare, William, "The Tempest". Ed. Anne Righter. Harmondsworth : Penguin, 1968.

Unpublished Dostoevsky, The—Diaries and Notebooks (1860-81), Vol-I. Ed. Carl. R. Proffer. Trans. Arline Boyer and Carl Proffer. Ann Arbor : Ardis, 1973.

9

Education in Human Values Amidst Diversities

S. L. Sharma

At a time when the value question is starting in our face and when social scientists seek to shy away from confronting it on one pretext or the other, discussion on value education is a bold initiative. The social scientists of both the hues, liberal as also leftists, continue to evade the value question by advancing their own rationalizations. The liberal intellectuals evade it by invoking the Weberian of value-free knowledge, while the leftists do so by consigning values to he realm of epiphenomenon, as in their view economy, not culture, is the prime determinant of social organization. I find both these positions untenable for the simple reason that values are basic to any social system and that they cannot be wished away in any meaningful social analysis.

The theme can be approached from either of the two end-points: from the vantage point of values or from that of diversities. The question of values has gained in criticality on account of aggravating problem of value decadence in our public life while the question of diversities has acquired topical relevance on account of discord in diversities. I propose to focus on the value question in relation to the context of diversities.

In the interest of systematic exposition of the theme, however, I would like to first touch upon the prevailing problem of value decadence. In Part II of my presentation, I will focus on the value problem in the context of cultural diversities in India. Part III of my presentation will be devoted to the analysis of the causes of value problem in contemporary India. Finally, Part IV will deal with the significance of education in human values, identification of the values that are relevant for cultural pluralism and the strategies of inculcating such values through education. In each part of my presentation I would like to advance some sociological hypotheses for the consideration of the readers.

PART—I

As a student of society, I would like to reiterate that values are of fundamental significance to any social organization. In fact, every human society is founded on values and it is the values that hold it together. Values indeed constitute the grammar of socio-cultural life.

It will in order here to clarify the meaning of value. In sociological parlance, value signifies a conception of the desirable. It represents a social preference, a collective choice, and a shared vision of the 'worth'. Let it also be noted in passing that it is not an inherent property of an object. It is indeed a quality endowed by the people upon an object. Stated in simple words, value is that which is regarded as a value by the members of a group or a community. Further, it has an objective and a subjective dimension, a collective and an individual facet. It has an objective and collective dimension insofar as it is 'out there' and is shared in common by the members. It has a subjective and an individual dimension in that it is subjectively internalized by an individual and is mediated through him/her. Furthermore, psychologically speaking, it has three dimensions: cognitive, affective and conative. In simple words, it represents an idea (a concept), a sentiment with an emotional charge, and a motivating force for action. In popular terms, value is an ideal which is within the realm of realizable.

There are various types of values, e.g., eternal and temporal, universal and relative, traditional and modern, etc. For the present purposes, I would like to distinguish between two kinds of values, i.e., moral and civil. Moral values are those that pertain to the realm of 'human good' (ought to), civil values on the other hand relate to the sphere of public life. In simple words, moral values are intrinsic to culture while civil values are basic to public life.

Based on this distinction, I would like to advance my first hypothesis which is as follows: We have had a glorious tradition of moral values but not so of civil values. Not only have the moral values been adored in our scriptures, they have also been transmitted through socialization from generation to generation. To appreciate this point we need only to recall the four *purusharthas*, i.e., *dharma* (moral obligation) *artha* (economic pursuit), *kaam* (sexual pleasure), and *moksha* (salvation) as the value goals of human life. Similarly, the values of truth, non-violence, transcendence, integrity, selflessness, altruism, curtailment of wants, etc., have been so much a part of our tradition of moral values. It is an irony though that today we are witnessing a disconcerting trend of decadence of moral values, as is evident from the phenomenal rise of corruption, criminalization of politics, violence, hypocrisy, self seeking, etc. The horrifying scale of the value decadence can be gathered from a survey undertaken by the Tribune on the value question in Chandigarh in June, 1996 which brought out that there were over 40 per cent aborted pregnancies involving school girls, besides rising cases of child murder, and teenagers becoming drug addicts and alcoholics, etc.

But that is not my main point. My primary contention is that we have not had a strong tradition of civil values. This is evident from the fact that the values of hierarchy, authoritarianism, elitism, etc., have dominated our public sphere. The value of hierarchy is so much reflected in our caste system as also in the structure of gender relations; the value of authoritarianism is symbolized by the authority of group over individual, teacher over students and man over woman. There cannot be a more telling proof of the lack of civil values in our tradition than the scars of untouchability and *sati*.

It may be noted at this point that we have incorporated in our Constitution the civil values of liberty, equality and fraternity only in the post-independence era. Here again I would like to advance another hypothesis which is as follows: While we have incorporated these civil values into our Constitution, they are not yet internalized in the people's psyche. This hiatus between incorporation and internalization is evident from the recurrent problem of communal and ethnic conflicts that we encounter these days.

What follows from the foregoing analysis is that even as our tradition of moral values is on decline, the culture of civil values has yet to strike roots in our social psyche.

PART—II

Turning to the context of cultural diversities, it may first be noted that the term diversity does not stand for individual differences. In fact it connotes collective differences, i.e., differences which mark off one group of people from another. These differences may be of any sort: biological, religious, linguistic, etc. Thus diversities refer to patterned differences between groups.

India is known for its rich stock of diversity, diversity of all sorts including ethnic, religious, linguistic and regional. One has only to refer to the book 'People of India: An Introduction' by K.S. Singh in order to grasp the full significance of the range and depth of diversities in India. He found more than 3500 communities in India, 325 community—specific languages and dialects and 25 scripts. While we have this amazing scale of diversities in India, it is also important to note that we have had a tradition of harmonious living together of the diverse ethnic, religious, linguistic and cultural groups in our land for so many centuries. Ravinder Kumar Sharma, a historian from Kurukshetra tells me that our history is full of documents testifying to the amicable and abiding relationship among the people of diverse, racial, religious and linguistic backgrounds. There happened something during the colonial period that led to the rise of mutual suspicion and distrust. The situation has aggravated even more in the post-independence era. Thus there has been a continuous and progressive erosion of the one and only great civil value of cultural tolerance that we have had as a part of our heritage.

PART—III

It is time of reflect on the causes of erosion of values in contemporary India. In this regard, I would like to advance the hypothesis of anomic development for explaining value crisis. In several of my earlier publications, I have consistently argued that the prevailing paradigm of development is faulty. It is faulty because it is premised on a faulty conception of human nature and social order. Because of its exclusive emphasis on economic growth, it reduced man to a mere economic species and society to a mere economic organization. This just is not true. For, man is a lot more than mere economic species and society is lot more than mere economic organization.

For the same reason perhaps Newt Gingrich, Speaker of U.S. Assembly of Representations has offered a perceptive indictment of the prevailing model of development. He is right when he observes: "It is very difficult to protect civilization with: 12 year olds having babies; 15 year olds killing each other; 17 year olds dieing of Aids and 18 year olds holding diploma that they cannot read.

Furthermore, the prevailing model of development represents a case of anomic development. Anomic is defined by Merton, a renowned American Sociologist, as a situation of socio-cultural breakdown which is characterized by overstress on the cultural goals to the neglect of institutional means. Thus anomic development is that which tends to overstress pursuit of goal over means, resources over rules and interest over values. The prevailing model of development is such that it overstresses the cultural goal of becoming wealthy as a success goal of life, with scant regard for the kind of means, legitimate or illegitimate, adopted to achieve it. Such a development is only expected to lead to decadence of moral values on the one hand and civil values on the other. The various explanations of ethnic and communal conflicts in contemporary India have highlighted the role of politico-economic factors. In short, forces of westernization, modernization and globalization which are organically linked to development have understandably led to marginalization of moral values and disruption of civil values. Little wonder that we now live in an ethos where a person's success is measured in terms of money rather than integrity. For all practical purposes, Crooks command greater respect today than men of integrity.

PART—IV

From the above it follows that there is an urgent need to save our values from further dissipations and to restore them to their old glory. And this need gains in further salience if we seek to build a pluralist society. There is a difference between a plural society and a pluralist society. A plural society is that which consists of plurality of cultural groups which co-exist in an uneasy relationship. A pluralist society, on the other hand, is marked by the culture of pluralism. The culture of pluralism signifies the centrality of two values, i.e., respect for cultural identity of each group and the value of equality. We are certainly trying to build a pluralist society out of a plural society. What role can education play in the creation of a pluralist society? In this context, it is important to cite Delor's Commission Report titled 'Learning: The Treasure Within'. This report has identified four goals of education: learning to know, learning to do, learning to live together and learning to be. Of these four, the third, i.e., learning to live together is of immediate importance for our purposes. Two questions arise at this point. One relates to identification of the values relevant for cultural pluralism. The other relates to devising the strategies of inculcating such values through education.

Attempts have been made to identify the values that need to be promoted today. International Institute of Educational Research, Japan organized more than half-a-dozen workshops to identify such values. The values that are identified in these workshops are as follows: caring for others; concern for society, nation and international community; concern for environment; concern for culture; self-esteem and self-realization; peaceful resolution of conflicts, freedom, justice, equality and love. Similarly, China has identified following five as principal values: love of mother land, people, labour, science and socialism. National Council of Educational Research and Training in India has also identified certain values which number as many as 84.

I would like to submit that for a proper identification of human values it will be rewarding to distinguish them into four sets: those pertaining to environment, self, collectivity and culture. With respect to environment, survival may be regarded as the first human value to be followed by positive health, environmental conservation and material prosperity. The values pertaining to self include human freedom, integrity, dignity and self-development. As regards, values concerning collectivity, peace and harmony, equality, respect for others' viewpoint are necessary for the smooth functioning of pluralist social order. Finally, the values pertaining to culture include such values as truth, beauty, bliss, which signify inner human sensibility. Equally important are the values of cultural identity, cultural tolerance and respect for other cultures.

The next question is how to imbibe these values: four social agencies at once come to mind: family, school, church and media. Of these four, for the present purposes, we are concerned with the role of education. Two observations merit consideration here: (1) Values cannot be taught, they are only caught. What it implies that it may not be an effective strategy to make values part of the curriculum. Experience shows that many a time it turns out to be counter-productive. (2) Observation, values can be imparted through education by making them part of the educational ethos. Practice carries greater effect than precept. It is through presenting a model of living by values that teachers can transmit values. Values thus can be transmitted more effectively through exemplification than through instruction.

Ways and means have to be devised to promote inter-cultural understanding. A Huxley in his book: "The Brave New World" has proposed certain ways of promoting inter-cultural understanding. The first step in that direction is to initiate inter-cultural communication. Once the channels of communication are activated between the diverse cultural groups it is bound to promote inter-cultural understanding.

10

Relationship between Diversity and Human Values

Suraj Pathak

Diversity is inherent in human society. It is said that no two men are alike. Diversity is multi-dimensional and there cannot be any exhaustive list that may enumerate all kinds of diversity. When we talk of human beings, we naturally talk about varied qualities and the resultant difference between man and man. People differ in their exterior appearances, as well as their inner content. The difference is to be seen in each part of the body, the structure of body, the complexion of the body and the marked difference of the facial expressions. Divergence of the inner content of human beings is all the more pronounced. Men differ in their urges, their aspirations, and their desires. There is a vast difference in the approaches adopted by the human beings for the attainment of their goals. They differ in their temperaments, their reactions towards others. The relationship between man and man is determined and governed by the different attitudes of human beings.

As everybody is different from the other, the attraction and repulsion is natural. Human beings have learnt a lot from nature. In nature the flora and fauna differ vastly from place to place yet it remains collective. Trees with diametrically opposite qualities are to be found in the same forest. The same soil gives birth to the trees with sweet fruits and the trees and creepers with poisonous juices. The environment is the same, the location is the same, the soil is the same and even the climate is the same. In the world of animals we find a wide range of difference—natural and inherent to their species. The hunter and the prey, the strong and the weak, the bullies and the tortured ones tend to live in the same forest. If the hawk is there, the sparrow also lives there. If the snakes are poisonous, there are harmless and even advantageous creatures like earthworms. If the fox lives with its cunningness there is also the elephant who lives with its wisdom.

The question arises as to how the plants and animal with vastly varied natures live together and human beings, the so-called Supreme creatures of the world find it difficult or rather impossible to live together. Why have they divided our mother earth into countries based on the diversity of racial, cultural, religious, linguistic and other acquired factors? Why does not man learn anything from nature? What, after all stands between man and man? Is he not mature enough to understand that diversity is the real recipe of life? Why cannot he understand that only things produced mechanically are bereft of diversity? Why is he not ready to accept and respect the otherness of others? How can he expect to have all men alike? These are perhaps the most difficult questions which defy easy answers. God created man in his own image and placed him with the best qualities of head and heart. He gave him not only the understanding and comprehension but also tolerance and perseverance. There must be some external force, some acquired knowledge, and unnatural imposed convictions that make it difficult for human being to live in peaceful co-existence.

It is shocking to note that the individuals like–plants, animals tend to understand, appreciate and absorb the diversity but in-organized system they become intolerant and do not behave in the manner in which they would have behaved in their individual capacity. Collectiveness and togetherness, strangely enough, bring with it intolerance whereas it should make them more aware and sensitive to the diversity which is inherent in man. Pt. Nehru says that organized religion has done much more harm to human society than the good it has done. The partition of the country in 1947, the recurring communal riots thereafter and the most recent incident of burning alive of the Kar Sewaks at Godhra and the resultant backlash thereto in Gujarat and other parts of the country are the worst examples of religious intolerance.

The caste based diversity played havoc with the young people of the country at the time when Mandal Commission Report was implemented. The linguistic diversity forced the Founders of modern India to divide the country into linguistic States. The further division and sub-division is demanded even today after more than 50 years of independence. Water disputes between different States, claims and counter claims of different States on particular towns and cities show the ugly face of regional diversity. The discrimination on the basis of colour is not a matter of yester years only. Even today in many parts of the western nations, non-whites are treated as savages and second-rate citizens.

Political diversity is perhaps now the worst sort of diversity. Everything has been politicized. Every incident gets coloured in political hues. Even the most inhuman acts are seen as political events and not the acts against humanity. In the campuses political diversity has taken a strong hold. Any quarrel between the two students assumes the shape of a dispute between the rival political factions and divide is on political lines. The political bosses try to take political mileage out of every act howsoever inhuman it may be.

Lust for power has aggravated the situation. The urge for domination over others through the animal in us keeps alive or rather strengthens these diversities.

The educationists of the world should pool their wisdom in finding a solution to this problem. At the present moment it seems to defy any solution but actually it is not so.

Our problem is that educationists of the world are busy in the teaching of science and materialism. Philosophy, human psychology on which the education was based in ancient times has been relegated to the lowest status. Any system of education which does not teach scientific adventurism and materialistic aggression is considered to be irrelevant and is being discarded. Materialism, in itself is nothing but mercantile barbarism with a cutthroat competition without taking into consideration the higher values of human life. Scientific adventurism is obsessed with the manipulation of information forgetting that knowledge gets lost in information and wisdom gets lost in knowledge.

The solution to this complex problem perhaps lies in the revivalism of values. Mahatma Gandhi was right when he said that the right objective can be achieved through right means. Man without values is an animal. Values like universalisation, tolerance, and humanism should not only be taught but also lived by the body corporate of educationalists.

I come from an institution where values are given importance and whose motto is 'to differ without divergence' and to make efforts 'to harmonize tradition and change.' The Founder of my College Late Raja Lalit Sen inspired the college family to pursue this ideal 'till hill and river vanish'—the logo of my institution. It is only through values that we can teach the younger generation the lesson of tolerance. They will have to be told to develop a habit of not only accepting but also respecting the otherness of others. Adjustment and not domination should be the way of life. All human being are one. We have been told time and again by the Saints and the Seers that there is no difference between man and man, *vasudev kutumbhkam* is the message of our scriptures. *Manas ki jaat sabhay eka pahachanvay* is the message of Guru Gobind Singh, *eak pita eaks ke hum varik tu mera guru bhai* is the wisdom of Sikh Gurus. Even the science teaches us the inherent oneness among all living things—plants, animals and human beings.

These values will have to be taught and education will have to take up this challenge. The word 'Education' in itself implies the teaching of values and there is actually nothing to state the obvious but as the things stand today we will have to tell the educationalists of the world that the word 'education' requires them to educate the minds of the young generation by teaching values. And values will come through the taming of the mind, the appreciation of the wisdom of the ages and not through scientific adventurism and materialism.

11

Value-Crisis, We and the Present Times

D.R. Vij

Terms Defined

Values may be defined as 'qualities that a person has learned to believe are important or worthwhile. They can be principles to live by or goals to be achieved.'

By 'Value', as used in the title of this paper, we mean those desirable ideals and goals which are intrinsic in themselves and which when achieved or attempted to be achieved, evoke a deep sense of fulfillment to one or many or all parts of what we consider the highest elements of our nature.

'Crisis' means a time of difficulty, danger or anxiety about the future.

And the word 'We' refers to the older generation of the present Indian society especially the teacher community.

The phrase 'The Present Times', refers especially to the period 1947 (when India became free) and after.

Value-Crisis: A Reality

As things are, value-crisis is a hard reality and a cause of serious concern to the country. What should be of greater concern, however, is the fact that in spite of our being alive to the gravity of the situation, things are going from bad to worse.

Aql Baarik Hui Jaati Hai
Rooh Tazarik Hui Jaati Hai

(The intellect is sharpening, but the spirit is becoming darker every day).

Value-crisis is deepening day by day with rapid advancement in knowledge, science and technology on the one hand and constant deterioration of values on the other. The very survival of man seems to be at stake.

Value-Erosion: A Problem of National Concern

The national document: "Challenge of Education—A Policy Perspective (August 1985)" brought out by the Ministry of Education, Government of India, New Delhi drew attention of the nation to this problem thus:

"Thoughtful people in all walks of life are greatly disturbed by a progressive right from the time India became free. National leaders and educationists have been seized of the situation at through. Consequently, all National Commissions and Committees on Education in the post-independence era have been emphasizing the importance of character formation in our educational institutions. Unfortunately recommendations in this regard were hardly put into practice. The downward journey of values continued without ever showing even the least sign of improvement."

Marz Barhta Gaya Jyon Jyon Dawa Ki.

(The more we treated the malady, the more it grew).

It was in 1960, therefore, that Sri Prakasha Committee on Religious and Moral Instruction had to report: "The many ills that our world of education and our society as a whole are suffering from, today, are mainly due to the gradual disappearance of the hold of basic principles of the religion on the hearts of the people. The old bonds that kept them together are fast loosening and the various new ideologies that are coming to us, are increasingly worsening the situation."

Top priority given to Value Education by the National Policy on Education (NPE, 1986) is a logical conclusion of the sad tale of the diminishing human values in our society. The NPE has clearly stated, "The growing concern over the erosion of essential values and an increasing cynicism in society has brought to focus the need for readjustments in the curriculum in order to make education a forceful tool for the cultivation of social and moral values. In our culturally plural society, education should foster universal and eternal values, oriented towards the unity and integration of our people."

National Programme of Action (POA)

For the first time, in history of free India, the Central Government had pledged itself to a Programme of Action (POA, August 1986) as a follow-up measure to make the NPE successful.

POA, to my mind, is a unique national document of great potential with a solid supportive and an optimistic approach. In its own words, "There is today, as never before, an upsurge in favour of national integration and adherence of certain national values and concerns." "If implemented with sensitivity, vigour and persistence, the proposals contained in the programme of Action ... will enable the educational system to move towards the democratic and socialist ideals enshrined in the Constitution."

The fundamental question which crops up once again, of course with greater concern and intensity is: Shall we succeed this time? Or to put it more bluntly, Shall we ever succeed?"

The answer to this question could range from a definite 'No' to a positive 'Yes'. Much would depend upon the type of person who is responding. Objectively speaking, NPE and POA will be successful only to the extent we implement the policy and programmes sincerely, efficiently and effectively. The document POA makes a million dollar point in this regard when it observes:

> "Implementation of N.P.E. has to being now wherever possible, in whichever way possible. Bigger schemes of quantitative expansion and quality improvement take time to get formulated and processed, and even longer to get understood and implemented. The process of preparation of these schemes has commenced and will be followed up with necessary urgency. Meanwhile, every institution, every centre of non-formal education and of adult education, every teacher and student and every member of the society must examine what they can do.... While the Central and State Governments will fully shoulder their responsibilities and will give an account of it to state legislature and Parliament, it is people's involvement in the educational reconstruction which will make the real difference. Time is of essence, and unless we act now, we stand in the danger of once again missing the opportunity of

educational reform, so critical not only for the development of our nation, but for our very survival."

Education for the 21st Century

Jaques Delors vested with the sacred responsibilities of giving a future direction to the society in matters relating to education highlights and emphasizes once again the immense and urgent need of Value Education/Value Development in all system of education. The Report entitled "learning: The Treasure Within" which he, as chairman of the International Commission, submitted to UNESCO in 1996 discusses among other things, the major tension facing the 21st century. In this connection, the Report goes on to say, "Lastly – another perennial factor – the tension between the spiritual and the material: often without realizing it, the world has a longing, often unexpressed, for an ideal and for values that we shall term 'moral'. It is thus education's noble task to encourage each and everyone, acting in accordance with their traditions and convictions and paying full respect to pluralism, to lift their minds and spirits to the plane of the universal and, in some measure, to transcend themselves. It is no exaggeration on the Commission's part to say that the survival of humanity depends thereon.

PART–III
TECHNIQUES AND APPROACHES TO VALUE EDUCATION

12

Approaches to Value Education

Anuradha Agnihotri

Education is an excellent tool for bringing about behavioural change in life. It helps an individual to live in harmony with the nature and strengthens his relationship with individual, family, society and nation.

Value-defined

The term 'value' comes from the Latin word 'valere' which means 'to be of worth.' Literally, value means something that has a price, and is precious or worthwhile. It may be described as an emotional attitude, which motivates a person directly, or indirectly to act in the most desirable way.

Value Education

It involves exposing students to a whole series of values in their complete totality, to bring about an improvement in child's thoughts, ideas, attitudes, interests, character and sentiments. It influences all aspects of a child's personality.

Why Value Education?

We are living in a world where we come across erosion of values due to industrialization, westernization and change in value system.

Education is an excellent tool for bringing about a behavioural change so that we may live in harmony with the nature and it also strengthens the relationship with individuals, family, society and nature.

Various Education Commissions and National Policy of Education have emphasized value education as an integral part of school curriculum.

Approaches to Value Education

The following approaches could be used for imparting value education:

1. Direct Approach or Direct Pedagogical Input (DPI).
2. Integrated Concurrent Approach (ICA) .
3. Critical Inquiry Approach (CIA).
4. Total Atmospheric Approach (TAA).

1. Direct Approach or Direct Pedagogical Input (DPI)

It is the most widely used approach to value education. The basic principle behind this approach is value should be taught rather than being caught. It focuses on cognitive domain mainly and is used in lower-classes. Main techniques of direct approach are:

- Lectures.
- Discussions.
- Stories.
- Reflective exercises.
- Dramatisation.

It is a suitable approach for lower-classes and aims at direct communication of values through a variety of commonly used techniques.

2. Integrated Concurrent Approach (ICA)

This approach focuses on imparting value education not through separate classes but by being incorporated into the contents of various subjects of the curriculum. It is also referred to an integral pedagogical model or integral pedagogy because it aims at providing values by a teaching learning process to develop the all round personality of the children. It has 5 basic steps:

Context of Learning

- Previously acquired concepts.
- Real contexts of child's life like family, peers, schools etc.
- Socio-economic, political and cultural context.
- Institutional context (school climate).

Learning Experience

There may be indirect experiences or direct experiences. The indirect experiences involve only cognitive domain of the child whereas direct experiences include reaching out to child's affective domain as well. This approach advocates use of direct experiences by following techniques:

- Role playing.
- Real life examples.
- Situational games.
- Activities.

Reflection

Reflection is a process whereby we try to find the meaning of learning experiences. Teachers should move from learning experience to action by properly reflecting on the learning experience or content, so that it may be reflected in their attitudes and feelings.

Action

It leads to internal as well as external improvement of behaviour. For example, a chapter in History, "First national struggle for freedom", may focus on imparting values like patriotism, national integration, etc.

The poem 'A Solitary Reaper' may be taught for inculcating the value of sensitivity. The topic 'Laws of Gravitation' may focus on the background on which these laws were made and so on.

Evaluation

If includes academic as well as non-academic evaluation and should focus on assessing the overall change in child's personality. This approach is an easy solution to the problem of providing value education within the course curriculum, without requiring much of input as in terms of specially trained teachers, special provision in the time table etc.

3. Critical Inquiry Approach (CIA)

This approach focuses on value inquiry undertaken by the child with the help of the teacher and it seeks to find a solution to a problem by child himself, so that it is really acceptable to the child and does not involve blind following. It is important because it involves an element of logical and critical reasoning, openness and critical awareness regarding the problem.

Certain examples can be taken from real life involving different situations and the student may be asked to give his thought, opinion or a viewpoint which may be totally different from the traditional viewpoint and then analyse it through open discussions. Main Techniques used in Critical Inquiry Approach are:

The media approach: Use of pictures, newspapers, films, magazines, posters, television, internet, etc.

The Simulation Model

In the simulation model, certain games to learn the consequences of one's behaviour and improving it by orienting, training, operating and debriefing the participants are used.

The Jurisprudential Inquiry Model (JIM)

This model has been developed by Donald Oliver and James, P. Shaver which helps to think systematically about contemporary issues by analysing them, raising questions and debating them openly, e.g., should India adopt war or peace as a measure for dealing with terrorism? Teacher may have discussions on this, in which one group may speak for 'war' and another for 'peace' and subsequently confrontation and argumentation may follow for each stance. This model can be effectively used to discuss important issues related to social, political and economic scenario with students to arrive at a rational decision.

Value Analysis Model (VAM)

In this, a situation is presented to the students through a chart, film or slide and the students are asked to identify, discuss and evaluate different courses of action and their consequences and thus arrive at a desirable, moral and most logical conclusion. This model helps to develop reasoning powers, value judgments and value clarification skills and enhances thinking, speaking, and reasoning powers. It is an interesting means of providing training to students to deal with social issues in a rational manner and also to deal with value conflicts effectively.

4. Total Atmospheric Approach (TAA)

This approach focuses on ensuring a favourable atmosphere for the child in the school, for the values should be caught rather than taught. This approach may also be called an "indirect approach" as the values are not inculcated through direct moral education classes but through curricular and co-curricular activities and in this approach the behaviour and personality of the teacher plays a crucial role.

Thus there are three main thrust areas for value inculcation in the school:

- Curricular activities.
- Co-curricular activities.
- Role of teacher and head of institution.

Different values may be inculcated by teaching of different subjects such as:

Subjects	*Values*
Science	Scientific temper, logical reasoning, critical thinking, observing, systematic work, reflective thinking, appreciating beauty of nature, etc.
Social Studies	Patriotism, loyalty, religious tolerance, national integration, truth, honesty, etc.
Mathematics	Logical thinking, reasoning, analysing, etc.
Health and Physical Education	Self-discipline, cleanliness.
Languages	Communication skills, beauty, appreciation, sensitivity.
Craft	Aesthetic beauty, perfection, dignity of labour, work ethics, cooperation, team spirit, etc.

Various co-curricular activities such as games, debates, poster making, quiz, declamation, creative writing, dance, music, drama, field trips, community service, exhibition and even morning assembly all help to shape the personality of the students in a desirable manner. Moreover, these activities inculcate values like aesthetic sense, appreciation, kindness towards everyone even animals.

In the words of Tagore, "a lamp cannot light another, unless it continues to burn its own flame," thus teachers should practice all the values themselves what they preach. The role of head of the institution is even more crucial as he/she has to be a role model and set an example before all the staff members and students, he should be dynamic, caring and democratic in approach. The management of the institution should maintain cordial relations with the principal, teaching staff, non- teaching staff and students and should try to understand and solve their problems in a democratic manner. It is not only important to run the programme for value education; its effectiveness within a fixed time frame should also be evaluated. Ultimately values get in built into the system and a value culture is formed within an institution.

Conclusion

Selection of any approach for value inculcation must be given a careful thought before it is practised. It depends upon so many factors such as school environment, social economic and political climate, interest of the child etc. Whatever approach may be used, the ultimate aim should be to develop desirable attitude, abilities, behaviour and feelings in the child so as to make them a complete wholesome personality; because the future of the nation is in the hands of children of today who will be responsible citizens of tomorrow.

13

Teaching Techniques for Value Education

Sucheta

In this era of Scientific and Technological Advancement, the psychological, cultural and environmental changes are affecting all aspects of social and personal life. Even the field of education did not remain untouched from the impact of these changes. This has brought lack of harmony between the outer life of action and inner life of emotions, because of which man is facing a grave crisis of moral and social values. The reflection of the same can be felt in the alarming discontentment and frustration of people all over the world. The reason for all this can be seen in gradually slipping away of values from the realm of human conscience and the whole world is grappling with the monster of terrorism. On the other side, education, instead of helping the students to develop meaningful and purpose of life, has become merely an instrument of filling the mind with certain information regarding science, technology, materials, places, planets, etc. This does not serve the purpose of true education. In order to eliminate obscurantism, religious fanaticism, superstitions and dogmatism, education is an effective instrument in the hands of a nation to prepare its people to meet the challenges of time through development of attitudes, values and capabilities both of knowledge and skill. Education can never be complete unless it equips the individual for making the real challenges of life, prepare him for his responsibilities as adults and helps him in achieving full growth. Only education can imbue people with knowledge, the sense of purpose and the confidence essential for building a dynamic, vibrant and cohesive nation. The existing crisis of political, social and economic level has prompted the nation to think deeply on value education.

Different committees and commissions set-up at the international, nation level such as Radhakrishnan Commissions (1948), Kothari Commission (1966), International Commission on Education (1972 and 1996), National Policy on Education (1986, 1990) etc., also emphasized the same with a remark that curriculum be readjusted to make education in forceful tool for cultivation of human values. Teacher, being the pivot of the educational process can play a significant role in shaping the future of a nation by using various instructional approaches in the classroom situation for inculcating human values amongst the children of different age groups. For this, he needs to be given training in integration of values with the content while teaching, in using instructional methods for giving a clear concept of the concept and the values integrated therein, in encouraging the pupils to analyse different situations in terms of values they reflect and in passing on values to his students through his behaviour. Lewis (1985) studied the academic and socio-cultural influences on the development of values among students and found that teacher ranked highest as contributes to values. Even the popularity of the teacher amongst their students is related to their value patterns. Kaul (1972), Combs (1971), Pascarell (1982), Sheela (1987) conducted studies to show that effectiveness of teacher is directly linked with his perceptual organization, including his beliefs, values, understandings and concepts. These studies imply that the teacher community has emerged as the most influential factor in our educational system to imbibe the desired values in students. Therefore, every teacher, whatever be the subject he teaches, must be accepted by the children. He can fully change the life setting and life experience of students through a wide mix of pedagogic strategies. Teachers, by their conduct can make students to appreciate to right values and attitudes. The researchers employed various approaches for developing values amongst children belonging to various age groups.

Singh (1971) suggests the following teaching techniques to improve the process of teaching values to the students. The first requisite is to establish warm friendly and harmonious relationship between the teacher and the students in the classroom. Secondly values to be discussed should be related to the interests, needs and experience of the group. Thirdly, discussions can be held about the philosophical viewpoints.

1. *Lecture method:* Lecture method is a traditional method of teaching for values inculcation. In this method, great personalities, professionals and teachers deliver the lecture or talk on various value topics of social and moral importance. The lecture may be in a daily routine or at certain occasions. Through this method, teachers try to inculcate values simply in the form of information. In this way, they get the idea of what is good or bad in a particular situation or what values they should live by. So, this is a passive approach of value inculcation among students.
2. *Goldfish bowl method:* As is obvious from its nomenclature when a fish goes sick, it is taken out from the bowl and the treated one by one and put back. In the similar way, children are subjected to physical punishment or moral exhortation whenever value problem arises. The children may also be referred to child guidance clinics or educational psychologists or send to special school. But problem with this method is that process of curing the value system goes on without making any change in environment where the child becomes sick (devalued).
3. *Providing religious education:* This is another way of imbibing values through oral preaching among the children. The emphasis is given to impart religious ethos and morality. But this type of education has become outdated with the mergence of pluralistic society. The colleges and schools have students from various sections of society. Even though, there is no denying of the fact that teaching of religion helps in retaining values, still the doubt exists that this makes the students fanatic, short-sighted and less rational.
4. *Role playing:* Role playing is also a technique for the development of values among the students. Through this technique, children play different roles in various situation and they gain insight into values and feelings. Role playing requires students to take on and act out the roles of real or imaginary individuals in various situations. According to Shaftel (1967), it involves nine steps. These are: *(i)* warm up (teacher introduction and reading of story); *(ii)* selecting role-players; *(iii)* preparing the audience to observe; *(iv)* setting the stage; *(v)* the enactment; *(vi)* discussion and evaluation;

(vii) further enactments; *(viii)* further discussion; and *(ix)* generalizing. To engage students in role playing, the teacher or a student reads a story in which an individual is faced with a problem that is personally important and relevant to the concerns of students in the classroom. Although it is an effective technique, yet is limited in implementation.

5. *Providing moral ideology:* In this method, ideologies are put before the students. These may be form religious fundamentalism or social or political philosophy. This approach indoctrinates rather than educates.
6. *Teacher behaviour:* This method is based on the assumption that ideal teacher and ideal school are the most powerful instruments of creating values. They have great influence on the child and indeed constitute elements of value education. Here, value acquisition is regarded as by-product of the totality of education with the result that it gets submerged in that totality. This approach has two major problems—one is that it is away from emotions and the second is that it is away from rationality.
7. *Books and supplementary reading:* The reading material is essential for it inspires and also clarifies the definition and nature of values. But this knowledge is more theoretical and is not likely to bring about desired behavioural change.
8. *Activities:* Now-a-days, most emphasized aspect of teaching values is activities like simulation, cultural activities, productive manual work oriented activities, etc. It is presumed that these activities help in moulding the character and bringing about behavioural change.
9. *Providing assembly programmes:* Certain programmes like morning prayer, meditation, talks on moral themes, quotations for today, narration of anecdotes from the biographies of great personality, etc., are the programmes through which various values can be inculcated among children. But these programmes have religious outlook rather than scientific.
10. *Social science programmes:* Programmes like NCC, NSS, *Shramdan* and other social service programmes have immense importance for imbibing values among students.

But, these programmes have become the source of getting certificates for further benefit in the career rather than the true service.

All these methods appeal to emotions and not to reason. The rational outlook is essential for making the man open-minded, relative and provisional in nature, dispassionate, cool and tolerant in opinion. The point is that rationality does not give us values, rather attempts to regulate our valuation, our feelings give us the values but the reasoning helps us to achieve those values. Therefore, such a method of teaching value is required which is conducive to imbibe values in students.

Value Clarification Approach

Value clarification is a process that may be used in schools/colleges to help students learn to make choices from alternative opinions based on individual belief systems and consideration of the consequences of choosing particular options. It is an approach that tells a person what value should be or what values should live by. Raths, Harmin and Simon (1966) first explicated this process in their book, "Values and Teaching" in which they described seven sub-processes that lead toward value clarity. These sub-processes are: *(i)* choosing from alternatives; *(ii)* thoughtfully considering the consequences of alternatives; *(iii)* choosing freely; *(iv)* prizing and cherishing; *(v)* publicly affirming; *(vi)* acting repeatedly; *(vii)* acting with a pattern or consistency. These seven sub-processes were also described as 'criteria' for a value.

Krishcenbaum, 1973 goes further in expanding the concept of valuing. According to him, the use of the valuing process does not guarantee a good decision for individual or society, it merely increases the likelihood. This valuing process has five dimensions, each containing several sub-processes. These five dimensions are: *(i)* thinking, *(ii)* feeling, *(iii)* choosing, *(iv)* acting and *(v)* communicating. These five dimensions are not discrete psychological processes; an individual can be engaged in all of them or some of them at the same time. These strategies of teaching values appear to be more effective in value orientation of students than conventional method as their focus is on the valuing process itself. These approaches are analytical in nature and use behaviour modification technology. Other methods that are very useful for clarifying one's own values are: Jurisprudential Inquiry Method (JIM) and Social Inquiry Method (SIM).

Jurisprudential Inquiry Method (JIM) of Teaching

Jurisprudential Inquiry Method, originated by Oliver and Shaver, is especially useful in helping the students for rethinking their position on important legal, ethical and social and more values. The JIM helps the students to participate in the definition and redefinition of values.

The dictionary meaning of Jurisprudence is science or philosophy of law, or the knowledge and skill to deal with issues in legal fashion. According to Oliver and Shaver (1966), it means Jury process of resolving complex controversial issues as is held by a Supreme Court judge. As the judge first of all listens the case which is followed by evidences, then analysis the legal position taken by both the sides, weighs their position and evidences, assesses the meaning and provisions of law and finally makes the best possible decision. Similar type of role is played in the classroom by the teacher with the students to analyse the social problems and public policy issues. This model helps the students in understanding the complexity of the problem so that they can be able to make their positions to reflect that complexity. The main purpose of this method is to help students learn how to formulate defensible stances on public policy issues. In this way, the main goal of the JIM is for students to develop public policy stances and dialogue skills by using three types of competence that is:

(i) an understanding of the value's framework of Indian creed;

(ii) mastery of the intellectual skills of legal reasoning; and

(iii) knowledge of contemporary and public issues.

This method involves conception of values and productive dialogue as well as curriculum and pedagogical consideration. During the process of dialogue, students take a position and the teacher challenges the position with question. The teacher's questions are designed to push student's thinking about their stance and to help them learn. The teacher orients the class to the case and students identify the values in conflict. By taking a stand and defend a position, students usually become emotionally involved in the analysis, making the discussion intense and personal. With more practice, it is hoped that their positions will become more complex and well-formulated. The method, however, has to be looked into from the point of view of its assumptions and characteristics.

Assumptions

The basic assumptions underlying the jurisprudential inquiry method are:

(i) This method is based on a conception of society in which people differ in their views and priorities and in which social values legitimately conflict with one another.

(ii) In order to resolve complex, controversial issues within the context of a productive social order requires citizen who can talk to one another and successfully negotiate their differences.

(iii) The process of rational consent is one of the free and open climate through which differences on values are negotiated.

Characteristics

The main characteristics of this method are: *(i)* Socratic dialogue; *(ii)* Conflicting values are taken; *(iii)* the students have to identify one or more public policy in the taken case in order to synthesize a controversy or case in terms of decision for action or choice; *(iv)* in order to analyze the public policy issue, the students have to identify the legal ethical issue underlying the public policy issue; *(v)* balancing values; *(vi)* the teacher uses analogies as means of contradicting students general statement and *(vii)* particular pattern of argumentation for policy stance.

Social Inquiry Method (SIM)

Another teaching method advocated in the direction of inculcating values is social inquiry method. Social inquiry method, originated by Byron Massialas and Benjamin Cox (1966) is concerned with the improvement of society and solution of societal problems. In this method, social problems are analyzed through academic and logical reasoning. The primary purpose of this method is to teach students how to reflect on significant social and moral problems and define those problems through genuine inquiry. In this method, a problem concerned with local people is taken; hypothesis is framed and then facts are gathered to support the hypothesis. Later on, the desired values are put forward. In this way, students are sensitized about the problems of social domain and then various value conflicts are solved through inquiry.

Assumptions

The basic assumptions underlying the social inquiry method are:

(i) Social values are controversial. This method is based on a conception that social values in a society change from time to time. So, one is required to learn and to think objectively regarding the social and moral values, so that one can participate in the process of change known as social reconstruction.

(ii) Another assumption of this method is genuine inquiry and logical thinking to resolve the controversial issue and to solve the issue of interest.

Characteristics

The main characteristic of this method is genuine inquiry. According to Massials and Cox (1966), inquiry has meant a general position toward child-centred learning and has referred to building most facets of education around the natural inquiry of the child. This stance towards inquiry is generated from a philosophical belief that the promotion of a reflective and inquiring frame or reference will improve the quality of personal and social existence.

Another feature of this method is the reflective classroom for inquiry. Massialas and Cox have given three essential characteristics of reflective classroom.

Firstly, they stress that the social aspects of the classroom are especially important, and an open climate or discussion is required. According to them, "All points of view and statements are solicited and accepted as propositions that merit examination." Secondly, they emphasize on hypothesis as the focus of inquiry. This is another characteristic of reflective classroom. In this method, the discussion revolves around hypothetical solution of problem situations and the nature of hypotheses themselves. The third distinguish aspect of the reflective classroom is the use of fact as evidence. The classroom is recognized as a platform where scientific inquiry is engaged. In the classroom, the validity and reliability of facts are considered as well as testing of a hypothesis. It is the validation of the facts that is given the greatest consideration.

During the process of social inquiry method, teacher acts as the counsellor to inquiry. He/She helps the students to clarify their position, improve the process of study and work out their plans. Another characteristic of this method is that it lends itself well to building on the prescribed course of study and the mechanics of the traditional classroom.

In short, it can be said that social inquiry method is a very useful approach to reflect on social problems. In this method, students learn how to clarify their values through genuine inquiry. Inquiry is the main characteristic of this method. In this method, the teacher initiates the inquiry and sees that it moves from phase to phase. Students, depending on their inquiry abilities, take major responsibility for the inquiry itself, and even carry it through the phases if they are able. The norms of inquiry call for free and open discussion among a body of equals.

Conclusion

The main characteristic of these approaches are that these expose the students to social problems by putting various value patterns in conflict. The students are made to rationalize their stand based on value framework. Here, the basic idea is that the individuals decide about the action when they are engrossed in various conflicting situation. In brief, we can say, value clarification approaches can be of some help to change the behaviour pattern of students and can inculcate the human values amongst the students.

REFERENCES

Combs, A.W., "The personal approach to Good Teaching", In Hyman R.T. (Ed.) Contemporary Thought on Teaching. New Jersey: Prentice Hall, Inc. Eaglewood Cliffs, 256-267, 1971.

Kavl, L. ,"Factorial study of certain personality variables of popular teachers in secondary schools."

Krischen Baum, H. ,"Beyond Values Clarification", Upper Joy, New York: National Humanistic Education Centre, (1973).

Lewis, J.T. "Academic and Socio-cultural influences on Development of Values among Students in two year colleges", Dissertation Abstreets International, 46(3), 593-A, 1985.

Massialas, B. and Cox, B. *Inquiry in Social Studies,* New York: McGraw-Hill, 1966.

Oliver, D. and Shaver, J.P. *Teaching Issues in the High School Boston:* Houghton Mifflin Company: re-issued by State University Press, Logan, UT, 1974.

Passcarelli, J.T., "A Study of characteristics and behaviour of four British open Education Teachers" Dissertation Abstracts, 43(3), 775-A, 1982.

Raths, L.E., Merill, H. and Simon, S.B., "Values and Teaching Working with values in the classroom" Ohio, Merrill, 1966.

Sheela, "Change in Teacher Behaviour as a Function of inculcation of Values predicting Teacher's Effectiveness", Ph.D. (Edu) P.U. Chandigarh, 1987.

Shaftel, F and Shaftel G. "Role playing of Social Values: Decision-making in the social studies," Englewood Cliffs, N.J.: Prentice Hall Inc., 1967.

Singh, A. "Teaching of Values in Schools", Progress of Education 45(10-11), 380-384, 1971.

14

Education in Human Values: Need and Techniques

Kirandeep Singh

The Indian education system has changed from *gurukul* education to cyberspace education. The last two decades have witnessed a paradigm shift in the process of imparting and learning education. We are more and more being drifted towards westernized education leaving aside our rich traditional values and ethics. The values and ethics, which promoted qualities that make an individual socially effective and happy, inculcate friendliness, co-operativeness compassionate, self-disciplined, tolerant fearless, honest, truthful, dependable, courteous and having love for social justice.

Human Values: A Changing Perspective

Religious epics and religious institutions are often being misinterpreted and presented before today's youth for serving self-interests of certain individual. This is leading towards erosion of spiritual and moral values. Young people are becoming more and more self-oriented and self-centred instead of being cooperative and moderate.

Guru, the teacher (who has been supposed to be the incarnation of *Brahma, Vishnu* and *Mahesh*) in the past was held in high esteem by the society. But in modern times, teacher is losing his status. The growing menace of indiscipline is not only spreading its tentacles among students, but has plagued the teaching community as well. Both keep on blaming each other for the present day situation.

Modern education, which involves learning or teaching of social, physical, biological, engineering or medical sciences, has undoubtedly done a great job by providing comfort to our bodies, but our minds and souls are still starving.

Need of the Hour

The growing concern over the erosion of essential values and pervasive cynicism have brought to focus the need for readjustments in the curriculum in order to make education a forceful tool for the cultivation of social and moral values. We need the education of the whole man—physical, vital, mental, intellectual and spiritual aspects, which would be liberating and life giving true-education. In our culturally plural society, education should be able to foster universal and eternal values oriented towards the unity and integration of our people.

Different commissions and committees at national and international levels viz. Radhakrishnan Commission (1948), Kothari Commission (1966), International Commission on Education (1972 and 1996), National Policy on Education (1986, 1990) have also recognized the need for values in educational system. Values which are rooted into culture are committed to progress. These values interwoven with knowledge create wisdom.

Role of Teacher in Value Inculcation

The art of ensuring moral development in secular, multi-religious, and multiethnic society needs to be cultivated through committed teachers. Teachers have to play a vital role in imparting education in human values. In the NCTE document, "Curriculum Framework for Quality Teacher Education (1998)" also, one of the main competencies highlighted in the 'Teacher Profile' is inculcating a sense of value judgment, value commitment and value transmission. A teacher in the words of Dr. Shankar Dayal Sharma, should succeed in conveying the larger ideals of service to the community, virtues of tolerance and respect for all faiths, the importance of character, integrity and discipline and the value humanism to his pupils.

The teacher in the 21st century should remember that the students of today will shape the new tomorrow. On the values we inculcate in them today, will depend the future of our world. A world, where we move together to develop common ideals and purposes, loves each other and co-exists to create a co-operative commonwealth. For this the teacher should concentrate to:

- create a healthy-environment of national unity, integration and communal harmony;
- develop the qualities of character and strong leadership;
- incorporate views of great sons of the soil whose ideas and ideals have moved the world;
- ensure social quality and justice;
- create a conducive atmosphere for intellectual rigor and freedom of expression and thought;
- emphasis the development of moral and character values;
- promote scientific temper through the knowledge of scientific methods of enquiry and their use in solving problems;
- develop capability of appreciating and tolerating differences and diversities of various sorts and the capacity to choose between alternative value system;
- attempt at development of non-cognitive areas of learning with emphasis on regularity and punctuality, cleanliness, sense of duty and service, responsibility, equality, co-operation, truthfulness and national identify for personal and social growth of children;
- encourage sports and cultural activities, NSS, NCC and yogic mediation.

How to Communicate Values?

Teacher can make effective use of techniques such as speech-based techniques, activity-based techniques, dramatization techniques, simulation techniques and co-curricular techniques to communicate values to students.

Techniques of Communicating Values

Speech-based Techniques	*Activity-based Techniques*	*Dramatisation Techniques*	*Simulation Techniques*	*Co-curricular Techniques*
Think-Tank Session	Preparation of Scrap Books	Role Play	Games	Organisation of Talent Contests
Panel Discussion	Preparation of Collages	Skits		Organisation of Career Days

(Contd.)

Speech-based Techniques	*Activity-based Techniques*	*Dramatisation Techniques*	*Simulation Techniques*	*Co-curricular Techniques*
Debates	Project Work/ Library	Mime		Organisation of Career Days
Round-Table Conference	Research			
Seminars	Nature Walks			
Symposia	Work Experience Programmes			
Photo Language Sessions	Creative Writing			
Case Studies and Problem-Solving	Surveys, Interviews, Field Trips			
Cine forum Discussion				

However, while communicating values the teacher should:

- know the dreams and aspirations, the needs and desires, problems and struggles of the young;
- understand the students language;
- be open in your dealing with the students;
- prepare the session carefully;
- be flexible;
- create an atmosphere of warmth joy and freedom;
- be firm but have faith in the young.

Teachers can thus train and equip their students with the knowledge, skills and attitudes they need to encounter the future with courage and confidence in conflicting situation. To conclude, education in human values can be powerful instrument that can eliminate obscurantism, religious fanaticism, violence, superstition and fatalism, foster harmony, peace and co-existence resulting in the blossoming of human excellence.

REFERENCES

1. Charles, E.N., 1999, *Value education—A Mannual for Teachers*. St. Xavier's Institute of Education Society, Mumbai.
2. MHRD, Department of Education, Government of India, 1986. National Policy on Education, New Delhi.
3. NCERT, 2000, *National Curriculum Framework for School Education—A Discussion Document*, New Delhi.
4. NCTE, 1998, *Curriculum Framework of Quality Teacher Education*, New Delhi.

UNESCO, 1996, *Learning: The Treasure Within*.

15

Education in Human Values: Some Techniques

S. Abdul Kareem

The Scenario

The society that rates market value, use value, esteem value, cost value and exchange value allows human values to go down the drain; hence the perpetual cry; erosion of human values. Society cannot hold them in its folds. They fall apart. Rare as are these attributes that set off human beings from the animal species, values have a tendency to slip through man's fingers and his humanity stands questioned. In the animal work, the tiger is ever sure of being a tiger, a fish of ever being a fish, but civilized man is never sure of being a human being. If the salt loseth its savour, where with it, then, shall be salted?

We gave unto ourselves a Constitution with a secular slant and banished the gods of our idolatry. Moral education remained a programme on paper; it never touched the outer fringes of our existence. In this mundane world, everything is weighed, measured but values get devalued and thus suffer gross neglect. Ultimately, values and mankind become aliens who have never met. Hence, the need to salvage them from the debris of civilization that crumbles into ruins as years roll by. With the last vestiges of respectability having given up their ghosts, the new generation id fed on the sop of sophistication. The glossy veneer covers up the many cracks within. Hence in men there is more of apes than of the glassy essence. Men with transparent values are hard to come by.

Nurseries of Values

Erosion of values, as of soil, makes the components crumble when the capacity to hold them together disappears. Naturally cohesion fails. As families grew in size, the nice bonds that once held them together came to be snapped. The values of mutuality of interest, inter-dependence and tolerance that the families in the past generated gave place to self-centredness, mistrust and impatience. The family as a living unit came to be splintered and became secluded owing to conditions of existence and survival. Thus, the family no longer remained the nursery of values.

Schools and colleges got crowded. The shift system could hardly manage the growing numbers, with classes swelling every year, as it were bursting at the seams. The loss of personal touch discredited the sacred ties of the master and disciple as of yore. The heavy syllabus made short work of moral education and those periods meant for ethics came to be usurped by mathematics. Citizenship to students outside the political science stream became a mumbo jumbo mouthed glibly but practiced hardly. With the blissful ignorance of the core contents of justice, liberty, equality and fraternity, we the people made ourselves sovereign. The drift led to disintegration.

Campus and Society Nexus

Students in their teenage are as exposed to the campus culture as they are to the societal mores. It has been virtually impossible to undo the damage done to our students in the urban conglomerations. Dr. Alexander Meiklejohan state in his work, *The Experimental College*: "The closeness of connection between the character of a society and the character of its education cannot be strongly stressed. Schools and colleges are not something apart from the social order to which they belong. They are in that order, trying to prepare its youth for participation in its own activities. And a society can only teach the hopes, the knowledge, the values, the beliefs which it has."

As a result the ways of the world and the practices prevalent in society do impinge on the consciousness of students. A society that rare on a sound value system and is saturated with sharp practices on a large scale, presents a conflicting arena for an idealist steeped in values. Ultimately what gets an upper hand is what works in the societal pattern obviating the design drawn on the young minds by an impressionable system of values.

Peace and tranquility are at best ideals hardly seen in our times. Everywhere there is the tumult and uncertainty. Man is beside himself and as such, he is incapable of drawing upon the resources of mind, withdrawing into himself or taking his stand inside himself, attending to his inwardness far from the exterior of this tumultuous world. Such a withdrawal is conducive to the formation of ideas, which bid fair to become ideals with the strength of conviction and character. With the innerself thus strengthened, man will not allow himself to be dominated by things but govern them himself imposing his will and design on them. Thus man can realize his ideas in this world harmonize it and impregnate it with ideals. Such a conception of man fortified with a system of values is analogous to that of Shakespeare when he created Ariel, the spirit of ideas at whose bidding even the winds would blow.

Strategic Withdrawal

It took thousands of years of man to achieve this inward concentration by withdrawing into himself, which is an indispensable condition of learning. Over the millennia, through cultivation and culture, man has been continually creating thought little by little. Being a volatile acquisition, there is the danger of man losing this gift of conceiving ideas and formulating thoughts. The destiny of man depends upon his retaining and maintaining that consciousness and concentration. It is not that man lives only to think but thinks so as to make his life purposeful by basing it in ideas and thoughts. Aristotle had said that Gods do nothing but think. By such a proposition, the Greeks projected that man's greatness lay in exercising his intellect and taking his stand within himself. Thus when such a reflective consciousness became man's forte, we had ages of reasons, enlightenment and culture.

If some had sought to isolate contemplation from action, others tended to reject contemplation completely and deify pure action. Bereft of ideas, man is likely to show the tendency to slip back into animality. Human life looses value when the figure of a pure human of action rises above the horizon. Without a strategic retreat into the self, we are likely to repeat the mistakes of the past. Founders of religion found enlightenment with such retreats, as did Buddha by withdrawing to the forest, Mohammad to his tent and cave, and Jesus to the desert. The moment mankind ceases to live by ideas it feels lost and demoralized.

Not all are capable of the reflective consciousness. Those who can turn ideas over days and nights are few and far between. While men in a group only feel, it is only an individual who can think positively and constructively. Creative individuals can provide the fertile ground for ideas and ideals to germinate. They can create new values for society, set up new moral standards to which life of community should endeavour to confirm. A man's value to the community depends upon how far his feelings, thoughts and actions are directed towards promoting the good of his fellows.

Attitudinal Change

Ideas and ideals are not enough. For the instruction of system of values, change in attitudes is desirable. It should begin with a change in our system of beliefs. With the impetus set in motion by the acquisition of knowledge and experience, our emotions provide motivational drives. When the predisposition of the human mind becomes more pronounced and inclination inevitable, it leads to attitude formation. More than anything, attitudes have an inherent sense of direction and bid fair to flow in positive channels, grow, blossom and bear fruit. To the fund of ideas and ideals, positive and constructive attitudes impart dynamism with a sense of right direction. It is the alchemy of right attitudes that transforms ideas into ideals, as they emerge pure and chaste, tested and tried in the ordeals of life. Karl Marx was well aware of the potency of ideas and ideals when he said: "No army in the world is as powerful as an idea whose time has come."

A Strategy Oblique

It is too much to think of reforming the youth in the process of informing their minds. Programmers of preaching more often generate a resistance, if not a reaction. Brainstorming as a strategy has an effect, which is short-lived. Idea stimulators may be part of the principles of applied imagination and creative techniques. Far from these direct approaches, which may not be rewarding, an oblique strategy may hold out a promise when the direct has not made any dent in the defenses of the people. The human psyche operates below the level of consciousness. The unconscious had all along being considered the repository of evil. It is interesting to discover what exists in the psyche outside of consciousness. Sigmund Freud had subjected such light on the dark and dirty psychic hinterland. Drops that fall directly do spatter, but those that descend obliquely bid fair to stay and sink into human consciousness. When man's conscious life has lost a system of values, there are compensations in the unconscious. Such is the psychic law.

The unconscious had a hold; it was believed, only on the sick. Even the healthy seem to be a fascinated by it. Dark as are those forces of human nature, Light is bound to emerge from this area of darkness. The stagnant pond may have dirt and filth but over night beautiful flowers may open as do lotuses. The unconscious is the veritable repository of true values. The psychic depths are, according to Carl Jung, nature and nature is creative life. Buck Rodgers in his recent book, *Getting the best out of self and others* (Harper and Row, New York 1987, p. 22) narrates an experiment conducted by an Australian psychiatrist who contracted three professional prostitutes to come to his apartment. When they showed up, he paid them their fee and told them to disrobe. Without any hesitation, the three women started undressing. He stopped them, told them to put on their clothes and informed them of his plan to hypnotize. He hypnotized them and trance was soon achieved. In that condition they carried out his orders most implicitly when he asked them to hop like kangaroos and stand on leg without moving a muscle. Then he, in that altered state of consciousness asked them to disrobe. Lo! They wouldn't do it. The psychiatrist concluded that people will not do anything under hypnosis that offends their true values.

To tap the potential of the unconscious and make it obey the orders of the conscious. Mind demands a discipline as strenuous as any. It is a heroic venture of salvaging wealth from the mental hinterland, as do pearls from the seabed. One can come to the pristine experience by exploring the realm of the unconscious as did Buddha sweeping aside his two million gods. The inculcation of values and their articulation sets guidelines for man's behaviours. Sometimes there may be a conflict between a value system and man's behaviour. One can identify areas of conflict by writing down on a sheet of paper one's values, ideals and beliefs. The next day the same man may record the way he spends his time and energy. By comparing the two lists, one can identify where the values are at variance with our behaviour.

'As man thinketh, so he is'. What we think, believe and feel affect the quality of life, which, in turn, influences our level of performance. The Education Commission had earlier stressed that "a search for the knowledge of self, of the meaning of life, of the relationship of man to other human beings and to the ultimate reality" must inform all our educational endeavours. The same view stands reflected and reiterated in the New Education Policy 1986. England had introduced religious education in schools by the Education Act of 1944. Since religion became the main basis of the great divide in the subcontinent, our Constitution framers distrusted its potential in a plural society like ours. While the lives and teachings of the religious reformers are included in the syllabus at the school level, it is imperative that comparative religion should find a place at higher level.

Human Values through Sciences

The projection of human values through appropriate life situations comes home to the students of literature with a grater degree of impact. Even the teaching of science organized imaginatively, can lay bare the broad spectrum of values to be cherished. The world of science, of our universe with planets in their respective orbits, does more than establish that it is a cosmos we live in and not chaos. The well marked regularity and precision can, at no count, be missed. In the plant world, the interdependence between the root system and the shoot system—the roots harbouring the bacterial nodules for fixing the subsoil nitrogen and the shoots providing the sap and succour for the bacteria—more than illustrates the principle of symbiosis, of mutuality of help prevalent in nature. The science of ecology lays bare nature's scheme of maintaining purity of our environment, of ensuring harmony between our flora and fauna, which man is seeking to disrupt in his haste to make the fast buck. The mysteries and perplexities of nature hold out an untapped potential of value system for man to profit by.

Foundation Lectures and Seminars

Despite the packed academic schedule, universities do cater to the felt need of organizing foundation lectures, at least six or eight in an academic year as is done in Karnataka University, Dharwad. On the same lines, science weeks and Jathas do create and sustain a refreshing awareness of the science potential of the country that gave to the world a prodigy like Shri Ramanujam and a genius like Sir C.V. Raman. Even religious functions could provide food for the minds shorn of rituals and ceremonies confined to the homes. The third component of our educational ventures namely extension, besides teaching and research, could throw a vast net to catch the rich treasures of our rare heritage. Such occasions impart vibrancy to the ideals of integration and harmony which hold out fair prospects of coming home to our business and bosoms so naturally.

The Directorate of Collegiate Education in Karnataka organized oneday regional seminars at Bangalore, Gulbarga, Dharwad, Mangalore and Devangere with the theme of human values in education. The participants in these seminars were the Principals and representatives teachers. Sometime 2, sometime even 5 from each Institution who were exposed to the thinking of practicing teachers from other regions thereby achieving integration through mobility thoughtfully mooted in the New Education Policy. Circular instructions were issued to follow these up with colloquia at the collegiate level.

Teacher's Role

More often we are driven to god men and saints to establish efficacy of values in modern times. This tendency generates in its wake a feeling that one need be a saint to have values, sinners as we are in this world, more sinned against than sinning. Since the exposure of these enlightened men to the youth is minimal, with their life more confined to isolation, it is necessary that men of wisdom and culture exemplify the values, as it were, by externalizing what is below the level of consciousness. Values must speak out, loud and bold through one's behaviour and conduct. Teachers as a community do provide a maximum exposure to the student community. Their attitudes and ideals impinge upon the nascent minds unmistakably. A teacher can radiate values as much through what he says as through what he is.

16

Inculcation of Values: The Crucial Role of Teachers

Kulwant Singh Pathania

Deterioration of values is a worldwide phenomenon in the present context. Despite its several thousand years old value-based cultural tradition, India is also subject to massive erosion of values. That is why political and economic corruption, scandals, scams, anti-social and anti-national activities are on the rise in the present national scenario. The rapid degradation of values in the Indian context has posed a heavy challenge before higher education. The Upanishads taught us the ideal of *Vasudhaiv Kutumbakam*—that is, the entire world is my family. Yet today we fight among ourselves in the name of religion, region, language or caste. The mosques, the temples or other religious structures are sought to be made more significant than the grinding poverty of Indian people, abysmal standards of nutrition, social injustice, etc. Jain and Patanjali taught us the ideal of *Aparigraha* (non-hoarding) but we use our power and authority for hoarding wealth by exploiting our helpless fellow-men. We advocate rationality as a guiding principle to be followed in private and public life but in our inner psyche we are still guided by blind rituals, superstitions, orthodoxy and egotism.

As noted educationist Kireet Joshi remarks: "Humanity today stands at a critical juncture. Hope and despair, pride and pessimism, comforts and confusion fill human hearts in unequal and unstable measure. Whereas the peaks of material progress scaled by some countries enthrall humanity as a whole, the depths of social degeneration in most part of the world make thinking people wonder if mankind can receive the light of recovery at all."

It is a recognized fact that modern education and training has failed to produce men and leaders of character and integrity who can make India attain its past glory. Not only in India, but also worldwide, there is a cry for "back to basic values." To help to produce enlightened citizens, different programmes on value education-human resource development, self-development, leadership and personality development—for students, teachers, executives based on time-tested Indian wisdom have been organised. The purpose of value education programmes will therefore be to help people become aware of their innate divinity and how to make its perfection and happiness manifest in every movement of life. Vivekananda had stressed the need for man-making, character-building education, whereby the beneficiary would be made a good citizen. He or she would be able to rise above all distinction and differences and would possess the spirit of *Tyaga* (sacrifice) and *Seva* (service).

In the era of LPG, the education system has ignored instructions in morals. It depends upon western education system which deals more with concepts and conjectures. Education is only on material or objective field of knowledge. Education is soaked in textual scholarships forgetting the values. The age old culture is ignored and materialism is prevailing in the society. Ramakrishnana Paramahansa has also laid great stress on real education with a view to making oneself as well as the entire world happy. His teachings envisage an education which teaches you the following:

How to live life well;
How to find happiness;
How to make others happy;
How to manage all kinds of people and happenings as well; and
How to grow and succeed in the right manner.

Value education is about nurturing the human spirit, exploring human freedom and realizing that education is never really complete. In the act of exercising our freedom, we do so in such a way as to make a difference in our world. Education without goodness, that its, without ethics is arrogant and dangerous. Unethical behaviour thrives in darkness, and can only exist when 'ethical' leaders remain silent. If we, who are in the business of educating the young, want to measure and assess our efforts we need to look at how our institutions nurture human freedom in the service of humanity.

Value is what an individual desires, likes or prefers. According to Milton Rokeach, "A value is an enduring belief that a specific mode of conduct or end state of existence is personally or socially preferable to an opposite or converse mode of conduct or end state of existence. A value system is an enduring organization of beliefs concerning preferable modes of conduct along with a continuum of relative importance."

Values can be classified in different ways under different categories. For example, they can be either intrinsic or instrumental, depending on whether they are desires for their own sake or are meant to be means to achieve something. Values like truthfulness, happiness, bliss and peace are intrinsic while desire for money and power is an instrumental value. Values can also be classified as moral and aesthetic. Moral values deal with perceptions of right and wrong while aesthetic values reflect beauty and ugliness. Values can again be classified as positive or negative depending on the ones a person wants and those he would like to avoid. They could also be considered as higher or lower. Higher values are intellectual, aesthetic, moral and spiritual while lower values are for material or physical gains.

Some advocate that values are subjective and relative to situation, place and time and their interpretations need to be changed or modified with variations in the socio-economic environment. There are, however, certain basic values which reflect morality and are eternal. Truth, goodness and beauty are eternal values, not created by man and are independent of his desires. Loyalty to one's country is a self-justified value. In the ultimate analysis, values to be cherished, nourished and promoted must be those which are a source of greatest good to the greatest number of people.

Values can also be grouped as theoretical, economic, aesthetic, social, political and religious. Theoretical value means having dominant interest in the discovery of truth and is empirical, critical, rational and intellectual in approach. Economical value means that an object commands a money price. People value money or material things not for their own sake but for the pleasure and enjoyment that they provide. Economic values are instrumental rather than intrinsic;

they are values of commodities in exchange and arise out of production and use of material goods.

Aesthetic values refer to the experience that a person has when he perceives an object as beautiful or conversely, ugly. One realizes an aesthetic value when one perceives an object as a unified expression of meaningful feelings. The aesthetic experience is a special kind of experience and is an interaction between an object and a subject. The subject that is the person contributes sense organs and also depends on his past experiences for appreciation or dislike of objects. One gets social values from friendship, love, family and participation in good activities. Political values represent interest in political matters and/or having alliance with a particular political party. Lastly, if a person considers an object divine, it is said to have a religious value and its experience is called religious experience which may be spiritual or divine.

After independence, a number of Committees and Commissions were constituted. They underline the importance of value education. In 1938, Mahatma Gandhi set up a committee on "Basic National Education" under the late Dr. Zakir Husain also emphasized the need for changing the system of education in India. In 1944, the Sargent Committee observed that without an ethical basis, any curricula would be barren. In 1945, Religious Education Committee of the Central Advisory Board of Education recommended that spiritual and moral teachings which are common to all religions, must be an integral part of curriculum. The University Education Commission, also known as the Radhakrishnan Commission (1948-49) stressed the need to incorporate spiritual training in the curriculum of educational institutions. The Mudaliar Commission (1952-53) also observed that growth of character of students would depend, to a very large extent, on religious and moral instruction. The well-documented and oft-quoted report entitled "Education and National Development" of the Education Commission, (1964-66) also known as Kothari Committee, listed many areas requiring immediate action—these included stress on moral education and inculcation of a sense of social responsibility in students. National Policy on Education (1986) stated that "Education in India stands at crossroads today", that "neither normal linear expansion nor the existing pace and nature of improvement can meet the needs of students", and that "Education has an acculturating role and it refines sensitivities that contribute to national cohesion, a scientific temper and independence of mind and spirit." It also recommended "conscious internalization of a healthy work ethos and of values of humane and composite culture." The Ramamurthy Committee (1990) also observed that education must nurture a set of values like love and compassion, build up a new social order based on truth and non-violence and prepare the ground for integration between science (truth), spirituality (unity of life) and democracy (non-violence) which is the link between the two. It may be gathered from the preceding discussion that the five basic human values which have been emphasized again and again are: truth, righteousness, peace, love and non-violence.

Why Value Education?

The overall crisis of values in the society at large has left a negative impact upon the mindset of the student community as well. The youngsters have fallen in the clasp of eroding values such as dishonesty, insincerity, lack of punctuality, disrespect for elders, disregard for work-culture and entrepreneurial activities resulting in gun-culture, greed for earning money and wealth by easy and foul means, lack of patience resulting in student unrest, absence of the value of true leadership, loss of compassion, lack of concern for the rural background from which they come, absence of sensitivity towards women as reflected in a plethora of rape cases involving women of all ages, and so on. Today's students are the citizens and nation-builders of tomorrow and the values they cherish or their transgression will certainly affect the nation, either positively or negatively. It is only the value oriented education that can minimize such problems by bringing about a change in the nature, vision, thought, character and conduct of students, individuals, politicians, administrators, executives and ultimately, the society, the nation and the world.

Crucial Role of Teachers—An Empirical Study

Teachers have crucial role in the development of fundamental human values in the students. The NCERT in its publication, Documents on Social, Moral, and Spiritual Values in Education 1979 had identified 84 instrumental values, attitudes, behaviour patterns, habits and sub-values. A Core Group if Planning Commission (1992) endorsed the regrouping these 84 sub-values into five basic Core

Universal human values like truth, right conduct, peace, love and non-violence. These five values form the subject-matter of integral education model of Sri Sathya Sai Baba, the Chancellor, Sri Sathya Sai Institute of Higher Learning. Schematic presentation of these is given as under.

Schematic Presentation of Core Values and Sub-values

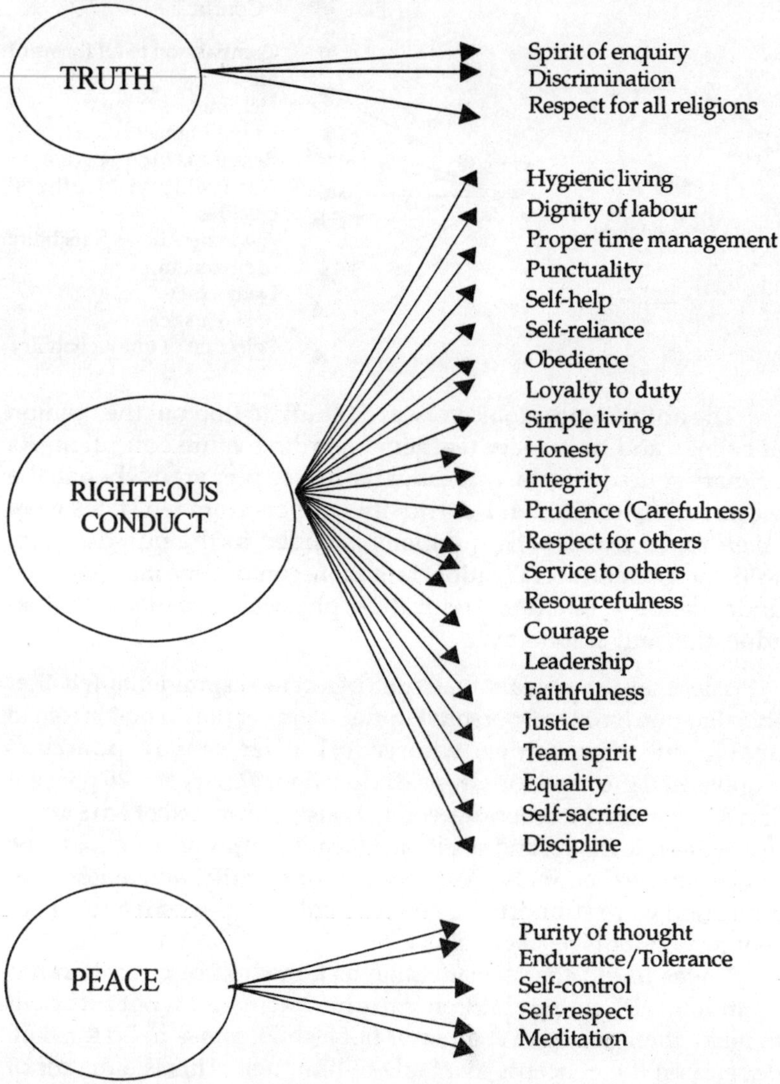

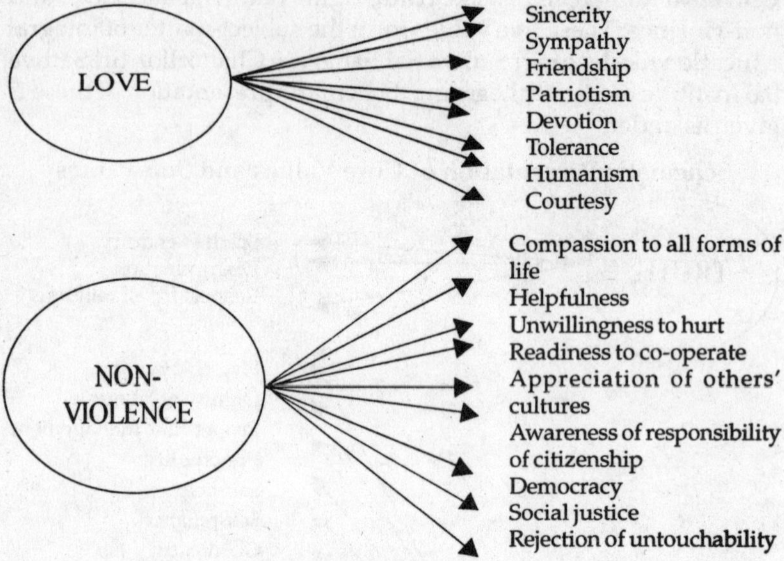

The author undertook a research study to find out the opinion of college and university teachers regarding value education. As primary source of data, a questionnaire was prepared wherein the views of fifty college and university teachers from ten states were taken for analysis. The questions included in the questionnaire were focussed on socialization, imitation, conformity, interpersonal understanding, emotional education, physical education, spiritual education and autonomy.

The analysis reveals that cent per cent respondents felt that socialization and interpersonal understanding play a major role in development of values, whereas 91.3 per cent respondents emphasized the need for physical education. 87 per cent, 85 per cent and 82.6 per cent teachers agreed to holistic approach of education, teacher as role model and spiritual education as foundation for value education respectively. Autonomy, conformity and emotional education were supported by 69 per cent, 65.2 per cent and 65 per cent respondents respectively.

It was found that socialization as a method of education has limitations. Plunging children into group activities is not sufficient to make them moral. Whether or not a child comes to do this will depend on the concepts available to him/her. This is a matter of cognitive learning, not simply getting the child to engage in group activities. For there is no reason why the child engaging in group activities should not see fellow group members as deadly rivals or despised 'non-starters'. Good teachers, of course, know this and intervene in group activities, encouraging the child to see his/her fellows in a certain way.

Again, without morality autonomy is also of no value. Great criminals, for instance are markedly autonomous men. The rise of autonomy to prominence in education certainly does not mark the eclipse of such other values as those of morality and truth.

If the proponents of socialization have a tendency to overstress consideration of the interests of others, autonomists tend to give undue weight to individualistic principles expressed in such notions as self-realization. In fact, neither can be made the stuff of basic morality and insisted on; both should be exhibited to pupils as possible ideals. Paul Gauguin must find his place alongside Gandhi; Wagner his, alongside Florence Nightingale; and those, in some ways more educative figures personally torn by both ideals, like Tolstoy and Goethe, must find a place too.

It was also observed that development of values is best stimulated when problems and challenges are presented before the student in a way in which the learner is gradually brought to see things for himself. Liberal education can in fact develop in the students the abilities to make relevant value judgments. This implies the ability of a student to bring the whole range of ideas upon the area of experience. It is the art of effectively relating theory to practice, of abstractions to facts; of thought to action. Liberal education also develops the ability to discriminate among values. This includes the distinction of various kinds of values and their relative importance, an awareness of the values of character like fair play and self-control, intellectual values like love of truth, aesthetic values like good taste, etc.

Pathways for the Teachers

1. Study the course content to find what it contains that is applicable to other subjects and outside the academic life too. For instance, while teaching Einstein's theory of Relativity, a science teacher can extend the concept to other subjects too. He may show that even values may be different

pertaining to different cultures, different societies, different times and situations.

2. Select instructional materials which are best suited to the job of making relationship apparent. For example, while teaching Romantic poetry, the teacher can create awareness about values relating to conservation of environment like love for Nature, bio-diversity, compassion for all animate and inanimate things, prevention of excessive use of natural resources, etc.

3. Use appropriate method of teaching (i.e., problem-solving, discussion, leading question, etc.) which will facilitate active learning of values like leadership, co-operation, group-harmony, mutual respect and so on.

4. Provide room for practice. It is not enough to point out relationship. Pupils should be given practice in finding relationships of their own. Values like punctuality and discipline, sympathy and tolerance, democratic rights and responsibilities may be taught in applied situations. There are many programmes that can be organised in educational institutions involving students as individual in groups or teams or on the sports field. It can be in the classroom or it can be in the hostel life, prayer or assembly hall, or meditation, community work, village extension work, celebration of natural, religious and social festivals—these are quite a few illustrative programmes that can, if planned and executed properly, help in the development of values.

5. Sound steps need to be devised by the Department of Education both at the centre and in the states to stop political interference in educational institutions. A rational transfer policy must be framed. It is, in fact, difficult to see how one trusts the teacher to foster values when his own strings are pulled by others.

6. Stories of great persons and values they cherished always have a salutary effect on the minds of young people. In this context, the following extract from a poem by H.W. Longfellow is relevant:

   "Lives of great men all remind us,
   we can make our lives sublime,

and departing, leave behind us,
foot-prints on the sands of time.
Foot-prints that perhaps another,
Sailing over life's solemn main,
Forlorn and ship-wrecked."

While commenting upon great persons, the important thing to bear in mind is to impress upon students the qualities of head and heart that made them as great as they were. It was not cnly intellect or intelligence but other virtues and qualities pursued with three P's, patience, perseverance and practice that made them great.

17

Value Development Among Students: Vital Role of Teachers

P. L. Gupta

"The actions of man are the best interpreter of his thoughts."

—Locks

Education is a "man-making" process, said Swami Vivekananda. It is, in fact, a multidimensional process with the specific purpose of achieving maximum self-realization for the person and of the optimal benefit of the society. When a person is educated, he/she is enabled to develop the cognitive, affective and psychomotor skills in accordance with the inherent capability of the individual. The main aim of education is to shape the character of the students as the best citizens of the nation, as well as to make them persons of high morality and highly spiritual individuals. All these qualities are related with character of an individual. These qualities are reflected through the behaviour of a person, but a continuous deterioration and decline in values can be observed in our youth and people of the country. The existing education system seems to be a failure in shaping the character of the youth. Values are the pillars of meaningful life and education is the tool which can bring a change.

One of the challenges before a modern teacher is how to make value education effective and interesting to the modern youth. The present-day youth with all its potential and goodwill to learn seem to concentrate on all other academic subjects except value education. This poses a challenge to all concerned with the all round development of the pupil through education.

Values: The Guiding Force in Life

Every aspect of our life has value. In fact, values permeate the whole of human existence and are a major factor in deciding what sort of human beings we are. Everyone of us has needs, urges and aspirations. Anything that satisfies the urges and helps us in realizing the aspirations has value.

An individual also internalizes values through the process of socialization. Values figure at the core of one's life and form the spring of human endeavours and actions. As such they are significant and fundamental dimensions of human life and indicate how one adheres, attaches and reacts in life situations or circumstances. Values also are the blueprints or action plans, which orient and decide the thinking, actions, feelings and behaviour itself. Value is a "conception explicit or implicit, distinctive of an individual or characteristic of a group of those desirable traits which influence the selection from available modes and ends of action." (Wuchohn, 1957). Rokeach (1973) defined values as an "enduring belief, a specific mode of conduct or end state existence along a continuum of relative importance." Therefore, values are the criteria for determining levels of goodness, worth or beauty. A widely accepted concept of value in traditional philosophy is, "Truth, Goodness, Beauty" or *Satyam, Shivam* and *Sundaram.*

Existing Environment and Need of Value System

Education is a powerful instrument of social change and human progress. It is also a powerful tool to cultivate moral and spiritual values in an individual. It has been said that *Vidya datati vinayam* but it has not been practiced in its entirety in the schools. Inspite of the ever-growing wonders of science and technology, we are living in a turbulent and worried world under the dark shadow of war and annihilation. Our growing progress in controlling our material world has not been matched by similar advance in human character and virtues. Many of the philosophers and educationists feel that human-values are disappearing in all walks of life, both public and personal. We may cite the following evidence of this disappearance:

1. Persistence of casteism and discrimination of various types in public and private institutions.
2. A decline in the strength and integrity of the family and alarming increase in separation, divorce and conflicts.

3. A decline in respect for parents, teachers and other civil and legal authorities.
4. Increase in the aggressive and destructive behaviour in the family, school, streets, playfield and entertainment centres.
5. Complete lack of purpose and direction pervading in today's youth resulting in unsatisfactory academic performance and other social evils.
6. An increasing destruction of animal and plant life and the population of our environment.
7. A growing desire for sense objects leading to exploitation of one section of society by another.

Today neither students nor teachers understand the true meaning of education. Education should foster morality, righteousness and character. It should fill the hearts of man with compassion. Then alone it acquires fullness. Education is not for living, it is for life. Students today turn a blind eye to the very basis of life. This leads to the loss of self-confidence causing many agitations and upheavals that man witnesses today. While making a frantic scramble for living, man today fails to realize the very meaning of life. Character is the very basis of life of man. Indian culture has always emphasized the need for cultivating and fostering character. But the students today pay no head to the excellence of Indian culture and allow themselves to be swayed by the superficial secular learning.

Education has become mechanical. It caters to mere intellectual development without catering to the blossoming of the human heart. The modern system of education makes man hard hearted and destroys the qualities of compassion and love in him. Once when Gandhiji was sitting gloomily, a foreigner came to him and asked, "Gandhiji, may I know what is the cause of your gloom." Gandhiji replied, "The education imparted today turns man into a hard-hearted person instead of instilling the qualities of love and compassion. The educated young men of today are totally devoid of sweetness and compassion."

The welfare and well being of the world today hinges on the education we impart. Education, which is the very breath of an individual, is very sadly neglected.

To correct the above imbalance and to renew individual commitment to an active value-based life, many distinguished thinkers like Mahatma Gandhi, Rabindra Nath Tagore, Vivekananda, Sri Aurobindo have made a plea for integrating human values in education. Values such as love, co-operation, trust, acceptance, joy, dignity, respect for individual differences, compromise, truth, understanding and reverence must be taught because they are key to the survival of man. Teaching human values is teaching survival skills.

India is known for its rich cultural and spiritual heritage, and the need for a value system through education, has been felt and recognized through the centuries. Various education commissions in the past have emphasized the need for value education.

The National Policy on Education NPE of 1986 and Programme of Action (1992) has very strongly recommended the need for value education due to the following reasons. Tremendous advance in Science and Technology has resulted into a complete change in the lifestyle of people. Science and Technology is being used to produce weapons of mass destruction endangering the very existence of the human race instead of using it for the betterment of human life.

Life in the future is going to be faster and more complex. The students of today have to face such moral situations in future in which instead of depending on others, they may be required to take their own decisions. The present youth has special problems. It has begun to question the conduct of elders especially leaders. They do not see the relevance of the values preached.

A glance at our educational system will reveal to us how far our educational institutions have been successful in making value education an integral part of education in the vast majority of our schools. Though attempts are being made towards it, the methods of value education are largely such that encourage memorization, moralizing and role learning rather than responsible personal decision-making. Main strategies for imparting value education could be child centered, teacher centered and experimental learning strategies.

The need for value education has been emphasized time and again. The question now is, "How do we go about helping our youth in value development through the process of value education?" Teaching values through moralizing and advising seems to be ineffective today, narrating stories has its charm only for the moment without any attitudinal change. The parents offer one set of values; schools project a different set of values, religion proposes yet another set of moralization. The modern communication media offers in very attractive ways all sorts of stimuli and inputs about what to believe, how to behave, what models to follow, what type of life-style to follow etc. The peer group influence, ideologies of the political leaders, film stars, and sports figures, each adding to the confusion to a confused mind, pose a dilemma to the young today.

In a world of confusion and conflict, we ourselves do not know where we are going? And where we are leading our pupils? We have to help our students to develop their own value system. This necessitates on the part of the teachers to use various strategies that facilitate the process of value development and value clarification.

Can Values be Taught?

Mazumdar (1983) said, "Values cannot be taught through formal and direct teaching. They can be inculcated only when the institutions provide activity for it and experiences inside and outside the school that promotes responsibility, co-operation, honesty, fair play and self-control. Education for values has to be based on the ideas of supremacy of reasoning over anything else and not only unintelligent conformity."

For inculcating values many experts in the field suggested different ideas, some of them are cited here:

- Provision of value-based education.
- Designing value-based curriculum.
- Designing special orientation programme for teachers.
- Values-based foundation courses.
- Publication of literature based on values.
- Necessity to develop code of conduct for teachers and students.
- Inculcation of philosophical view towards life among teachers and students.

- Infusion of values in the teaching of subjects.

However, values cannot be taught but caught. There are various difficulties we face in developing the human values among students. It is due to the nature of human values. The following points are to be kept in mind while inculcating the human values among the students.

1. Our first difficulty is about the very conception of moral education, for moral education is often misconceived by most of us. The first misconception ensues when we happen to relate moral education with religious education, while the fact remains that the two are distinct and separate without any essential linkage. And if there is any linkage it is only contingent.
2. Our second problem is in regard to content and form of morality. Moral behaviour has in fact both a 'form' and a 'concept'. Our mistake in defining the moral worth of an action has been that we take cognizance of the content (such as speaking the truth, helping others, not killing, non-stealing, etc.) and not its form (the reason that led to the particular action). We mistakenly think that morality is a set of principles or virtues to be instilled in the child's mind by processes of reinforcement (reward and punishment). We take them as 'bag of virtues' to be followed unconditionally in all situations. But experience and analysis also show that there are no principles or virtues, which can be unconditionally followed always.
3. The third difficulty is about the way the content of morality is to be taught. There is enough empirical evidence to show that all attempts at direct moral teaching resulted in failure in regard to development of moral behaviour. Moral traits like honesty, truthfulness and consideration for others etc., cannot be effectively inculcated by direct instructions.
4. Then there are difficulties about treating moral education as a separate and distinct subject in the curriculum.
5. There are further problems that could arise in regard to the teachers teaching moral values.
6. There are also considerations about educating the teachers

in moral education before the same can be introduced in our schools.

Value—A Matter of Affective Domain

Actually the value education is related to the affective domain of the education. E. Lyall has very rightly said "Morale or character is not ready made but it is created bit by bit and day by day." Therefore, it is not sufficient to give only the knowledge of values but it is necessary that value system must be integrated into the personality of an individual so that it may be characterized. Hence it is said that values are not taught but caught. It is required that a person should live in the atmosphere of desired value system. In fact, there is no need to use word desirable. Value itself has an essence of desirability. To acquire a value, a person should go through the following five stages that are levels of affective domain. These stages are:

(a) *Receiving:* Getting aware of value.

(b) *Responding:* Responding value in appropriate situation.

(c) *Valuing:* Making judgment on preferences.

(d) *Organizing:* Organize it to make stable in value system of mind.

(e) *Characterization:* Making value as a part of character.

Role of Schools in Developing Value System

The environment of the institution plays a vital role in shaping the personalities of the students. When we consider education as a system, all the elements of the institution are equally responsible for the development of values among the students. All the elements whether teachers, administrators, parents of the students, pupils and the environment, constitute the institutional climate where the students spends 6-8 hours per day. Further discussion reflects how do they affect the school climate? What should be their roles? etc.

Role of Teachers

The teaching community today faces an endless and challenging task of imparting value education and value based education. The impact of inculcating values among students by the teachers is in fact colossal and quite lasting, as A.P.Sharma has pointed out in the *University News* of 15 May 1995, "Against many destructive non-values such as egotism, arrogance, domination, corruption and money-power in the society today, there is still the longing for ushering in and striving for a new society based on justice, equality and common fellowship. As teachers have always claimed a special capacity to influence conduct and to shape moral character, the society expects them to develop not only knowledge but also ethical values among students thus creating an environment that would foster fraternity amongst mankind."

It is teacher who creates the reputation of the institution. Main responsibility of shaping the behaviour of students is in the hands of teachers. Teachers in fact, are the designers of the future of their students. Directly or indirectly they influence their students, hence teachers should present themselves as ideals. They should have a clear and clean image among students. They should be honest, sincere, and punctual, and should follow the professional ethics. They must devote time for discussion with the students. Discussion should be made informal, outside the classrooms also, not only academic but also on social problems, individual problems faced by the students and on social values. Teachers should be sensitive, sympathetic and have positive attitude towards students' emotions. It is the role of a teacher to make students realize the depth, magnitude and significance of values.

Teaching Strategies

Human values are taught as well as caught. There are certain techniques suggested by different educationists. Almost all commissions and committees on value education recommend both formal and informal or direct and indirect approaches to education in values. The direct method aims at teaching values by setting apart one period or two periods in a week. It makes use of five major techniques such as: prayer, silent sitting, group singing, story telling and group activities. The indirect method (integrating values with curricular subjects) must supplement the direct method, so that inculcation of values does not remain an isolated attempt. Rather, the entire school should be full of an atmosphere in which pupils can breathe in and imbibe values with natural ease. The other techniques are critical inquiry method, case study, role-playing, value clarification technique, value analysis model etc., the main purpose of these techniques is to develop rationality among the students. In all these techniques some issues are raised and with the help of discussion the students try to judge their values. To reach the generalizations is not the aim of these techniques. Community extension work or community based projects are also useful, where students go to the people, discuss with them and see the reality of life. In this way these methods are useful in developing instructive awareness among students.

School Climate

School climate is one of the most important factors, which directly influence the affective domain of the students. The following points may be taken into consideration while creating value-oriented environment in the institution:

1. School should provide the pleasant atmosphere. Cleanliness and aesthetic aspects should be incorporated. The principles of campus beautification should be followed.
2. Teacher should live in touch with students as much as possible. He should be affectionate and helpful to the students.
3. School should have democratic and transparent atmosphere where everyone can express himself or herself without any fear.
4. Teacher-student relationship and all other relationships should be made friendly, respectable and should be based upon faith.
5. Administrators and other members of the school should have concern with each other and take care of others also.
6. Important National days and festivals should be organized in the school and the students should be allowed to take part freely in the celebration of the festivals etc.

Co-curricular Activities

School may organize extra co-curricular activities, which can help in developing human values among the students. These activities may be:

- Discussion and talks on special events or problems.
- Community participation.
- Organizing debate, symposium and panel discussion etc.

- Organization of cultural programmes.
- Organization of different competitions.
- Activities for aesthetic values.
- Educational tours and excursion etc.
- Organizing social welfare activities etc.

MTA and PTA Conferences

This is an alternative to develop instructive consciousness. In schools, we have MTA and PTA. These should be functional so that community comes closer to each other for exchange of ideas and the solution of common problems. Students can also take part in it.

Situational Analysis Approach

In our daily life, we meet innumerable situations/encounter problems/dilemmas. These situations/dilemmas emanate from conflicts between individual needs and social values. Further these conflicts among needs and values occur at various levels—intra personal, the family, workplace, community, groups etc. There are two approaches for presenting these situations/problems to learners. In the first case, situations/problems are presented with possible solutions/responses/behaviours. The situation is analyzed highlighting the consequences/effects of each opinion. In the second approach, the situation is presented with consequences of following a particular approach. The situation is analyzed psychologically and philosophically and leaves the learners to accept and own a particular option/behaviour or reject all of them. The approach should be suggestive it should not be prescriptive in any way.

These approaches are quite useful to inculcate the value of 'service' to others. Similarly teachers can develop suitable situations to promote requisite values among their learners. However, it is stressed that in value education, teachers should not search for ready-made tricks, prescriptions or recipes for application in teaching-learning contexts. They must evolve their own strategies suiting their contexts.

Concluding Remarks

If the destiny of India is being shaped in the classrooms then teachers have to play a vital role in inspiring and moulding the personal and national character of the learners. One of the major aims of education is to initiate the students into worthwhile ways of thinking and doing, and thereby foster an all-round growth of the learners. And this can be achieved to a great extent, if values are given due importance in educational institutions. Value-components/ strategies, therefore, ought to be exercised, practiced and appreciated by the teachers. It is the moral duty of the teachers to put values in day-to-day operations and transactions of the institution. If this happens, then academic complexes will succeed in their educational venture of man-making.

In short, values cannot be developed through teaching only. Value system is related with the affective domain of the person hence it is necessary that a person should live in the atmosphere of value-consciousness. The teachers should be responsible to create such atmosphere. Developing value consciousness is the major step towards value development.

REFERENCES

Chilana M.R., *Value Orientation of Education*, Chandigarh: Youth Delik, 1998.

Dhanavel.P., "Importance of Value-based Teachers", *University News*, Vol.38, No. 18, May, 2000.

Mazumdar, H.B., "A Quest for Values in Education", *Journal of Indian Education*, 8(5), 1983.

Reddy, N.K., Man, *Education and Values*, Delhi: B.R. Publishing Corporation 1979.

Ruhela, S.P., *Human Values and Education*, Sterling Publishers, 1990.

18

Trinity of Learning: Parents, Teacher and Child

Anant Ram Thakur

Introduction

The growing concern over the erosion of values in public life has brought to focus the need to critically examine the various aspects of value education at the school stage. A new orientation has to be given to education to bring it in tune with the emerging needs and aspirations. The curriculum, instructional materials and technology methods should be directed to inculcate values of humanism, socialism, national integration as well as ethical and moral values in general education. Life-long learning should aim at the pursuit of excellence and the attainment of quality life. Therefore, value-oriented education is essential for balanced personality and harmonious society. It helps a person in unfolding his personality by bringing it forth and revealing the potentials and qualities in him.

Children as White Marbles

Children's minds are innocent and pure. Each child is a white marble for the teacher and the parents to mould into an image of God. To instill in the minds of the children the values of truthfulness, humility, goodness and loving service to others—the homes where they grow, have to be the first schools. It is a known and universally accepted fact that the first and foremost teacher of a child is his 'mother', so have the parents put in their child what we call, *sanskaras*. The child is a product of heredity and environmental factors as child learns what he sees at home and around. So our actions should be proper so that it does not leave bad impressions on their minds.

Today, the child has I.Q. (Intelligent Quotient) more than that of previous generation. We have to recognize the great potentials of the child and help him to let him glow in an open environment. The objective of education should be imprinted on the children's minds.

Parent's Role in Shaping the Child

Ninety per cent of blame for spoiling the behaviour and character of children go to the parents because they show unnecessary affections and give too indiscriminate freedom to them. The endearing nature of parents is fading out rapidly in a mist of affected nature. Most of the patents pay no head to the anxieties of the growing child. It is not all to shift the responsibility by admitting the child in a 'Top School' and washing their hands off the child. The problems faced by children affect the smooth running of school-life what is learnt at school turns out to be quite contrary to what actually happens at home. Whatever parents have to do, cannot be overdone at school, however, responsible teachers may be. Knowledge can be given by the teachers; however, the discipline, the rigorous control of the senses and behaviour must be administered by the parents so that the later also practise the human values and reform their children. Then the children become sacred souls and holy individuals.

Sri Sathya Sai Baba, rightly says, "The homes in which children grow have to be clean and with vibrations free from hatred, envy, greed, spite and hypocrisy. Mothers should promote respectful behaviour to the elders in the family. They should be careful how they themselves behave in the presence of children, for young learn a lot from emulation. A spirit of understanding and sympathy has to pervade the home. The food that the child takes in has to be pure. From the age of two to five the child looks upon its mother, and so the mothers' behaviour has to be proper."

Role of a Teacher

The role of a teacher is very vital for he/ she has the greatest share in moulding the future of a country. Of all professions, his is the noblest, the most different and the most important. He has to cultivate in himself humility, compassion and the spirit of loving service, much more than those belonging to other professions, for he is an ideal and an example to his pupils. But if a teacher has a vice, thousands are polluted. A school should not be considered to be just a common place arrangement designed for teaching and learning. It is a place where consciousness is aroused and illumined, purified and strengthened, the place where the seeds of discipline, duty and devotion are planted and fostered into fruition. A constructive companionship between teachers and students must be developed. Gurus like Parshuram, Bhishma and Drona influenced their students by practicing what they preached.

Teachers as a Role Model

A teacher in real sense is he who practices himself the human values. He should quote such examples in class which leave everlasting impressions. Once a lady along with her child went to Ramkrishan Paramhansa and requested the Guru to make her child leave the habit of eating molasses. Ramkrishan Paramhansa asked the lady to come after one week. After that period the lady went to him Paramhansa said to the child, "Beta leave this habit." The lady was astonished to hear it said that you could have told me all this on that veryday why did you take one week to tell this sentence? Ramkrishan Paramhana said, "Because I had also the same habit and I took one week to leave this habit so I could now ask the child to do so." It means a teacher himself should be the example.

System of Education Required

The solution lies in the type of educational system having five elements:

(a) *Knowledge:* Truth which is intellectually apprehended.

(b) Skills of various kinds.

(c) Righteous conduct in personal behaviour.

(d) *Equipoise:* Balanced intellect controversies and reconciliation of opposites.

(e) *Understanding:* Awareness of cognitive tendency towards action.

These qualities are intimately connected with the faculties of man and his soul. These come from his intellect, will and heart, which combine to produce understanding in a joint response to environment. Such understanding is called "Felt Thought." To develop this, a teacher must understand the child fully and gauge his intelligence by holding discussions and debates, etc., in the class.

A teacher must love his students as a mother loves her child. He should teach like a Guru and behave like a friend.

Man-making—The True Aim of Education

The substance of education should lead to the creation of a complete man in the sense of having a person capable of positive interaction with the environment. The latent resources and potential energies dwelling deep within the people should be evoked through operational, scientific and rational organization. "Man-making" as Swami Vivekananda call it, should be the aim of education.

Each child should have the opportunity, under competent guidance to develop fully and richly as an individual and as a cooperating member of an inter-dependent society, full of manifold social, religious, economic, community and governmental agencies.

Conclusion

The academic education of today is shallow and useless because it has no value orientation bringing no transformation in them. If children of today are fortunate enough to have ideal teachers along with ideal parents, their progress towards development is smoothened. Teachers and parents ought to keep in touch and exchange views. The teachers should establish contacts with parents for welfare of children. Periodic meetings should be there, they should realize that mere cribbing and shifting blames will have its heavy toll on the young ones. There ought to be a healthy rapport between teachers, parents and children.

19

Development of Values: Some Practical Approaches

Yadavendra Kumar Sharma

The Present Crisis

Lot of concern is being expressed by every section of the society for the steep fall in our moral standards. Contemporary Indian situation witnesses ambivalence if not complete confusion of values. The character of the Indian has degenerated to such an extent that our social workers, enlightened citizens and statesmen whosoever have a genuine concern about the future of country have been giving alarm signals and calling for immediate remedial measures. India of Gandhi's dream has become a country of violence, bribery, corruption, nepotism, adulteration, smuggling, hoarding and social vices of all kinds. Far from being a spiritual heaven for the rest of the world, India has now become one of the most hardened materialistically oriented societies in the world. Money power has gradually taken over the moral power. It has become a common belief that those who have money can get any thing done in India, can get out of turn admission in schools, and colleges, get jobs without requisite qualification, get transfer to places of one's choice, can secure promotion even if one does not excel in work, get criminal cases dropped, get exempted from punishment and fines, evade income tax, buy bridegrooms and what not. A stage has reached when everything can be secured through money.

The huge election expenditures of candidates of various political parties alone give a clue to the ever-expanding spiral of corruption. Why would or how could an MLA or an MP spend so much money in his or her election, unless he or she was sure of getting a return of multiples of his election expenditure once he gets into assembly or parliament? This political corruption has so penetrated and corroded our entire social fabric that an average Indian has become a valueless, characterless ego-centric brute devoid of any concern for the rest of the society or for high values of life. It would become impossible to stop this fast developing degeneration of Indian social order unless immediate remedial measures are undertaken. Political parties have used corruption, religion and caste in their strategies to gain political power. This has bred violence, and communalism that has led to over 3500 communal riots since 1947. We then have to set-up expensive and elaborate committees to solve the problem?

Rise in crime rate, chaos in the society, an increasing sense of insecurity are the fallouts of this problem. A common man is feeling totally helpless, being a silent spectator without assuming any significant role in the amelioration of the present situation. Daily we read the disturbing news of heinous crimes being committed in the society around us. However, even a sensitive person usually reacts inside only without being able to do something substantial to improve the situation. The sad commentary is that we become sensitive only when we are directly affected. When the similar incident happens with someone else, it is no more than thrilling news item for us. Therefore, education in values becomes of paramount importance in the Indian context.

Why Value Crisis?

Where have all our values gone? Surely, our values are cherished as our great heritage enshrined in our sacred texts and safely treasured in our bookshelves and libraries, only to be referred to on occasions when we need them in support of our egocentric demands. We never miss any opportunity to shower lectures on morality whenever an incident of immoral act committed by people comes to our notice through electronic, print media or through the medium of rumour. It gives us lot of contentment to criticise those allegedly involved in immoral acts. Perhaps belittling others is the only way left with us to increase our stature, as we seldom bother for developing those values, which in reality make us taller. We fail to notice that while raising one finger on others three fingers point towards self and warn us for introspection. Right from the first informal agency of education i.e., the family the child watches tokenism in the concern for the values. Parents give a heavy dose of lectures to their children on moral values without practising themselves. School, community, political leadership, educational leadership in majority of cases is talking about ideals for public consumption only. We are in the habit of presenting ourselves in the form, which is appreciated by the masses, but what we do or want to do is what pleases us. Thus our thoughts, words and deeds are always in conflict. We praise non-violence and practise violence, we preach socialism, but we indulge in all sorts of corrupt practices, we preach morality but do not hesitate to commit immoral and unethical acts, we pretend spirituality, but practise materialism, we advocate equality and social justice, but practise exploitation, we teach values but act without them. In short we have become hypocrites.

Another reason for value crisis is that some of the values whether they belong to the category of self-oriented, society oriented or altruistic values go contrary to the values that are internalised by the children from the cultural settings of the groups that they belong to. If the children grow in the traditional socio-cultural milieu, they will imbibe the values of non-egalitarianism, egocentrism and ethnocentrism, which are opposed to values of equality, fraternity, cosmopolitanism and altruism.

Another related question which usually bothers a layman is, "why value based life?" If values based life really leads to a better life what prevents us to adopt and live such a life? And if valueless life is better than the value-based life, why do we feel so concerned abut inculcating values? Experiences from the immediate environment sometimes send strong signals that those leading a life with wrong values are leading a better and happy life. Unless this image is dismantled inculcation of right values will remain a difficult proposition.

It is in this context that there is an urgent need to inculcate values at all levels in our society, without which we will not be in a position to arrest our accelerating social degradation. How can we develop it as a part of habit to live in values? What changes are immediately required in our society and in our educational system? These are some of the questions, which need to be addressed on priority. It is concluded that the values can be nurtured in the society by way of socialisation process at the family level, introduction of universal human values in the curriculum, teachers training, cleaning of social and public life, spiritualization of life in general etc. This requires multi-dimensional overhauling of societal systems, which is possible only with unshakeable public and political will.

Need for Value Education

Value crisis and its consequences on the life of each one of us have forced different sections of the society to focus their attention on this crucial issue. Educationists, politicians, social workers, the wise community members all are raising their voice in unison to express their worries and seriousness to ameliorate the present situation. Various commissions, committees and policy documents on education have invariably highlighted the need to take immediate steps to improve the fast deteriorating situation of moral standards in the society.

Radhakrishnan Commission (1948-49) has pointed out, "The fundamental principles of our constitution call for spiritual training. How can we build values in human mind? Our attempt should be to suggest and persuade, not command or impose. The method of suggestion is by personal examples, daily life and works and books read from day to-day."

Kothari Commission (1964-66) has pointed out, "A serious defect in the school curriculum is the absence of provision for the education in social, moral and spiritual values. In the life of a majority of Indians religion is a great motivating force and is intimately bound up with the formation of character and inculcation of ethical values. A national system of education that is related to the life, needs and aspirations of the people cannot afford to ignore these very useful forces. We recommend, therefore that conscious and organized attempts be made for imparting education in social, moral and spiritual values with the help, wherever possible of the ethical teaching of great religions."

The National Policy on Education (NPE) 1986, embodies the aspirations of a national consensus to infuse values into the contents of our educational inputs. While explicitly value education is indicated in the Part VIII of the policy from para 4 to 6, implicitly it is emphasised throughout the Policy Statement. References are also given in Parts II, III and IX. Thus, the entire policy in a way is a declaration of our intention to make our educational system value based. The policy document has clearly stated, "The growing concern over the erosion of essential values and an increasing cynicism in society has brought to focus the need for readjustments in the curriculum in order to make education a forceful tool for the cultivation of social and moral values."

The UGC's view on the matter is well reflected in the recommendations of the conference of Vice-Chancellors of Indian Universities organised by UGC in Delhi in May 1984:

"Value orientation should be the primary objective of education at all levels. Since the objective of education has to be primarily, the development of the personality of the individual so that he or she may play a meaningful and effective role in the society and the country, it has to be value oriented. Value oriented education does not merely imply an intellectual discussion on the theme of value as an integral part of the syllabus in various disciplines, but also the practice of those values in the day to day life by the teachers and the students, which should be considered the final goal.

The group therefore recommended that besides including value oriented subjects in the foundation courses at the first degree level, attempts should be made to introduce value oriented concepts in all subjects of studies. The group further emphasised that steps will have to be taken to introduce value oriented concepts as part and parcel of the life of the individual in primary and secondary education and even in teacher education. It should form an important part of continuing education.

Since then the UGC has helped in the organization of two more conferences of Vice-Chancellors—one at the University of Rajsthan (Jan., 1985) Jaipur and other at Sri Sathya Sai Institute of Higher Learning Prasanthinilayam (Sept. 1987) in district Ananthpur of Andhra Pradesh to consider ways to promote value oriented education.

Another important step in this direction was the organization of an International Conference on "Strengthening Value Education" which was also held in Prasanthinilayam from September 25-29, 2000. In this conference 600 delegates from 78 countries contemplated on the issues related to strengthening the value education. After five days of hectic deliberations following important recommendations were made:

1. All children have a right to equal opportunity to receive the best and free education that would bring about good character and excellence.

2. Human values must be an integral part of all subjects taught in the education system of the world.
3. All governments all over the world should be encouraged to develop and implement laws and policies, which enable values in education to be an integral component of teacher education, professional development and student learning experiences.
4. Education in human values, peace and international understanding should be taught across the entire teacher education curriculum.
5. In order to implement the above, a voluntary network of educators sharing the education goal of human excellence will be established for educators to exchange ideas, experiences and promote values education.

These recommendations later formed the Prasanthi Nilayam Declaration. The 'Prasanthi Nilayam Declaration' was submitted to UNESCO, the United Nations and other International organization for further consideration and action at the global level.

The process of these intellectual exercises is still continuing and it reflects the need of value education that has always been felt even from the pre-independence period till date. Thus people have been aware of the threats of a society with low moral standards. The efforts in this direction will continue in order to evolve strategies to impart value education to the coming generation in a manner which may prove to be most relevant in the present context.

Which Values Need to be Inculcated?

The world of values is rich and variegated. There are certain basic universal perennial human values applicable to mankind anywhere in the world. On the other hand, there are values specific to different socio-cultural entities at different periods of time. A list of values may include: truthfulness, sincerity, integrity, honesty, goodness, beauty, love, non-violence, conscientiousness, compassion, endurance, perseverance, self-restraint, independence of thought, righteousness, courage, friendliness, generosity, selflessness, equanimity in thought, feeling and action; concern for natural environment, concern for other living beings, empathy, excellence, grace, decency, tolerance, confidence, self-esteem, honour, simplicity, being responsible, innovative, being adventurous, democratic way of living and acting, secularism, socialism, equality, co-operation, secularism, equality, co-operation, national integration, international brotherhood, removal of poverty, caste, illiteracy, ill health and backwardness, upliftment of the weaker section of the society, pride in own heritage and culture, peace, incorruptibility, law abiding, community orientation and public duty concern for public property, civil sense, and responsibility, stability, self, reliance, scientific temper, social justice, etc. They can be classified as universal and particularistic, basic or core and peripheral values etc.

The classification that suits the value education the most is a classification of values into three categories: (1) Self-oriented, (2) Society oriented and (3) altruistic (Selfless, humane, philanthropic). The self-oriented values are those values the inculcation of which is important for the development of one's character like truthfulness, non-violence, punctuality, dignity of labour, cleanliness, patience, self-reliance and equanimity. Society oriented values are those values which relate to better social relationships as for example courtesy, gratitude, duty towards others, tolerance, magnanimity, co-operation, understanding, compromise, compassion, kindness and non-violence. Altruistic values when internalised should help the individual to transcend his personal interest in favour of the good of others. The examples of altruistic values are fraternity, sacrifice, forgiveness, concern for others, empathy, service, sharing sympathy, hospitality, justice and love.

Some of these values go contrary to the values internalised by children from the cultural settings of the groups they belong to. If the children grow in the traditional socio-cultural milieu, they will imbibe the values of non-egalitarianism, sectarianism, egocentrism and ethnocentrism, which are opposed to values of equality, fraternity, cosmopolitanism and altruism. Therefore, the task of educational institutions assumes greater significance. Opportunities have to be provided to unlearn the wrong values imbibed and simultaneously to learn positive human values, which are conducive to social development. Socialization is essentially a learning process aided by primary and secondary groups of association. The education is also a learning process the difference being only in elements of voluntariness and directionality. Through educational strategies the individual has to be motivated and provided opportunities to imbibe positive human values, which will be helpful to him and the society at large.

Sri Sathya Sai Education in Human Values Trust emphasizes five basic human values in their value education programme. These are truth, righteousness, love, peace, and non-violence. These five values basically encompass all other values. A Gandhian programme of value will add to it the value of dignity of labour and self-reliance.

Methodology for Imparting Values

Values are something, which, normally an individual has to think through for himself, and not something which he can depend on his environment to bestow upon him or others to impose on him. Also, the inner, personal exercise of identifying and determining values is better undertaken early in life, not postponed to follow life's experience. When an individual has taken the trouble of personally thinking through a clearly defined scale of values for himself, he equips himself intellectually, morally and in operational terms for performance truly attuned to his highest priorities.

It has been observed that even a large amount of knowledge about values does not necessary ensure their inculcation. There is very little to guide us as to what methodology is effective in the promotion of values. Even the available programmes like moral education have hardly been assessed in terms of actual assimilation of values in one's personality system and improvement of character and behaviour. Values cannot be taught as the knowledge can be. Methods, which are valid and appropriate in the field of learning in regard to knowledge, are not applicable to the field of learning in regard to values. Great philosopher Plato has not recommended the dialogue method for young people but for mature over 30. "Young minds instead of searching for the truth would be distracted by the excitement of the debate, and thus instead of becoming good persons they would become good at the rationalization", was his advice. "Virtues", said the Aristotle, "are acquired primarily through habit and practice and not through discussion." It has been rightly said, " As swimming can be learnt not by listening to lectures on swimming but by plunging into water, similarly one can learn values only by living in values." It is the behavioural manifestation of the value that indicates value of a person. A man becomes just by performing just acts, brave by performing brave acts and temperate (self-controlled) only by performing acts of temperance.

Value development is a continuous process starting from childhood. Role of family, and educational institutions is important. Besides, community, religion and culture also play important role in the development of values.

Family

Value inculcation has to start from the family level which is the first social institution of education. The foundation of values is laid down at home during the tender years of the child. Parents are the custodian of the children, hence it is important to first consider the role of the parents. If the parents tend to be over indulgent or giving too much freedom, they must bear the major share of the blame for ruining the character of the children. Parents must prove to be an example of honesty, sense control and discipline. Knowledge can also be imparted by the teacher but the discipline, the rigorous control of the senses and the behaviour of the child must be administered by the parents. Then only the children can become sacred souls, holy and sanctified individual. Children learn a lot from the example. The child watches with curiosity the actions and words of the elder members of the family especially that of the parents and tries to imitate much of it. Therefore instead of preaching the values to the children, parents must act as role model for them. They should themselves exemplify the values through their own conduct, which they want to inculcate in their children. The parents whose behaviour and conduct is contrary to what is spoken or taught to their children create a storm of doubt and a dichotomy is raised in the child's minds.

The homes in which the child grows, as indeed all homes, should therefore be clear and with vibrations free from hatred, envy, greed, spite and hypocrisy. Parents should be careful how they should behave in the presence of the children. Instead of taking care of big events they should concentrate on small acts, which should be in conformity with the preached values.

In order to instill the habit of prayer and the values of humility and loving service to others in the minds of the children, the parents have a very important role to play. Parents should not be seen by the children to be worried, helpless and discontented, distressed and having no faith in God. This situation does not lead to the development of balanced personality with a strong value system.

However, this is not an easy proposition, as majority of parents are not found with such qualities. To develop competencies in the parents to perform such roles effectively is of course a challenging task. For creating a situation conducive to develop such competencies in the parents, there is a need of an effective education system that may produce citizen with such qualities. Leaders in the society should exhibit exemplary behaviour, which can be followed by common man. However, we find that there is no harmony in the words, thoughts and action of people who are supposed to give lead. Common man leading a value based life finds it difficult to survive in such an environment and sometimes succumbs to the pressures of the environment. How such people can be expected to inculcate values among their progeny?

The School

The schools and the teachers working in the schools have an important role to play in the development of the values. Foundation of values should be laid through a proper methodology of teaching–learning the course in value education should start right from the lower-classes, which should be almost entirely practical. This may be continued more with the objective of creating passion and dedication for living a value based life rather than merely its theoretical knowledge.

The value education should not remain a syllabus, a textbook, an examination with marks, but be a genuine consideration for a life based on values. Value education does not merely imply an intellectual discussion on the theme of value as an integral part of the syllabus in various disciplines, but also the practice of those values in the day-to-day life by the students and teachers. Attempts should be made to introduce value oriented concepts as a part and parcel of the life of the individual in primary and secondary education and also in teacher education.

In the school system the teacher is the kingpin. His role is always crucial in the inculcation of values. Therefore, he has to play his role with all sincerity. Swami Vivekanand strongly felt that true teacher is one who can immediately come down to the level of the students, and transfer his soul to the student's soul and see through and understand through his mind. Such a teacher can really teach and none else. For preparing teachers to perform their role effectively in the inculcation of values, it is important that there should be well designed programmes of value education in the teacher education programmes. The teacher as a person should also be convinced that value-based life is better life. The negative notions about values need to be dismantled.

The teachers, though considered builder of the nation are selected for this vital role with least care, proper screening is required so as to ensure that they are fit to perform the assigned role effectively. Only scholastic dimensions are evaluated whereas co-scholastic dimensions which play a decisive role in making a better human being are hardly assessed during the selection of the teacher. It would be impractical to visualize an ideal system of education conducive to development of good human being without providing requisite inputs in the system of education in terms of teachers with a strong value system.

Head of the institution also plays a crucial role in this direction. The value system at the top percolates down to the teachers working in the institution and thereby to the students. However, the selection of the head is sometimes guided by consideration other than his being a person of strong values. Till the norms for the selection of the head and the teachers are objectively observed, valued based education will remain restricted to theory and examination only with out any inkling in the behaviour.

School can apply certain approaches for the inculcation of values among the students. Direct approach for value inculcation has been found quite effective especially at the school level. It is being successfully tried out in Sri Sathya Sai system of education. The techniques includes silent sitting, prayer, group singing, story telling, and group work. These techniques can be applied in the other schools of the country too. However, the success will depend upon the sincerity, commitment and dedication for implementation. For the effective use of these approaches teachers equipped with necessary skills to implement these approaches effectively are needed. School can also make use of indirect approach including incidental approach and contrived situation. In the incidental approach any incident taking place in the institution is an occasion for the development of values. In the contrived situation, a situation is rather created to test the values of the students and incase it is found that the behaviour of the students is not in accordance with the desired values the remedial action is initiated accordingly for the development of values.

Values cannot be taught in the same way as lessons of information. Instruction should form a minor role and a major role should be assigned to intimate contact and individual guidance. The role of the teacher is to put the child on the right road to his perfection and to encourage him in his growth by watching, suggestions and helping but not imposing or interfering. The reason for a poor state of affairs is probably lack of a strong will to change the system. Perhaps we give priority to education only in our speeches and written documents whereas in practice education continues to be one of the most neglected area. Vast quantitative expansion in school education witnessed by us during the last half century though was essential, it should have been accompanied by improvement in the quality in the same magnitude.

All occasions of daily life should be utilized by the teacher to bring his student nearer to the realization of the ideals. There are occasions when children express wild impulses and passions, and often they are in revolt. Children have their own daily battles of loyalties and friendship, and there are moments of desperate depression and of violent enthusiasm. All these occasions are occasions for value oriented education. With patience and perseverance, the teacher can utilize all these occasions to show the truth and light and to awaken among the children the right sense and the right direction of true progress.

The teacher can help and guide the children keeping in view the following guidelines:

- A good many children are usually under the influence of their inner psychic and spiritual being which is manifested at times in their spontaneous turning to truth, beauty and goodness. To recognize this turning and to encourage it wisely and with a deep sympathy would be the first indispensable step.
- The undesirable habits should not be treated harshly. The child should not be scolded. Particularly, care should be taken not to rebuke a child for a fault which one commits oneself. Children are very keen observer and note such lapses very minutely.

- A child should be encouraged to think of wrong impulses not as sins or offences but as symptoms of curable disease, which can be remedied by a steady and sustained effort of the will. Falsehood has to be replaced and rejected by truth, fear by courage, selfishness by sacrifice, malice by love.
- The teacher should ensure that the student gradually begins to become aware of his deeper self and that with this growing awareness the student is able to harmonize and resolve the conflict.
- Great care should be taken to see that unformed virtues are not rejected as faults. The wildness and recklessness of many young natures are only overflowing of an excessive strength, greatness and nobility. They should be purified, not discouraged.
- The questions asked by the child as a result of curiosity should not be set aside by saying that it is foolish or stupid. Curiosity cannot be postponed and an effort must be made to answer questions truthfully and in such a way as to make the answer comprehensible to the student's mental capacity.
- Opportunities should be given or created which would enable students to embody progressively higher and nobler values.

Portals of Higher Education

Colleges and universities constitute the institutions imparting higher education to the youth of the country. These institutions are considered important as it is in these institutions that the finishing touches are given to the personalities of the youth. It is at this stage that the students start realizing that they are responsible individual and perceives their independence, slowly moving away from the state of dependency. Although the foundation of the values is laid in the early years of the school, colleges and universities have to play their roles in strengthening the desired values developed during school years. Further, it is never late to dismantle the negative values imbibed from the adverse environmental influences. The role of these institutions is thus considered important in nullifying the ill effects of various influences like that of peer group, society, media etc.

The teacher occupies a pivotal role in imparting value education to the students. If the teacher meets pupils only in the classes where some particular area of the academic matter is the central point for discussion, their understanding of pupils will be quite inadequate for a relationship in which the complex value interests of pupils are seriously handled. A tutorial house or counselling system is a must because it helps teachers to understand pupils properly. Since there is no pre-service training for the teachers teaching at higher education level, the sole responsibility rests with the Academic Staff Colleges which organize orientation programmes and refresher courses for these teachers. The teachers should be trained to integrate values with the subject of their teaching in these programmes. A large number of activities have been designed for such teachers which should be effectively put into practice during these programmes. In the value education as in any other area what is asked of the teacher is a total commitment to the development of rational autonomy in both thought and action.

The teacher has to sacrifice his petty interests in order to prove himself as the role model for the students who may then willingly follow his examples. It has been observed that teacher do involve themselves in the politics of the campus for serving their trivial interests. They use students to serve their ends and alternatively, students use them. This vicious circle continues and the teacher looses the authority, which he otherwise enjoys automatically while playing his role ideally.

Pecuniary considerations, though as important for the teacher as for any other member of the society, should not however render teacher helpless to compromise with the long cherished values. This is a danger sign and it will make the whole edifice to crumble. In the absence of teachers who can really make a dent on the personality of the student, his natural alternative (*guru*) remains media both print and electronics. A couple of incidents of acid throwing on the faces of girls reported recently in the newspapers are sequel to similar incidents shown in the television serials and thus stand as testimony for this fact. Young minds instead of receiving a moral lesson out of such situations learn how to perform such immoral acts. The thrill in such acts allures the youth. The type of sex and violence being portrayed in films and television as a cheap mean of minting money has degenerated the values of the society and youth in particular is the victim of it. The talk of censorship on media appears to be only for public consumption without any commitment for the same. It is in this context that the colleges and universities have added responsibilities of strongly influencing the value system of the youth so that such extraneous influences are negated.

At college and university level, work of community service should get the importance it rightly deserves and should be included as a part of the total educational process. But to make the community service truly value oriented, emphasis should be laid on the true spirit with which the proposed work is to be done. Work should be done with ever showing skill and perfection. Value oriented education should particularly include subjects like international understanding and peace, Human Rights, Knowledge of India and Indian Culture, Indian Values and National Heritage.

The curriculum at all levels should provide enough opportunities for pupils to acquire a considerable amount of knowledge that is essential for morally responsible living in our democratic society. Value education should prepare individuals for participation in social life and acceptance of social rules. Lastly what is important in value education is that the institution should provide a healthy climate for sharing responsibilities, community life and relationship.

Conclusion

Present scenario thus depicts a gloomy picture. India, the spiritual heaven of yesterday is gradually loosing its ability to lead the world on the path of the spirituality. The materialism is fast overshadowing spiritualism, which has been a rich heritage of this country. An urgent need is being felt to anchor our social system on a strong value system. This is reflected in the emphasis given to moral education or value oriented education in the reports of various commissions and policy documents. A large number of values of universal nature have been identified. The need is to internalize these values. This goal can only be achieved if various segments of the society come forward to play their role with all sincerity. We need leaders with a strong character and strong will. Commitment and sincerity, rather than ostentation is needed to reestablish a system based on universal values. Social institutions starting from family to schools and institutions of higher learning all have to shoulder their responsibilities to the best of their abilities. The teachers teaching in these institutions will have to act as vital instruments in the accomplishment of this stupendous task of man making. The quality of the coming generation to a large extent will be decided by the quality of the teacher selected to play this role. The world can become a better place to live only if it is inhabited by better human being and for that development of a proper value system is pre-requisite.

REFERENCES

Gokak, V.K. (1982), *Teacher's Handbook for Education in Human Values*, (Ed.) Sri Sathya Sai EHV trust, Prasanthinilayam, (A.P.).

Joshi, Kireet (1998), *Urgency of Value Education*, in Subhash C. Kashyap (Ed.) Urgency of Value Education and Primacy of Girl Child. Uppal Publishing House, New Delhi.

Mascranahas, M. and H. R. Justa (1989), *Value Education in Schools and other Essays*. Konark Publishers, Pvt. Ltd.

Report of Kothari Commission (1964-66), *Ministry of Education*, Government of India, New Delhi.

Report of Religious and Moral Instruction (1959), *Ministry of Education*, Government of India, New Delhi.

Report of University Education Commission (1948-49), *Ministry of Education*, Government of India, New Delhi.

Ruhela, S.P. (1986), *Human Values and Education* (Ed.) Sterling Publishing House, Pvt. Ltd., New Delhi.

Sanathana Sarathi (Oct. , 2000), *International Conference on Strengthening Values Education*, Sri Sathya Sai Books and Publication Trust, Prasanthi Nilayam, Distt. Anantpur, (A.P.), p. 320.

Saraf, S. (1993), *Bhagwan Sri Sathya Ŝai Baba: The Eternal Educator*. M.K. Rajan, Typographic, Wadala, Bombay.

Seshadari, C., M. A. Khadekar and G.L. Adhya (1992), *Education in Human Values: A Source Book* (Ed.), NCERT Publication, Sri Aurobindo Road, New Delhi.

Yadav, D.S. (1994), *Education of the Complete Man* (Ed.), Nirmal Publications, New Delhi.

PART–IV
TEACHER EDUCATION AND HUMAN VALUES

20
Value Oriented Teacher Education

Ramachandra Jantli

India is a country with rich culture and heritage. Indians are well known for kind hearted and broad mindedness. This is mainly because of value based education imparted in the past. In ancient times education for attainment for Mukti was main objective of education. Our great epic Rigveda rightly depicted "Sarve janoho Sukhnobhavantu" which means all creatures on this earth should lead happy and peace life.

At the end of medieval period in India Foreign invaders started establishing their kingdom and up to the British Empire the Indian people lost political, social, economical and educational values as a result of which the Indian culture and spiritual character of Indians faded away. The Indians slowly started imitation of western culture. As a result of which today we see everywhere violence disturbances and conflicts and also communal disharmony among our own people. This is mainly because of lack of value-based education.

The relationship between education and values is the most talked about issue in Indian education today. 'Value education' and 'Value oriented education' have become the buzz words. Various committees, commissions and national policy on education have drawn attention to the need for moral and spiritual values in education. Although there is a general acceptance that education has to have a thrust on the development of values. It is not clear as to how this is to be achieved. What values are to be inculcated in education and how.

'Value' is a difficult concept to define. Some philosophers have even argued that it is an indefinable, a fundamental category. An approach towards understanding the meaning of values is to recognize the distinction between a *statement of fact and a judgement of value.*

Indian philosophy accords the pride of place to values. Philosophy in India did not originate in wonder but as a practical need arising from the presence of moral and physical evil in life. Its aim is not the disinterested pursuit of truth but to serve as a practical aid that showed the right way of living.

Inculcation of values or value education is a much discussed issue. Although national consensus has emerged on the need for value orientation of education, differences continue on the kind of educational intervention and curricular prescription demanded by it. The content of value education also remains a continuous issue. Perceptions also varying about the compendium of values which school should promote. Any proposal value education package is looked upon with suspension of hidden agenda.

Value education is also education in the sense that it is education for 'becoming'. It is concerned with the development of the total personality of the individual, intellectual, social, emotional, aesthetic, moral and spiritual. It involves developing sensitivity to the good, the right and the beautiful, ability to choose the right values in accordance with the biggest ideals of life and internalizing and releasing them in thought and action. As such the process calls in to play all human faculties—knowing, feeling and doing. Not only should the learner be enabled to know the right and the good, but also to care, to feel the appropriate emotions, concern and commitment and exercise the will to do the right thing. This is not to suggest that these factors function independently. In other words, value education spans the entire gamut of learning, developing rational critical thinking, education of the emotions, and cultivation of imagination, strengthening of will and training of character.

Teacher education in India should be centred on development of values. In ancient times if we see the glory of educational system in India, it is quite clear that it was fully spiritual and value oriented. Guru has highest place in the Gurukula.

Great epics of India like Vedas, Upanishad clearly explains that

"Guru Brahma, Guru Vishnu, Guru devo maheshwara, Guru Sakhsatha Parabrahma" Tasmai Sri Gurve Namaha" ....
"Na Guror adhikam Tatwam Na Guror adhikum Tapahha "
"Tawta Gnanat Parm nasti Tasmai Sri Gurve Namaha"................

The Guru was fully embedded with all values so as to call him a dedicated complete human being with all round development. The students were also equally responsible to develop the values to become perfect human being and use to grow more than his teacher. That is how Guru used to say *Shishyad Ichheda Parajayat*. This means Guru wanted his student to grow more than himself.

One of the main objectives of teacher education in India is to develop human values among the prospective teachers. For this purpose the present teacher education curriculum should be re-framed to suit the need for the present generation. Today we see many young graduates and postgraduate persons after obtaining good marks aspire to become the teacher. They join either primary teacher training course or secondary teacher training course without any professional values. Such persons need to be trained for inculcation of values.

Usually we see two types of teachers. One who teaches for teaching sake. Such teachers refer only the textbooks and finish his portion. Another type of teacher inspires the student and develops values among the children along with subject and gives proper attitude towards the future. Such teachers are said to be *Friend—Philosopher and Guide.* In India, there are lakhs and lakhs of teachers available but there is hardly any teacher Dr. S. Radhakrishna. Dr.Radhakrishana was an ideal teacher and a great philosopher embedded with human values. Teacher-students today are to be trained to become like Dr. Radhakrishna.

Value Oriented Teacher Education Curriculum

Value Education is not only religious education but also education for good health, habits, developing social nature and training for mind. It also develops sound body in sound mind. That is to say, it is harmonious development of an individual. It also develops quest for truth and passion for excellence. For one's upliftment, the refinement of *panchakosha*, viz. *annamay kosha, pranamay kosha, manomay kosha, vigayanamay kosha* and *anandamay kosha* is must. This can be achieved by attaining *dharama, artha, kama* and *moksha* which are the essence of values.

India is fast developing country where in scientific and industrial development is considered as main aspects. But we have forgotten that the glory of India remains in the spiritual and moral development. Sir E.M.Foster a great English Writer explains "Indians have to manage with old morality and new economy." This means one should not forgot the moral and spiritual ideals of our country. In the name of modernity we should not forget our culture and heritage. This should be reflected in the teacher education curriculum. The teacher education curriculum contains four main aspects.

1. Curricular subjects like
   (a) Educational Philosophy and Sociology.
   (b) Educational Psychology.
   (c) Educational Technology.
   (d) Special Methods of Teaching.
   (e) Optional subjects.
2. Practice Teaching Programme
   (a) Stray Lessons.
   (b) Unit Plan of Teaching.
   (c) Internship programme.
3. Co-curricular Activities like
   (a) Stage Activities (Cultural).
   (b) Sports and Games.
   (c) Community Service Activities.
4. Projects and Assignments
   (a) Subject-based Projects and Assignments.
   (b) Profession linked Projects and Assignment.

Important Values to be Inculcated in Teacher Education

Following values are quite essential for student teachers:

1. Moral Values
2. Intellectual Values
3. Cultural Values
4. Social Values

5. Economic Values
6. Disciplinary Values
7. Ethical Values
8. Aesthetic Values
9. Scientific Temper
10. National and International Understanding

The above values are to be included in the four aspects of teacher education programme given earlier.

The values are not developed through pressure but will be realized through experiences in the individual life. This requires sincere struggle in life for searching eternal truth. Following aspects are necessary for value process in life:

1. Imitation—Following the foot steps of the noble people.
2. Taking the advise from the ideal people—discourses.
3. Identifying the facts and figure and events in the past.
4. Self-experience in the life.

Methods through which values may be developed

1. *Direct method*: Preaching, explaining, narration of events of epics, etc.
2. *Indirect method*: Teaching different subjects like History, Logic, Geography, Science, etc.
3. *Accidental method*: Events that happen accidentally through which Teacher/Parents can develop the values.

It is very easy to include the unit values in the curricular subjects. Educational Philosophy should necessarily contain a unit on values—the meaning, definition and the relationship between education and values. The first impact of values on education and life of a human being may be included. In the educational psychology intellectual value and ethical and aesthetical values may be included. Similarly in the educational technology disciplinary values and scientific temper and scientific attitude are included. The special methods of teaching include scientific temper moral values and cultural values development. In some of the Universities there is a separate optional paper as Value education or Moral education for Teacher Education Programme. In which the development of values can be achieved to the maximum extent.

The second aspect of teacher education programme is that of practice teaching where in development of values is most effectively realized. The student-teacher while preparing the lessons should also write the values that are realized along with objectives of teaching for the particular lesson. They also can give good examples for realisation of particular values

The third aspect of Teacher Training Programme is fully devoted to the Co-curricular aspects. There is lot of scope for realisation of different values. Speeches and debates and essay competition on development values may be arranged in the college. Similarly Dramas' on Epics' of India (*Mahabharata* and *Ramayana*) may be arranged for realising cultural and moral values. Sports and games will develop social and disciplinary values. Observation and celebration national festivals and days of Great Theosophical and Epoch making personalities will develop national integration and emotional integration.

The projects and assignments may be given on values for the student-teachers to develop desirable attitude towards profession. The community service activities like:

(*a*) Blood Donation Camp.

(*b*) Eye Donation.

(*c*) Echo Club.

(*d*) Literacy Camp.

(*e*) Citizenship Training Camp.

(*e*) Health Care Camp.

Such activities will develop necessary values among the prospective teachers.

Conclusion

"Values are not taught but caught." Today we want value oriented teacher education, to mould the prospective teachers to become well worsted with moral and spiritual and other values. Such teachers can only be able to bring about the desirable changes amongst the children who can in term change the whole world of tomorrow in to the world of peace and prosperity.

21

Human Values and Teacher Education

A. S. Sethi

Teaching, says Sri Sathya Sai Baba, "is the noblest of professions. For, it involves the cultivation of selfless Love and the showering and sharing of that Love. The teacher moulds a generation into self-confident, self-reliant Atma-conscious people. He is the architect of happy homes, prosperous communities and peaceful nations. He has not only to equip himself with knowledge and skills to inform and instruct, but also the vision and insight, to inspire and transform. Children absorb from teachers and elders, their habits and manners, behaviour and beliefs. Therefore, the teacher has to be a constant example of the ideals he has to implant in their hearts. He must excel in humility, simplicity, morality and integrity, so that education results in excellence. Such a teacher can be a beacon of Truth, Love and Reverence. The children who grow under his wise care will shine as Lamps of love in their homes, radiating courage, joy and hope. Let the Beacons never fade. Let the Lamps be ever bright. Good Teachers = good students = Good Nation."

There could be no better statement than this about the personality and role of teachers. This must be taken as the Character for teacher education in the country.

This statement emphasizes inclusion of at least three essential components in teacher education programme. The first component relates to the development of a sound knowledge. This will mean a sound knowledge of philosophy, sociology, and psychology as they bear upon the practice of education, as well as of the subject, which the pupil teacher will teach. The second component would refer to the development of teaching competence and other pedagogical skills. The third component, which is rather neglected at present, calls for the development of the personality of the prospective teacher, and of human values in his thoughts, feelings and behaviour. Gokak (1973) and Saraf (1993) speak of five human values of Truth, Righteous conduct, Peace, Love and Non-violence. These values include in a balanced way the profound moral insights of all the world's great civilizations. Other values too are important, such as compassion, fear of sin, forbearance, patience, honesty, responsibility, and hard work. These and others like these may be included as sub-values of the five core values mentioned. Taken together, these values encompass the full vision of human potential—physical, emotional, intellectual, psychic and spiritual.

Strategies for Value Orientation in Teacher Education

One may visualize at least five major strategies through which value orientation to teacher education may be brought about. These are: (1) Selective admissions, (2) Modeling, (3) Direct input of values, (4) Value integration with subjects and (5) Experiential assimilation of values.

Selective Admissions

The candidates to be admitted to teacher education programme should not only possess teaching aptitude, but they should also exhibit a modicum of commitment to ethical, moral and human values (Jacbowitz, 1994). Apart from having superior mental ability and subject mastery, they should possess the zeal to bring out the best in their students—body, mind and soul.

However, the admission process will not achieve everything. It will have to be supplemented with educational programmes to help the future teachers to unlearn a whole lot of dysfunctional behaviours and attitudes, and to consolidate and develop what is valuable.

Modeling

Modeling implies learning by example in which individuals acquire new forms of behaviour merely by observing the actions of others (Baron & Byrne, 1993). The teacher education has to inculcate values in the prospective teachers by his own example. His life ought to be his message. No amount of telling, talking, or reading, will inculcate values and character in pupils. It is only what the teacher is and what he does which will have an impact on pupils, minds. The teacher is like a tank. The pupils are like taps. Pure water in tank will bring pure water in taps. The teacher himself has to imbibe values first and practise them in his life. The character of the teacher and what he teaches are inseparable. His mannerism, voice, bearing, attitude and approach to students in classroom, laboratories, library, workshop and at the campus in general should be imbued with a deep concern for inculcating values in pupils through modeling or personal example.

Direct Input of Values

The addition, the pupil teachers may be provided direct input of human values to enable them to assimilate them at the cognitive and reflective level. This could partly be achieved through the study of a specialized course in Education in Human Values. Such a — would provide a framework for understanding the meaning, rationale, and relevance of human values to one's personal development as well as to the peace and progress of the mankind. This course will also aim at the pupil teacher acquiring insight into the process of value development in the individual in the background of diverse view points of psychoanalytic, cognitive, and behaviouristic psychology. In addition, the pupil teachers will be involved in a series of practical activities like group discussions, role plays, seminar readings, and value clarifying exercise (Raths *et al.*, 1966; Singh and Singh, 1986) in the context of various kinds of moral dilemmas and value conflicts as they prevail in contemporary society. This course will also emphasise development of self-reliance and altruism through such activities as cleaning and beautification of the campus, socially useful productive work, animal and plant welfare and classroom cooperation. Besides these micro programmes for value internalization and personality development, a macro approach too is needed. This will consist of creating a suitable and environment, which exudes values and fosters them. The teacher educators should demonstrate human values though their day-to-day dealings with the pupil teachers. They should be models of patience, tolerance, love, discipline and character. Exhibitions and display of value-oriented writings, pictures and posters should be organized regularly in teacher education institutions. Visits to places of art, science, and culture should be a part of the education of teachers.

Value Integration with Subjects

Another source of providing theoretical understanding of human values is their integration with the formal teaching of regular theory courses. Education is a pluralistic and poly dimensional subject. It encompasses a broad spectrum of knowledge domains such as philosophy, psychology, sociology, administration, science, technology and pedagogy. Therefore, it ideally lends itself to relating and highlighting values in very wide context. Apart from teachers informally bringing out values inherent in their subject, a student may himself raise questions of an ethical nature in the class while a topic is being dealt within any subject. Or students may do extra reading related to various subjects. They may place before the teacher situations or information, which call forth value discussion.

Further, the pupil teachers themselves should integrate human values with their practice of teaching. Here not only they themselves discover how everything is vibrant with values but in turn lead their class to do so. As Tamlinson and Quinton (1986) and Kirschenbaum (1976) tell us, in each subject the content and knowledge are intertwined with values and all of it is redolent with a score of elevating ideas, which transcend the vicissitudes of time and man. These ideas and values as well as the knowledge come in a symbiotic form, one is not separate from the other. Any knowledge if it is worth anything must be soaked in human values. Knowledge devoid of values is fragile and vulnerable. The students should assimilate both as a composite whole. Moreover, the learning or understanding of subject-matter does not have to precede the valuing process. They usually proceed best when they proceed together. Neither should wait until the other is accomplished. Subject-mater in fact forms part of the value lesson. Here teacher's skill and insight play a very important role. Literature and language, for example, should highlight sublimity of human conduct, beauty of feelings and sympathy for all creation. History can bring out heroism, patriotism, courtesy, chivalry, service, compassion and consideration for others. Science should reveal the harmony, order and unity in nature. These examples are a pointer to infinite possibilities of integrating values with the teaching of traditional subjects.

Experiential Assimilation of Values

To be effective the human values must not only be seen and observed in others or comprehended by the intellect but they must also reach the heart of the student and provide opportunities for direct intuitive experience in addition to providing theoretical understanding. Such opportunities could come in the form of morning prayers, mediation sessions, group singing and Yogasanas. In a non-residential campus, universal prayers and silent sitting should be incorporated in the morning assembly along with spiritual readings and group singing of patriotic and devotional songs. The Yogasanas in this case may be combined with games and sports programmes. In addition, community and social service in the form of village and slum adoption, loving care of the diseased and distressed, and teaching a few children who have no one to guide them could be introduced as a regular programme in all teacher education institutions.

Besides, co-curricular activities are an excellent vehicle for journeying into the world of values and experiencing them in fullness of the term involving all the domains of personality, namely, physical, intellectual, emotional, psychic and spiritual. Field events, stage activities, literary activities, art and craft, and a large number of extra mural activities could be build on the foundation of human values. The value-oriented activities in the co-curricular field would lend spontaneity and deeper and broader perspective to the process of acquiring and practising values.

Evaluation

Unless value education for teachers is put under the scheme of evaluation there will be only a lip service both by the teacher educators and the pupil teachers. However, it is necessary to have a broad-based evaluation for value education. Oral presentations, group discussions, practicals, and observations by a panel of judges should be given due weightage besides written tests, assignments, quizzes, seminar readings, and tutorials in which the pupil teachers are evaluated on continuous basis. This procedure will be used not only to rate the level of pupil teachers' attainment but also to monitor their growth along value dimensions and provide required guidance.

In short, the evaluation process should be broad-based encompassing multi-facets of knowledge, understanding, skills, attitudes and behaviour. It should have both formative and summative phases, utilize both oral and written testing as well as observation of the prospective teachers in classroom and in a variety of other situations.

Summing-Up

To integrate human values in teacher education programme should get our top priority. Our teacher education institutions should go beyond producing technicians or purveyors of knowledge and information only. Their primary objective should be man making. Their first responsibility and justification for existence should be to produce Gurus who are removers of ignorance. Gurus can destroy ignorance if they themselves are not ignorant. In this context, we must remember that the teacher who is entrusted with the task of carrying illumination into tender minds has to become aware of light within so that he may inspire the pupils under his care. "Who am I?" It is the question the answer to which must be known and experienced by each teacher. The answer to this question need not be an esoteric or mystical one. It is enough if the question makes one realize that one is a human being and not an animal. It calls for the removal of the animal traits in man and establishing of sacred thoughts about oneself and about others. Unless the pupil and teachers are led to develop an insight into the truth of their self and being and therefore a sense of self-efficacy to practise values, value orientation in teacher education cannot happen.

REFERENCES

1. Baron, R.A. & Donn Byrne (1993), *Social Psychology: Understanding Human Interaction*. New Delhi: Prentice-Hall of India.
2. Gokak, V.K. (1973), *A Value Orientation to our System of Education.*
3. Jacbowitz, Tina (1994), *Admission to Teacher Education Programmes. Journal of Teacher Education*, Vol. 45, No. 1, pp. 46-52.
4. Kasturi, N. (ed.)(1986), *Satya Sai Speaks—Vol. IX,* Prasanthi Nilayam Sri Sathya Sai Books and Publications Trust.
5. Krischenbaum, H. (1976), *Advance Value Clarification*. New York: University Associates.
6. Raths, L.E., M. Harmin and P. Simon (1966), *Values and Teaching*. Ohio: E. Merril Book Inc.
7. Saraf, S.N. (1993), *Bhagwan Sri Sathya Sai Baba—The Eternal Educator*. Bombay: M.D. Rajan Typographic.
8. Singh, L.C. & L.P. Singh (1986), *Effectiveness of Value Clarifying Strategies in value Orientation of B.Ed. Students*. New Delhi: NCERT.
9. Tamlinson, R. & N. Quinton (1986), *Values Across the Curriculum,* London: The Falmer Press.

22

Teacher Training in Values: Some Thoughts

Kalplata Pandey

The identity of any country may be very well perceived by its citizens. A country is not only known by its geographical surroundings but by its roots of rich cultural heritage, civilization, traditions and above all by its value preferences. It is our proud privilege that we are the citizens of that great nation which was rewarded by the title 'vishwa guru' on the basis of its role of torchbearer of knowledge, values, cultural heritage and feeling of universal brotherhood. Unfortunately, we had to regress gradually from that top position due to some known or unknown reasons. This downfall had badly affected our rich traditional value dominated way of living.

The past five decades after political independence have witnessed constant erosion of the essential social, moral and spiritual values and an increase in cynicism at all levels. Situation is becoming worse day by day as such to save the country; we have to find out the right path to come out of the prevailing darkness. This path can only be found out by spreading the light of knowledge through value education as value based education can help the nation to fight against all kinds of fanaticism, violence, dishonesty, corruption, exploitation and right prone behaviour patterns. As far as the recommendations of various policies regarding value education are concerned, the National Policy on Education (1986) has laid emphasis on equity, and social justice in education to promote the country's unique socio-cultural identity and to contribute national cohesion, promoting tolerance, scientific temper and the concerns enshrined in the Indian constitution. The recommendations of Justice J.S. Verma committee on fundamental duties of citizens pave the way for strong commitment to basic human values and social justice. Some of the duties mentioned in the article 51A are—to abide by the constitution and respect its ideals and institutions, National Flag and National Anthem; to cherish and follow the noble ideals which inspired sovereignty, unity and integrity of India; to value and preserve the rich heritage of our composite culture etc. The 42nd Constitutional Amendment of 1976 incorporating these ten fundamental duties of citizens is a valuable pointer to what the country expects from its citizens. All these values must find a prominent place in the total education system of India. In the present day's socio-cultural scenario of our country where the voice of right and duties oriented education has become must for the future prosperity of the country.

Now the question arises here that how these values should be taught to our students studying in educational institutions to make them more duty bound rather then right prone citizens? Who will teach values related with the fundamental duties to the students? Which strategies and techniques should be adopted for the inculcation and adherence of values and duties among the students as future citizens of our country? Among all the questions raised above, the most important question to be answered is, who will teach to live values dominated, duty based life with having full respect to human rights and here comes the role of teachers. As we all know, teacher plays a pivotal role in teaching-learning process. Therefore, in order to make our education system more effective on the one hand and to make learner a real democratic citizen on the other hand, it becomes imperative to know how teachers are abiding by those behaviour patterns, which they feel essential to inculcate among their students. These days it is in the air that most of the teachers belonging to any level of education are not performing their duties, as they ought to do. We all know that it is the teacher who, up to some extent, is accountable for the value erosion among his/her students. It is an irony that most of the teachers hesitate to change their behaviour patterns whether it is cognitive, affective or psychomotor one. We can justify this observation by the ill fate of the recommendations and suggestions given by the commissions and committees on educational reforms. One of the major causes of lacunae in the implementation of the same lies in the harsh fact that most of the teachers were not ready to come out from their age old conventional conformity living shells, to even appreciate these recommendations. This reluctance on the part of teachers as well as their tendency to raise voice against any reform is one of the major causes of the present day's situation.

Therefore in order to solve the problem of value erosion and right prone behaviour of the teachers, a well-designed teacher training is essential for pre-service as well as for in service teachers. In other words, we can say that through teacher education programme, the task of inculcating values can be substantially accomplished. Along with this, teacher training must be planned in the manner that after going through the training, the teacher must have commitment to values related with their duties also along with their other commitments to the learner, to the professional to attaining excellence for professional action etc. For this, teacher education has to be conceived as an integral part of educational and social system and must primarily respond to the requirement of the educational institution. It can no longer remain conventional and static but should transform itself to a progressive, dynamic and responsive system of education National values and goals need to be meaning fully reflected and their inculcation has to be attempted with care and caution. Along with this, the theoretical and practical components need to be balanced appropriately. While it is essential to develop identified competencies to prepare effective teachers, it is equally necessary to develop commitment and build capacity to perform as integral part of teacher preparation. A national concerned with erosion of values needs teachers who are professionally committed and prepared to present a value based model of interaction with their learners.

Thus, it is evident from the above mentioned fact that teacher should be very well trained for the role they have committed to perform for the learner as well as for the society. We know that professional development of teachers begins with pre-service and gets renewed through in-service programmes. Generally in-service teacher education programmes are being conducted by District Institution of Education and Training (DIETS), National Council of Education Research and Training (NCERT), Colleges of Teachers Education, UGC—academic staff colleges, etc., to upgrade qualifications of under qualified and untrained teachers as well as to upgrade qualifications of under qualified and untrained teachers as well as to upgrade serving teachers in both content and pedagogy.

They are also trained to cope themselves with the new roles assigned to them or new issues relating to policy initiatives. The training for value inculcation among teachers should also be added in this arena.

The present proposed training programme is planned for in-service teachers for inculcating, and adherence of values related to the duties mentioned in the constitution in them the detailed description of this proposed programme is as follows:

The major objectives of this programme would be to find out the level of awareness among in-service teachers regarding duties mentioned in the constitution; to train the teachers to live in value dominated bound life having full awareness of human rights and respect for the same and to conduct follow-up studies to ascertain the sustenance of this training. The target clientele of this proposed training will be the teacher trainers who are teaching in teacher training institutions. The duration of this specific training programme will be of six weeks. There will be 20 to 25 teacher trainers in each group. The selection of teachers for training will be done on the selection pattern of teachers for academic staff college's orientation programme. The co-ordinator of the programme will judiciously select an appropriate training strategy or a mix of training strategies keeping in view the theme, programme duration, background of participants, availability of resource persons, support material and technologies of training in hand. Training strategies would range from lecture-cum-discussion to methods like role playing, brain storming, socio-drama, gaming and project work. Along with this, library work, visit to relevant places, situation analysis, ethnographic enquiry would also be used as training methods and devices. Content of this training programme would be centered in the inculcation and adherence of values inherent in the duties mentioned in the constitution. Along with this, values mentioned in S.B. Chavan Committee Report (1999) will also be included in the content. The Committee has recommended that foundation for building the value based education programme, the social values like friendliness cooperativeness, compassion, self-discipline, courage, love for social justice etc., should be inculcated among learners. Similarly truth, righteous conduct, peace, love and non-violence are the core universal values that also are included in the list. Values related with the duties mentioned in the constitution and the values mentioned in the Chavan Committee report would be properly analyzed and after this analysis, following values may be finalized as the content of this programme: Patriotic value, social value; knowledge value; environmental value; constitutional value; value for excellence; value for self-discipline, peace, truth and righteous conduct etc.

Values and the duties related to these values are as follows:

Patriotic value: Having great affection towards country and regarding country as mother. Always ready to uphold and protect the sovereignty, unity and integrity of India, respecting the ideals of National Flag, National Anthem and National monuments, and defending the country and rendering national service when called upon to do so.

Social value: Having a spirit of harmony and common brotherhood and remaining active to serve the society and not using others for own sake.

Cultural value: Having reverence for rich heritage of composite culture, saints, patriots and national language. Respective ancient scripture of our country moral values like respect and honour toward teacher, parents, guest and ladies along with the feeling of unity in diversity respect for all religions.

Spiritual value: Believing in the doctrine that the world is one and therefore the entire world to be reflection of God, and serving God selflessly.

Knowledge value: Giving more importance to discover truth, gathering knowledge, developing spirit of reform for progress, using scientific outlook and gathering knowledge for the sake of humanity and its conservation.

Environmental value: Remaining quite alert regarding protection of psychological and natural environment including forests, lakes, rivers and wildlife and having compassion for living creatures.

Constitutional value: Having great faith in constitution and respect its ideals and never going against constitutional law in the individual, social and political spheres.

Values of excellence: Striving towards excellence in all spheres of individual and collective activities and intending to achieve the highest levels of endeavour.

Value for self-discipline: Having faith in self-discipline and respecting peace truth peace and righteous and righteous conduct.

The content of this programme may include topics like constitution, human rights, struggle for freedom and freedom fighters, national symbols, Indian society, violence and peace, philosophical and psychological aspects of Indian living, scientific temper and spirit of inquiry, Indian way of environmental protection professional ethics, excellence, social cohesion, etc.

As mentioned earlier, contents related with values mentioned above would be taught by print and non-print media according to need and nature of the content. On the whole, more emphasis would be given to the behavioural changes related to affective and psychomotor domains rather than cognitive domain. However, cognition of the content will be done by organizing lectures of specialists from various fields of knowledge. Along with this, various spiritual leaders will also be invited deliver lectures on specialties of various religions. As far as the use of media is concerned, an integrated approach will be followed. For this, Indian and western models of teaching for value inculcation and adherence will be used. Three-fourth of the allotted time will be devoted for practicing values through non-formal mode of teaching such as group discussion, brain storming sessions, role playing, gaming and video-cassettes related to the topics like environmental protection, violence, social cohesion, freedom movement, new inventions showing excellence etc. Teachers have to stay in the hostel during their training period and have to follow the daily routine fixed beforehand. As mentioned earlier, this programme will intend to touch cognitive, affective as well as psychomotor domain as far as inculcation and adherence of values, duties and personality development is concerned. The time budgeting of this orientation programme may be as follows:

Duration of course will be of six weeks or 40 days

Formal working hours = 40 × 5 = 200 hours

Lectures delivered by specialists on different topics = 75 hours

Other activities = 125 hours

Along with this, teachers will utilize the remaining time by visiting places to know the real situation and they will conduct ethnographic researches to have a first hand information about the existing situation. Inculcation of value related to self-discipline, truth, peace and righteous conduct will be done by implementing the daily routine strictly. This will include morning prayer, yoga, moun, prayers of all religions, group interaction etc. The above said value inculcation would be kept in mind while preparing the daily schedule for teachers.

We know that without follow-up programme, the implementation of any programme cannot be made full proof. Therefore, a follow-up study would be conducted to know that whether teachers are practicing those inculcated values or not. For this, an ethnographic inquiry will be done. Head of the institutions, students and other related persons will also be interviewed to have an authentic and objective report of the teacher. On the basis of this report the teacher will be given certificate of attending the orientation-cum-training programme. Teacher trainers would be trained in such a manner that they can teach pre-service as well as in-service teachers to live a value dominated, duty prone life. In this way, this orientation programme will help in improving the present condition of educational institutions, which are suffering from the curse of value erosion.

23

Sri Sathya Sai Education in Human Values for Teacher Education Programme: Teachers as Role Models

Madhu Kapani

Introduction

There are millions of teachers in the world today who no doubt believe they are doing the best they can for the children under their care, yet the troubles besetting our youth day by day continue to increase. Perhaps one significant cause of student unrest today is the fact that teachers are not able to command respect of young by invigorating their minds into creative patterns of dynamic thought.

The examples, teachers have to hold before them should be of those men and women who have learnt and practiced value education. Unless the teachers transform the knowledge into wisdom and help wisdom to express itself in character, the educational process would be an utter waste. If education could confer this gift of transformation of human personality, then surely life will become peaceful, happy and full of mutual help and co-operation. The minds of the young have to be vigilantly guarded against the inroads of corrupt ideologies and the budding citizens have to be actively helped to grow into noble specimens of manhood and womanhood. Brick and mortar do not make a school efficient and useful, nor are books in the library or appliances in the laboratory so essential. Teachers make the school or mar it.

It can necessary for teachers under training to be thoroughly exposed to values in their colleges of education. It presupposes that the teacher education also have a serious commitment to human values in life. Only then can they inspire the future teachers.

Education must not consist only in transmission through communication but also in transformation through assimilation and accommodation. The objective should be to educate teachers so that their human excellence blossoms forth and they imbibe right attitudes and values, besides being proficient in the skills related to teaching. A pupil learns more from what a teacher is and does than from what a teacher teaches.

Behaviour and attitudes are 'contagious' in a psychological sense, and there is much truth in the maxim that morals and values are caught and not taught; and personal example is the highest form of education. Hence, the teacher ought to be exemplary. Teachers should put into practice what they teach to the students. The ultimate factor at all times and in all places is the teacher. They are the most important assets of an educational institution and society at large. Sri Sathya Sai Baba (1985) compares the teacher with the water storage tank. If there is good and clean water in the tank, you will find good water in taps. Students are like the taps and will prove to be good only when the teachers are good. Teachers should have lofty ideals so that these can be reflected in their students, who are the future citizens and leaders. Teachers should first practise themselves what they want to teach to the students. They should have a feeling of *Tyaga* or sacrifice for the sake of the well being of the nation so that the students will have a similar ideal. Before they try to correct the students they should first correct themselves. Human values are not commodities to be sold in the market. They should be reflected in one's behaviour and one's way of life. They should be taught not as academic subjects but as the basis on which right living should be build up. The teacher should do *Sadhana* to ensure control of senses and achieve harmony in thought, word and deed. "When you achieve this harmony, you will become an ideal teacher." Teachers should identify their role, their responsibility and accountability towards their profession.

Good Teacher + Good student = Good Nation!

Some Related Studies

Sri Sathya Sai Baba has classified teachers into 3 categories, namely complaining teacher, explaining teacher and inspiriting teacher. It is imperative on the part of the teacher educators to produce inspiring teachers. The point has been clearly visualized by the National Council for Teacher Education (NCTE, 1996), which has prepared a new framework of teacher education curriculum for the country. This curriculum is based on the values and goals relevant to the Indian society.

According to Goodlad (1990), the challenge before teacher educators is indeed multifold and the task quite uphill because it can be achieved only when the teacher educators are enlightened and encouraged to improve their profile and make teacher education programmes worthy of their role performance and responsibilities as nation builders in pursuit of excellence in human life. Adiseshiah (1978) rightly states, "those that are entrusted with the responsibility of teaching the teachers have naturally to be men and women of high caliber whose influence would prove to be the greatest asset for prospective teachers." As Peck and Tucker (1973) have observed, 'teacher educators should practice what they teach. When teachers are treated in the same way they are supposed to treat their pupils, they are more likely to adopt the desired style of teaching behaviour'. Similarly, Vaughan (1996) observed, "without competent, creative and caring teachers who expect and demand the best from themselves and from all their students, other changes will have little effect. Teachers must model the content mastery, the inquiry skills, the responsibility, the character and the excitement for learning that they expect from their students. In turn, those who educate teachers must be models of exemplary practice." According to Futrell (1996), it may be difficult to meet for the "cataclysmic and colossal challenges of the twenty-first century unless teacher educators recommit themselves to finding more effective ways to prepare teachers to prepare future generation to address those changes and challenges." Perceiving the magnitude of the new challenges and tasks before teacher education, the United Nations Educational Social and Cultural Organization (UNESCO) report of the International Commission on Education for the Twenty-first Century (1996) strongly believes, "rethinking of teacher education is necessary, in order for it to bring out in future teachers, precisely those human and intellectual qualities that will facilitate a fresh approach to teaching." National Council for Teacher Education (1999), observes that "Inculcation of such qualities, values and virtues belong to the domain of Excellence in Education which primarily becomes the motivating force for a teacher education programme to be effective and tangible to the realization of the high ideals perceived globally. The profile of teacher education system and its teacher educators needs to be transparent to promote and permeate the cause of the educational excellence, more in practice than merely in precept."

Like-wise Ramji (1973) expressed that personal example of the teacher is perhaps the most important factor in any value-oriented education in the school. To quote Futrell (1996), "The goal of teacher preparation and professional development clearly articulates that reform of elementary and secondary education cannot occur unless the nation has teachers and teacher educators capable of teaching in restructured classrooms, of teaching a very pluralistic student population, and of teaching that population to meet higher educational standards that any previous generation has met," indeed lays down the very matrix of excellence in the educational parlance. There has occurred an urgency to develop national standards for each discipline, more particularly for teacher education as excellence in teacher education begets excellence in the quality of school education.

Similarly, Sanhodhan, the research and advocacy wing of Society for Integrated Development of Himalayas (SIDH) have conducted "A study of people's perceptions and Expectations from Schooling in Rural and Urban Areas of Uttarkhand" where they observed that most parents were unhappy with the impact of the present education system upon their children. Parents felt that the children must develop into 'good' human beings. Parents not only expected the children to imbibe values and ethics, but they also expected schools to teach them to do so, by internalizing qualities of good character (*gunas*) and the stress was on 'being' (*hona*) rather than 'appearance' (*dikhana*). In their perception true education is that which strengthens the moral character of children.

Sri Sathya Sai Philosophy of Integral Education

Right from the fifties, Sri Sathya Sai Baba has been emphatically declaring that good students are vital for the well being of a nation, and good character is a *sine qua non* for developing good students. Thus character development is at the core of the mission of Sri Sathya Sai Institute of Higher Learning. The stress laid on character development is no personal fad, as Sri Sathya Sai Baba often reminds that a human being is a composite of the body, the mind and the spirit. Hence true education must address all three components and not focus merely on communicating textual information. If mere job market is the goal, then character could perhaps be ignored but if nation is the goal then character moulding becomes primary. Keeping in view the vision of Sri Sathya Sai Baba, the Revered Chancellor, the Institute has consciously veered away from the purely textbook approach to the concept of integral education that aims at the simultaneous and coherent development of the body, the mind and the spirit. It is believed that such integral education alone can produce spirited citizens with farm belief in ethics and morals, and who are firmly committed to society and the nation.

The methodology for imparting integral education draws inspiration both from the best of modern practices as well as the virtues of our ancient education (*Gurukula*) system. Thus, education is not regarded as a mere classroom affair but a serious 24-hour business. In other words, the student is moulded not only in the classroom but also in the hotel, on the playground, and in the prayer hall as well.

In the hostels, students lead a spartan life with minimum comforts. Students from diverse backgrounds are brought together. This teaches them to adjust, co-operate and respect fellow beings. Several activities of the hostel are managed by the students themselves, like maintenance of hostel library, the general stores, the sick room, maintenance of the equipment, taking turns to serve food in the dining hall, managing the mess, helping weaker students in studies. The hostel becomes a veritable nursery where character building actually is initiated. It is here that spiritual living is actually practiced. Delors Report 'Learning the treasure within' (1996) too has emphasized learning to live together in the following words "Formal education must therefore provide enough time and opportunity in its programmes to introduce the young from childhood to co-operative undertakings thorough participation in sports or in cultural activities, and also through participation in social activities such as neighbourhood renovation, helping the under privileged, humanitarian work, inter-generational assistance, etc."

The founding fathers of our nation took care to stress the importance of values by making *Sathyameva Jayate* the national motto and giving central place to the Wheel of Dharma in the National

Flag. The founder Chancellor of the Institute Sri Sathya Sai Baba goes even further to declare that not only Truth (*Sathya*) and Righteousness (*Dharma*) but also Peace (*Shanthi*), Love (*Prema*) and Non-violence (*Ahimsa*) must from the basis of all human actions both at the individual and the collective level whether they relate to an organization, society as a whole or the nation.

B.Ed. Programme

When the B.Ed. programme was started in 1986, the Revered Chancellor took personal interest and care in giving shape to the philosophy of the teacher education programme, drawing the attention to numerous examples of the principles of good and great teachers available in our ancient tradition and history.

The B.Ed. programme at the Institute differs from the usual ones by the integration of instruction in the theory and practice with personality and character development, leadership training and training in discovering once own self. The approach is holistic catering to the body, the mind and the sprit of the students.

The cardinal values of Sri Sathya Sai Baba's philosophy directly lead us to his theory and practice of education. The five values of Truth, Righteous conduct, Peace, Love and Non-Violence are linked with the five facets of the human personality namely intellect, physical, emotion, psychic and spiritual respectively.

Gokak (1987) has given a logical correspondence between the five human values of Sri Sathya Sai Baba's philosophy, the five ideals of education and the five aspects of personality as shown in the tabular form.

Sl. No.	*Five Values*	*Five Aspects of Personality*	*Five Ideals of Education*
1.	Truth	Intellect	Knowledge
2.	Righteous Conduct	Physical	Skill
3.	Peace	Emotion	Balance
4.	Love	Psychic	Insight/Vision
5.	Non-violence	Spiritual	Identity/Oneness

Sri Aurobindo's concept of integral education is not different from Sri Sathya Sai Baba's integral education. Both have stressed that educational institutions are the appropriate agencies through which such values can be inculcated and internalized. The fundamental aim of education is the integration of the five aspects of human personality.

To bring about value component in education. Teacher training institutions will have to play a key role in preparing teachers for this need. The emphasis should be on the teacher imbibing the human values in their personality and behaviour to become a role model along with developing teaching competencies and professional skills.

Here I would like to present that whatever has been recommended by different national and international committees and commissions, is actually being practiced in the Sri Sathya Sai Education in Human Values for teacher education programme. Unlike the other conventional teacher training institutions, the Sri Sathya Sai model has the following features: Special course in Education in Human Values which is compulsory, of 4 credits and evaluated for 100 marks. Its objectives are to enable the trainees:

- To understand the importance of values in life and education;
- To develop awareness in trainees about self and society;
- To integrate desirable values of truth, honesty, character, self-reliance and self-discipline in their day to day work;
- To provide opportunities for broader personal outlook and positive social attitude;
- To provide awareness about education and its role in national development and international peace;
- To appreciate basic values underlying major religions of the world;
- To understand and appreciate Indian History and culture;
- To integrate human values in the lessons taught at school;
- To make teachers sensitive to the value needs of children and their full adjustment to society of future.

Based on the above objectives and replying on various educational reports, and various discourses of the founder Chancellor—Sri Sathya Sai Baba, a model syllabus has been drawn in Human values, which is being implemented since the inception of the teacher education programme at the Institute.

The second feature of the teacher-training programme is the practice teaching programme, which is unique because the trainees are trained to develop value, oriented lesson plans i.e., highlighting value inherent in their respective subjects both incidentally and in contrived situations.

In addition to the formal academic course, there is a systematic programme of integral items which encompass:

(a) *Yogasanas*, games and sports.

(b) Morning prayer and meditation.

(c) Morning assembly (Universal prayer).

(d) Attendance at classes.

(e) Social work/self-reliance programme.

Education

The grades awarded for these items are taken into account and it figures in the final grade statement. Unless value education for trainees is put under the scheme of evaluation there will be only a lip service both by the teacher educators and the trainees. However, it is necessary to have a broad-based evaluation for testing value education, 50 per cent by continuous internal evaluation and 50 per cent by external examination. Each trainee is awarded grades at the end of the course evaluated on a five-point grade scale.

The integral items as mentioned earlier namely, sports, yoga, morning assembly, etc., are evaluated keeping in view the following main components:

Punctuality, Willingness, Initiative, Team work, Mastery over skills, Regularity.

Departmental Study

To find the impact of value education in teacher education programme, a UGC sponsored Project was taken up by the faculty of education, Sri Sathya Sai Institute of Higher Learning Anantapur Campus, to study "The effect of value education on Teacher Trainees at B.Ed. Level."

The objectives of this study were:

(i) To identify the existing values in teacher trainees at the time of the admission to the B.Ed. course.

(ii) To develop the tools for assessing values.

(iii) To assess the values of teacher trainees after the completion of the course.

(iv) To compare the assessment of the teacher trainees of experimental group and the teacher trainees of the control group.

(v) To study the effect of value education in their professional field.

The findings of the study were:

(i) There is no significant difference in the performance in the performance of both the groups at the time of the admission to the B.Ed. course.

(ii) There is statistically significant difference in the performance of the trainees with value education and the trainees of the conventional training college.

(iii) The ex-student teachers also show exemplary behaviour in their professional field.

Follow up Survey

To further know the impact of value education on the B.Ed. alumni working in different parts of the contrary, a self-evaluation survey was sent to 100 teachers of whom 80 responded.

The findings of this follow up survey revealed high positive response in all the 3 categories. Category 1 'Teacher and Student' has questions pertaining to teacher's personal contact and rapport with students and their development. Category II is about 'Teacher and Herself' which deals with teacher's own self-evaluation and her role as a model. The responses are highly positive. The teachers are able to influence students and indirectly their parents resulting in behaviour and attitudinal changes in both. Category III deals with 'Teacher and Organizations' positive questions relating to the attitude of the administrator and the colleagues towards the implementation of value education. The response is highly positive. Many teachers are able to integrate values in their day to day teaching irrespective of the period allotted/not allotted for human values/ moral education in the institutions as shown in tabular form below: This is in response to question number 19.

Human Values or moral science class	*Once a week*	*Twice a week*	*Thrice a week*	*Everyday week*	*No period allotted*
	11%	20%	2%	56%	11%

The three categories are graphically represented below:

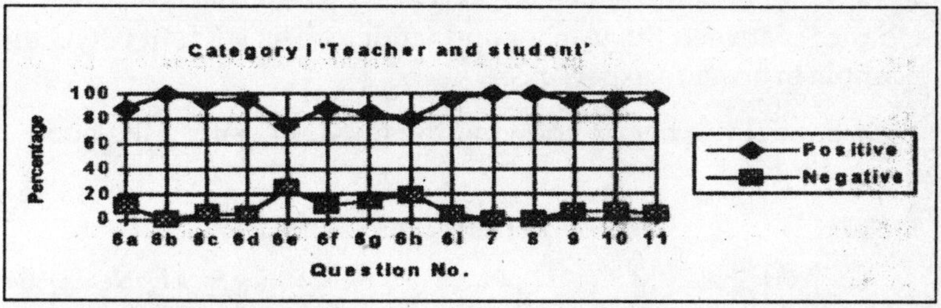

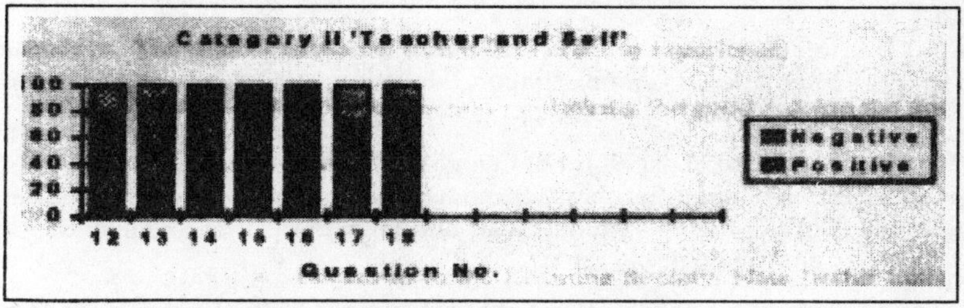

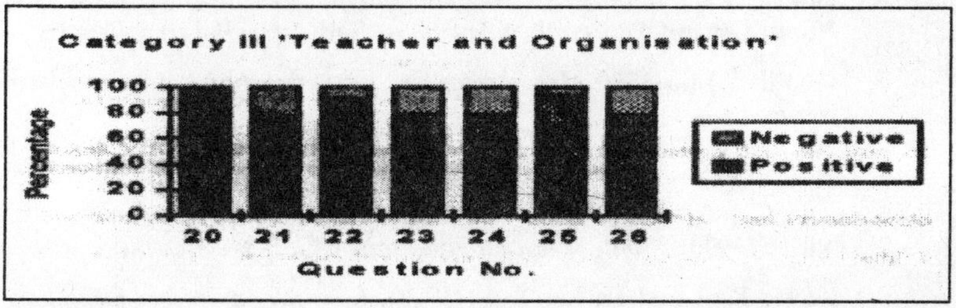

The high positive trend of the follow up study in implementation of human value by the alumni has revealed positive impact and supported that values can be integrated in teaching of subjects, by citing day to day examples and through direct and indirect methods of teaching.

Conclusion

This paper has highlighted teacher as a role model, based on Sri Sathya Sai Education in Human Value for teacher education programme with special feature of compulsory course in Education in Human Values and value-based practice teaching programme along with the integral education which is the major feature of Sri Sathya Sai Philosophy of Education, catering to the 3 HV-Head, Heart and Hands. The Founder Chancellor (1993) has emphasized on—"First be, do and then tell." This is an immense task and can only be achieved through sacrifice and dedication by the teacher to become a role model which is a two way process that is involved in a 'dance' between the teacher and student. The student needs the example in order to experience.

A model teacher = knowing the good + desiring the good + doing the good.

REFERENCES

1. Adiseshaiah, M.S. (1978), *Backdrop to the Learning Society*, New Delhi: Indian Council for Social Science Research.
2. Delors, J. (1996), *Learning the Treasure within*. Report to UNESCO of the International Commission on Education for 'Twenty First Century. UNESCO.
3. Futrell, M.H., (1996), *The Courage to Change*. In L. Kaplan and R.A. Edelfelt.(eds), Teachers for the New Millennium—Aligning Teacher Development, National Goals and High Standards for all students, California: Corwin Press.
4. Gokak, V.K. (1987), *The First Four Years of Sri Sathya Sai Institute of Higher Learning, Prasanthi Nilayam:* Sri Sathya Sai Balvikas Trust.
5. Goodlad, J.L., (1990), *Teachers for Our Nation's Schools*. San Francisco: Jossey-Bass.
6. NCTE (1996), *Curriculum Framework for Teacher Education*, New Delhi: NCTE.
7. NCTE (1999), *Profile of Teacher Educators*. NCTE, New Delhi.
8. Peeck, R. F. and Tucker, J. A. (1973), *Research on Teacher Education*, R.M.W. Travers (ed.), Second Handbook of Research on Teaching. Chicago: Rand McNally Publishing Co.
9. Ramji, M.T. (1973), *Value Oriented School Education*, New Delhi: NCERT.
10. Sanshodhan (2000), *A Mater of Quality—A Study of People's Perception and Expectations from Schooling in Rural and Urban Areas of Uttarkhand.* Research and Advocacy Wing. Society for Integrated Development of Himahalays. (SIDH). Mussoorie.
11. Sri Sathya Sai Baba (1985), *Sanathan Sarathi*—February, 1985, p. 31.
12. Sri Sathya Sai Baba (1993), *Divine Discourse* 20.11.1993. In Hand Book for Sai Teachers, the Sathya Sai Human Values Programme by Dr. R. Farmer and S. Farmer, p. 146.

13. UNESCO: 'Report of the International Commission on Education for the Twenty-First Century' (1996), *Learning the Treasure Within*, Paris: UNESCO.

14. Vaughan, J.C. (1996), *Foreword. Leonard Kaplan and R.A. Edelfelt (eds.)* Teachers for the New Millennium—Aligning Teacher Development, National Goals, and High Standards for All Students, California: Corwin Press.

24

Value Based Teacher Development in Higher Education

Yoginder Verma

We are living in the era of science and technology that has provided human life more avenues for availing comforts. It has opened up new horizons to explore into the physical domain of cosmos and utilize these opportunities for human happiness. Further, the material affluence and information revolution have brought the world much closer. There is more possibility for establishing close relationships with surroundings and the international community. But at the same time, it is being largely realized that modern man, even amidst plentiful milieu considered to be source of happiness, is more susceptible to physical diseases, mental disorders and emotional breakdowns. It is perhaps due to the fact that the man stands less developed in his inner strength to judiciously utilize the material affluence. It is only through education that man could be made stronger, from within and without.

Aim of Education

Education arises out of the need to perpetuate the society, to provide continuity in its ways of doing, thinking and behaving and to reinforce its value structure and to establish conformity to those norms that it sees as consequential and sustaining. It must reconstruct and transform the social order. International Commission on Education (1972) underlined the deficiency of modern education as a gap between its contents and living experience of its pupils, between the system of values that it preaches and the goals set-up by the society. It emphasized that the aim of education is to transform a person into a complete man, which results in a perfect integration of physical, intellectual, emotional and spiritual capabilities. Good education, according to Mahatma Gandhi, is "that which draws out and stimulates the spiritual, intellectual and physical faculties of children." (Gandhi, 1937)

Sri Sathya Sai Baba, Chancellor, Sri Sathya Sai Institute of Higher Learning (Deemed University) rightly states, "Education is for life and not for mere living." J Krishnamurti describes education on similar lines. He says "Education is not merely acquiring knowledge, gathering and correlating facts; it is to see the significance of life as a whole... The function of education is to create human beings who are integrated and therefore intelligent" (Krishnamurti, 1956). The outcome of true education is development of superior human capital with theoretical and practical knowledge, skills and high character. To Swami Vivekananda, "Education is not the amount of information that is put into your brain and runs riot there, undigested, all your life. We must have life-building, man-making, character-making assimilation of ideas. If education were identical with information, the libraries would be the greatest sages of the world and encyclopaedias the rishis." Education can be understood as liberation of oneself into new levels of intellect and emotion, as means of achieving new capacities and insights.

University Commission (1948) headed by Dr. Radhakrishnan made a pointed reference to the deeper goals of education by reminding us how our ancient teachers taught subjects and imparted wisdom. It stressed that education is both training of mind and soul and it should give both knowledge and wisdom. Einstein forcefully pleaded for striving morality in our actions for quenching our thrust for wisdom through knowledge. Education must liberate man from the shackles of cowardice, pettiness greed, hate, and narrow-mindedness, from the limits of "I" and "mine". Realizing the fact that for human fulfillment material comforts alone are not enough, the first Prime Minister of India Pt. Jawaharlal Nehru eloquently stated, "a university stands for humanism, for tolerance, for reason, for progress, for the adventure of ideas and for the search for truth, it stands for the onward march of the human race towards even higher objectives."

Values in Education—Some Initiatives

The contemporary scenario of education is contrary to the high ideals sought from it. According to Crowther (2003), "the explosion of higher education throughout the world has been subsumed within the worship of the forces of the free market and the unquestioned assumption that this will be of benefit to all. The marketisation of education, treating it as a commodity subject to the forces of market, has betrayed its objective. The social responsible ethos of higher education have been subordinated to the forces of marketisation." The ills arising out of such education system are reflected through the chaos, violence, exploitation of various kinds, indiscipline at all levels and immoral behaviour in the society. It is rightly said that if all is well with the Universities, all will be well with the society, but it is also true that a university cannot function as an island of high ideals if the society adores anti-values, awards immoral behaviour and tolerates injustice and prejudices. "Higher education institutions have been home to moral cowardice as well as to moral courage.... Failures notwithstanding, societies have historically looked to higher education as a venue for reasoned discourse rather than partisanship, for tolerance rather than discrimination, for free and open search for truth rather than secrecy or deception. For these reasons, universities are frequently the first targets of dictators." (World Bank, 2000)

A critical look at the educational scenario in the country reveals that there are more dry and barren mountains and gutters rather than plain and fertile fields nurturing the educational ideals ensuring a prosperous and peaceful society. Despite repeated references in various commissions, committees and policy documents of Government of India incorporating values in the whole educational process, the actual outcome is dismal. In this country there are counted oasis dedicated to realize the goal of education i.e., to build up a child into a complete man, who is suffused with knowledge, wisdom, skills and human values.

Unfortunately, our colleges and universities are over emphasizing the revision of curricula, and introduction of new subjects as necessitated by information revolution but have little concern to modify the same for inculcation of values aimed at making of integrated personality. In the recent years, Ministry of Human Resource Development, Govt. of India has taken initiative by introducing the component of values at different levels of education, including IITs and IIMs. Different national level institutions, such as NCERT, NIEPA, UGC-ASCs, etc., have been asked to incorporate contents of human values in their curricula. These efforts need to be understood in proper perspective so that education everywhere can be kept on an even keel of techno-informative knowledge and human values. These efforts will fructify only when the educational management is value-based and teachers are competent to integrate values in teaching.

Role of Teacher

Teachers have to develop themselves as role models whose interaction itself inadvertently passes on values to the students. It is the competent teacher possessing theoretical knowledge, practical wisdom, multiple skills and a strong value system who would be able to transform students into persons of high character and competence.

The role of teacher engaged in higher education is very crucial as higher education not only develops manpower for nation building but also prepares teachers for other levels of education. Sri Sathya Sai Baba rightly says:

> A teacher can be compared to a water tank and students to taps connected to it. As is the water in the tank, so is the water that flows from the taps. Therefore, the teacher must have a pure heart and virtues like adherence to truth, good conduct, duty, devotion and discipline, so that he can impart the same to the students. He/she alone is a teacher in the true sense, who imparts these virtues to the students. He/she is a student in the true sense, who cultivates these sacred qualities. If the teachers are ideal, the system of education too would be ideal. If the teachers do not possess moral, ethical and spiritual values, the entire system of education will go astray. Teacher moulds the rising generation into self-confident, self-reliant, atma-conscious persons. He is the architect of happy homes, prosperous communities and peaceful nations. He has not only to equip himself with the knowledge and skills to inform and instruct, but also the vision and insight, to inspire and transform. Children absorb from teachers and elders their habits and manners, behaviour and beliefs. Therefore, the teacher has to be a constant example of the ideals he has to implant in their hearts. He must excel in humility, simplicity, morality and integrity. So that education results in excellence. Such a teacher can be a beacon of truth, love and reverence.

The teacher has more than one role to play. He has to play the role of a facilitator, of a leader and of a parent substitute. "The teacher is not an instructor or task-master, he is a helper and a guide. His business is to suggest and not to impose.... The idea of hammering the child into the shape desired by the parent or teacher is a barbarous and ignorant superstition"(Sri Aurobindo, 1960). If he does not have a set of values, if he is not a communicator of love, knowledge, power and beauty, he would neither be able to put new life and energy into those who follow him nor approve honest endeavour, and cheer those who find their burdens heavy. According to Tagore (1924) "...only he can teach who can love. The greatest teachers of men have been lovers of men. The real teaching is a gift; it is a sacrifice; it is not a manufactured article of routine work; and because it is a living thing, it is the fulfillment of knowledge for the teacher himself".

Sheer parrot type teaching in the classroom cannot inculcate values. It is only through teachers and elders who are themselves embodiment of human values and live disciplined and regulated life that the values are imbibed. If they become role models, the students will automatically follow them. Hence, the teacher has to be fully developed on all counts.

Teacher Development in Higher Education

Earlier, there was no systematic training for teachers in higher education. It is only after the recommendations of NPE (1986) that the UGC launched Academic Staff Orientation Scheme in 1987 with the purpose of producing professionally competent teachers for higher education. Under this scheme, the UGC has established fifty-one UGC-Academic Staff Colleges (ASC) and fifty Refresher Course Centres. The Academic Staff Colleges are inter-university institutes operating within the university system. They are expected to develop overall competence of teachers through orientation programmes and knowledge upgradation through refresher courses.

From 1987-88 to March 2003, the Academic Staff Colleges have conducted 2,344 Orientation Programmes (each of 4 weeks duration) and 5,849 Refresher Courses (each of 3 weeks duration) in which 76,433 and 1, 85,388 teachers respectively have participated. Out of an estimated 4,75,000 teachers in the colleges and universities 2,61,821 teachers including 83190 women have undergone training (UGC-ASC, Mysore, 2003). During these programmes, emphasis is laid on the inculcation of certain values empowering teachers to perform role and responsibilities effectively. They are also sensitized and motivated to practice values in their professional life. The Academic Staff Colleges adopt both direct and indirect approaches for developing values.

Direct Approach

Lectures, group discussions, role-plays, quiz, project work, etc., are organized for providing understanding about the meaning, concept and types of values. Teachers are also given knowledge about the techniques and methods required for inculcation and enrichment of values. Some ASCs are also organizing 3-week Refresher Courses in Values. This enables teachers to understand the relevance of values in building up a prosperous society, sources of values, teachers' role in building up of high character students, values inherent in Indian heritage and culture, methods of teaching values, etc.

Indirect Approach

ASCs inculcate values through indirect approach by undertaking certain activities and exercises focussing at developing the values of discipline, co-operation, scientific temper, compassion, equality, humility, commitment, etc.

But these efforts are isolated without specific vision or perspective. Through these efforts, the values are being passed on to the teachers incidentally through the contents, organizers and the resource persons. After a reasonably good time of their establishment, now the ASCs should seriously think of systematic and planned inculcation of values essential for realizing the goals of higher education.

Toward Value-Based Teacher Development

Teacher development in higher education means empowerment of teacher by improving knowledge of subject and inter-disciplinary fields, sharpening of teaching and managerial skills, enrichment of values and improving confidence, enhancing sensitivity to societal needs and problems, so as to enable him to execute his role effectively. This task is very complex and gigantic. It can only be accomplished by creating an enabling environment with the active support of government; forceful intervention of quality assurance agencies and value based academic leadership of the host university. The entire process of value based teacher development is determined by various multi dimensional issues, which require proper understanding and thorough analysis. In this paper, an attempt has been made to present a design for value based teacher development with the purpose of realizing the aim of higher education. This design is based on the experiments conducted at the UGC-Academic Staff College, Himachal Pradesh University, Shimla. Essential elements of the design are discussed as under:

1. Choosing Appropriate Development Perspective

First of all, the Academic Staff College should develop an appropriate perspective for teacher development. There can be two perspectives of value inculcation in teacher development. Under traditional perspective, nurturance and cultivation of values is treated separately as one of the teaching components as is shown in Figure-A. Here, the process of inculcating values is undertaken as a separate activity and the effects are also measured accordingly. Undoubtedly, this perspective has been able to increase awareness about values; however, it has not entirely equipped the teachers to manifest values in their teaching behaviour. Perhaps, it is due to the fact that under this perspective, values are not considered as driving force for the development of other teaching components. Therefore, an eclectic perspective is suggested wherein values assume the role of underlying current that determines the direction and intensity of other components as is shown in Figure-B.

Figure A

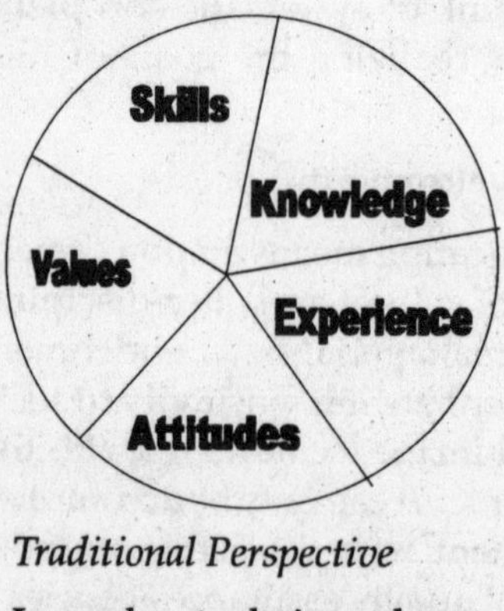

Traditional Perspective

Figure-B

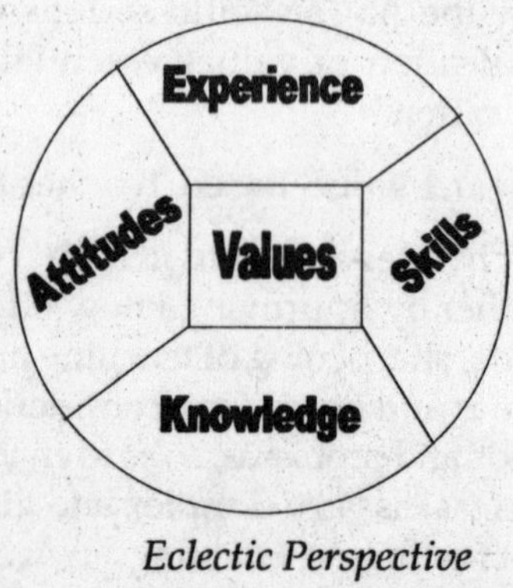

Eclectic Perspective

In order to bring about desired transformation, eclectic perspective for value based teacher development is suggested. This will prepare teachers for integrating values in teaching of social sciences, physical and live sciences, commerce and management, ethics and other branches of knowledge. Whole thinking should be guided by the assumption that the values are transcendental and all pervasive.

2. *Vision and Mission for Teacher Development*

The Academic Staff College should be devoted to the philosophy of value-based teacher development. It should have clarity about its vision and reflect in the form of mission statements. "Usually, the mission statements include values and the aspects of culture. Mission statements are used first and foremost in an internal role facilitating the communication of managerial beliefs and to indicate standards of expected behaviour, with lesser use externally"(Klemm *et al.*, 1991). The mission statements of ASC may be derived from the philosophy of establishing ASCs in the country; aims of Indian higher education; and benchmarks drawn from performance of the world class or the best practice standard. The sharing of vision and mission with the institutional members and stakeholders would ensure their commitment to various activities undertaken for teacher development. The participants would understand the direction, which the facilitators have planned for them..

3. *Selection of Facilitators and Training Staff*

It is value driven leadership, both at managerial and training level that ensures value-based teacher development. A good leader, demonstrating high ideals and values in his work and behaviour would be able to create facilitating environment for imbibing values. Value inculcation requires transformation of heart and modification of attitudes, which cannot happen with mere lessons in the classroom. It requires competent persons including Director and members of core staff who will provide stimulus and encouragement for development of values. Hence, the selection of quality personnel suffused with strong value system becomes prerequisite for value-based training. Core staff of ASC should be given training for organizing value based teacher development programmes. They should visit the institutions imparting value-based education so that they understand the fundamentals of conducting such programmes.

4. *Development of Value-Based Institutional Culture*

The ASC should develop ennobling and facilitating organizational culture, which helps participants in understanding the vitality of values in determining the effectiveness of an organization and effective teaching. Organizational culture includes the vision, norms, symbols, etiquettes, ambiance, interactions, the manner in which people greet and serve each other, etc. In the routine working of the ASC, even small acts exhibit the nature of prevalent culture. Every ASC envelops certain patterns in its institutional management. This sprouts into an institutional culture emitting certain values, which are internalized by the participants consciously or unconsciously. Value-based education cannot be imparted without institutionalization of basic tenets essential for producing desired value system.

5. Identification of Values Essential for Teacher Development

The Academic Staff Colleges should have clear understanding about the values to be developed during professional development programmes. They may draw the desired values from the basic philosophy of Academic Staff Orientation Scheme and also from the Guidelines for Academic Staff Colleges as circulated by the UGC. According to these Guidelines:

> "The orientation programme envisaged under this scheme must not be rigid. Under the programme, it is intended to inculcate in young lecturers the quality of self-reliance through their awareness of the social, intellectual and moral environment. The programme should enable the teachers to discover themselves and their potential through a positive appreciation of their role in the total social, intellectual and moral universe within which they function and of which they are important members. In a country where teachers are able to fulfill their responsibility with awareness and confidence, the educational system becomes relevant and dynamic"(UGC, 200 and www.ugc.ac.in).

With the perspective of value-based teacher development, the ASC may have to understand and enlist values by grouping them broadly under two categories.

(a) *Temporal values*: These include cultural values, political values, economic values, institutional values, and societal values. An elaborate exercise is needed to identify these values. These values in the context of teacher development should be identified by an elaborate study of the following:

- Guidelines for UGC-Academic Staff Colleges.

- Constitution of India.
- Indian culture and national heritage.
- Prevailing societal environment.
- Stakeholders' expectations from the teachers.
- Teachers' opinion about the highly cherished values in teaching profession.

(b) *Universal values:* We find that there are certain universal values.

"There are certain values, which are universal in their nature. They are relevant in all the times and at all the places. India is a plural society with a variety of religions, languages and regions. Formulation of social values would essentially necessitate taking into account the needs and sensitivities of different types of people living in this country. In a plural society like India, there has to be a constant endeavour to identify generally acceptable values and promote them. So far as the individual values are concerned they may vary from society to society, religion to religion. But the basic-values such as Sathya (Truth), *Dharma* (Righteous Conduct), *Shaanthi* (Peace), *Prema* (Love) and Ahimsa (Non-violence) should be free from controversy; and hence should be acceptable to all the people living in this country" (K. Sudha Rao, 2000).

These basic values may further be elaborated and grouped as *human values* comprising of freedom, responsibility, equity, self-control and co-operation; *moral values* including honesty, integrity, non-violence, fair-play and justice; and *spiritual values* namely— love, peace, purity, humility, truth, compassion, respect, tolerance, forgiveness, harmony, unity, happiness and detachment. These values germinate in spirituality. They are universal and imperishable and their results are experienced over long period of time. These values are truly called core values for they originate from all the religious and philosophical concepts. Thus, they are valued, shared and appreciated by all people, whether across cultures or down through the generations. One can understand and imbibe these values only by developing untainted and firm faith in the self or God. Values flourish when the thought, word and deed of man are sacred and are in unison. The heart is not polluted by malice, the tongue is not infected by lie and the body is not driven by the acts of violence.

The five human values of truth, righteous conduct, peace, love and non-violence have emerged from the integral philosophy of Sri Sathya Sai Baba. Baba says,

> "There is an organic link between the human values and the human personality. Mental happiness comes from peace, peace comes from love, love is linked with non-violence, non-violence is the outcome of righteous conduct, righteous conduct without truth cannot be thought of. Thus, the five values of love, peace, non-violence, righteous conduct and truth representing five major facets of the human personality, are the petals of the same flower" (Sri Sathya Sai Institute of Higher Learning, 2000).

While identifying values for teacher development, it should be ensured that temporal values are rooted in the universal human values. This requires deeper insight and rigorous monitoring.

6. Planning for the Programme

The ASC should develop a mechanism for the conduct of various programmes. It may constitute a co-ordinating team with defined purpose and guidelines. The team should deliberate over the theme selected for the conduct of a particular orientation/refresher course. The inputs, procedures, methods and activities are selected and designed in view of the mission and intended value inculcation. Sharing of experiences by ASC staff with coordinating team is found to be very rewarding exercise. It helps co-ordinating team in identification of values, determining performance standards and chalking out detailed programme for implementing value-based activities. Good planning itself demonstrates the values of discipline, sincerity, intuition, commitment, hard work, etc. Pre-programme planning should be enriched by time-to-time review and modifications as required. This inculcates the values of team spirit, participation, spirit of inquiry, synthesis, perseverance and tolerance.

7. Execution of the Programme

In a value-based programme, each activity should be designed with certain purpose and inherent value in it. The process of execution will itself nurture the value system of the participants. With a sense of accomplishment, they will feel more confident about the worth of values. Based on the experiments carried out in UGC-Academic Staff College, Himachal Pradesh University, Shimla, in a value-based teacher development programme, the planned activities should be executed with pinpointed purpose and value focus. Selected activities undertaken for conducting value-based teacher development programme, with an expected value addition are presented in Annexure-A.

8. Monitoring and Feedback

In order to ensure that the desired value enrichment is carried on, the programme team should develop a mechanism for measuring the performance and identification of the gap between the actual and expected responses in thoughts, words and deeds of participants. After examining the level of change, necessary corrective action should be initiated. The feedback should be taken at the end of day, week and whole programme. A close interaction between the members of programme team and the participants can provide certain essential cues which may not be quantified but substantially help in working out value driven activities. Techniques like *Think Tank* and *Review Over the Week* would not only provide feedback but also planned reinforcement of desired values.

At the end of the programme, the participants may be asked to provide feedback particularly on—strengths of the programmes, the message taken from the programme and description of the programme in few words. The experience of the author shows that at the end of a value based programme, most of the responses confirm the pervasiveness of planned values and resolve to adopt them in their personal and professional life.

9. The Aftermath

The process of inculcation of values should not stop with the conclusion of the programme but continue even after. The participants should be followed and observed for change in their thoughts, attitudes and actions. A survey of some cases will provide further feedback for reinforcement. Such survey should be planned to study the responses from all those who are in direct contact with the teacher. Feedback from the teachers in the form of reflections, after their joining in the parent department, would provide important information about the impact of value-based activities.

To illustrate, the Academic Staff College, Shimla, has been asking the participants to reflect over what they have learned during the programme and also what they have put into practice. It is observed that most of the responses were pertaining to value laden teaching conceptions. These responses were published in different issues of *Academe*, a journal of ASC, Shimla. Some excerpts of these responses are presented in Annexure–B. Research studies will further help in designing value-based programmes. In his Ph.D work while comparing the working of different ASCs, Joshi (2000), found that the Academic Staff College of H.P. University, Shimla has work culture with "Insistence on values of commitment, devotion, punctuality, humility and tolerance."

The focus in all teacher development programmes must shift from teaching as a unidirectional, teacher-centered, knowledge oriented activity to learning as learner-centered, value-based, experience-oriented, interactional activity, involving sub-activities like problem-solving, community living, drawing inferences, making generalizations, and moving from the mundane to the sublime, from the trivial to the enduring. This will be possible only when conscious efforts are undertaken to execute value-based teacher development programmes.

REFERENCES

1. Crowther, David (2003), Social Responsibility and the Marketisation of Higher Education, *Staff and Educational Development International*, New Delhi, Indira Gandhi National Open University, pp. 23-40.
2. Gandhi, M. K. (1937), *Harijan*, September 1.
3. Joshi, D.K. (2000), *Evaluative Study of Academic Staff Colleges*, New Delhi, Associated Publishing Company, p. 132.
4. K. Sudha Rao, *Best Practices in Higher Education – Integral Education; A Mission to Integrate Values in Education*, National Institute of Educational Planning and Administration (NIEPA), New Delhi, p. 1.
5. Klemm, M.S., Sanderson, S.G. and Luffman, G. (1991), *Mission Statement: Selling Corporate Values to Employees*, Long Range Planning, pp. 73-78.
6. Krishnamurti, J. (1956), *Education and Significance of Life*, London, Victor Gollancz, p. 14.
7. Sri Aurobindo (1960), *Sri Aurobindo and the Mother on Education*, Pondicherry, Sri Aurobindo International Centre, pp. 15-16.

8. Sri Sathya Sai Institute of Higher Learning (2000), *Sri Sathya Sai System of Integral Education*, Prasanthi Nilayam, p. 55.

9. Tagore, R.N. (1924), *Letters from Abroad*, Madras, S. Ganesan, p. 24.

10. UGC (2002), *The Guidelines for Academic Staff Colleges*, New Delhi, UGC.

11. UGC-Academic Staff College (2003), *A Report: All India UGC-Academic Staff College Directors' Meet*, held at Mysore on June 2-3, 2003, Mysore, University of Mysore, p. 36.

12. World Bank (2000), *Higher Education in Developing Countries – Peril and Promise*, Washington, World Bank, p. 44.

ANNEXURE—A

Value-Based Professional Development—Some Suggested Activities

Description of Activity	*Purpose*	*Values*
Setting the Tone: The participants are informed about the contents, resource persons and procedure of conducting the programme besides the details of various activities planned by the programme team. After critical interaction the suggestions given by participants are incorporated.	■ Share details about the 'programme package' ■ Seek comments and suggestions of the participants ■ Ensure participation and commitment of the participants ■ Convey the rules and norms of conducting the course	* Participative decision-making * Team spirit * Transparency and objectivity * Motivation * Curiosity·
Know Thy Group: Every participant is asked to develop familiarity with all those who are not known to him/her, to begin with and also to know their likings, strengths, subject specialization, etc..	■ Know the liking, strengths and distinctions of the group members ■ Explore opportunities for learning ■ Ensure fruitful interaction	* Respect for others * Friendship * Good manners * Caring * Compassion * Brotherhoodness
Breaking the Ice: Each participant is sensitized to the virtues and goodness of the group members and also about the sacrifice made for gaining the present opportunity.	■ Fulfill social and recognition need ■ Develop seriousness toward the goal of the programme ■ Understand others ■ Work as Team	* Friendliness * Compassion * Dignity of individual * Team spirit * Sharing * Optimism

(Contd.)

A Look Within: Participants are required to prepare their own profile including strengths and weaknesses.	■ Learn to introspect ■ Develop self-reliance and self-confidence ■ Overcome superiority and inferiority complex	* Self-confidence * Self-introspection * Discrimination * Self-discipline
Know Thy Profession: Participants respond to questions relating to the purpose of teaching, components of teaching, teaching conceptions, ethics of teaching, etc.	■ Understand the dimensions of teaching and learning ■ Clarify assumptions about teaching ■ Develop respect for teaching profession ■ Identify areas for development	* Self-analysis * Self-confidence * Dignity * Self-respect * Social Justice * Humility * Dedication
Help Thyself: Every participant is expected to associate himself/herself with one of the task groups constituted for the management of the programme.	■ Take group decisions ■ Increase group involvement and commitment ■ Utilize synergistic effect of pooling the group resources ■ Make optimum utilization of each person's talent and capacities	* Self-reliance * Team spirit * Discipline * Co-operation * Concern for others * Equality * Dependability * Helpfulness * Duty
Group Song: The participants select and sing together group song in the beginning of the day and national anthem at the close of the day.	■ Provide soothing effect ■ Integrate thoughts and feelings of the group members ■ Develop productive work culture	* Peace * Claim * Happiness

(Contd.)

	■ Create readiness for serious work ■ Nurture Talent	* Love * Respect for others * Concentration * Patriotism * Universal Love
Silent Sitting: All the participants observe two minutes silence in the warming up session.	■ Consolidate inner energies ■ Establish connection between inner and the outer environment ■ Get prepared for day's work ■ Tune toward committed activities ■ Learn to think before action	* Concentration * Self-control * Peace * Tolerance * Inner silence * Humility * Endurance * Understanding * Perseverance
Thought for the Day: Participants reflect over the thought for the day, given by one of the participants with different points of view.	■ Focus mind at good thoughts ■ Learn to assimilate ■ Be Broadminded ■ Develop Reflective Thinking ■ Be creative	* Reason * Intuition * Tolerance * Discrimination * Appreciating others * Spirit of inquiry * Quest for knowledge * Curiosity

(Contd.)

Mutual Evaluation: Participants evaluate each other on certain performance parameters.	■ Be open to evaluation by others ■ Accept evaluation by colleagues ■ Enrich evaluating skill ■ Learn to appreciate others' accomplishment	* Objectivity and fairness * Tolerance * Dignity of individual * Self-acceptance * Truthfulness * Self-knowledge
Self-Encounter: Participants evaluate their own pre-recorded lecturing styles/ behaviour manifestations.	■ Develop understanding about own behaviour ■ To judge oneself vis-à-vis other colleagues ■ Identify opportunities for self-development	* Self-introspection * Self-sufficiency * Appreciation of others * Self-respect * Self-confidence
Programme Evaluation: Each participant evaluates the quality of programme on daily basis and also the performance of each resource persons on certain identified criteria.	■ Develop critical thinking ■ Understand the dimensions of evaluation ■ Realize ones' contribution in programme effectiveness	* Fairness * Sincerity * Discipline * Honesty * Discrimination * Integrity
Simulation/Role Plays: Participants perform various roles in teaching games/role plays and simulation situations.	■ Sensitize to classroom and societal realities ■ Learn to adopt to environmental settings	* Consideration * Appreciation of other cultures * Kindness

(Contd.)

	■ Develop decision-making skills and attitudes ■ Be empathetic to others	* Confidence * Team spirit * Fellow feelings * Helpfulness
Field Visits: Participants visit various environmental, institutional and societal settings depending upon their subject of study.	■ Enhance observation skills ■ Seek solutions to real life problems and find opportunities for development ■ Learn to integrate theory with the practice ■ Be familiar to realities ■ Develop we-ness	* Self-sacrifice * Helpfulness * Respect for all * Discrimination * Curiosity * Quest for knowledge * Synthesis * Discipline * Optimism * Understanding * Compassion
Brain Storming: Participants give various views on a topic, even if not relevant.	■ Identify problems and issues ■ Develop creativity ■ Seek creative solutions ■ Utilize group resources ■ Nurture interaction among all	* Courage * Tolerance * Broadmindedness * Attention * Focus * Reflection * Optimism

(Contd.)

Panel/Group Discussion: A group of participants interact on a given theme/topic.	■ Generate rate new ideas and solutions to the problems ■ Learn to make group decisions ■ Assimilate ideas ■ Develop habit of critical thinking	* Team spirit * Courage * Appreciation * Tolerance * Initiative * Quest for knowledge * Perseverance
Hidden Talent: Participants are motivated to demonstrate the hidden talent which is otherwise not visible in the routine working.	■ Share creativity ■ Create accepting and enabling environment ■ Accept others ■ Nurture food feelings	* Appreciating others * Self-acceptance * Humanism * Forgiveness * Friendship * Inner happiness
Project Work: Each participant is assigned the task of preparing a project during the programme.	■ Development practical insight ■ Understand the environment relevant to a subject ■ Development active learners ■ Seek creative solutions ■ Learn to develop practical acknowledge among students	* Social service * Initiative * Sincerity * Spirit of inquiry * Quest for knowledge * Truthfulness * National Awareness
Leadership Roles: Each participant assumes the role of chairperson/reporter of the session and also group leader under different situations.	■ Develop managerial skills ■ Enhance leadership qualities ■ Realize role of teacher beyond classroom also	* Self-Confidence * Courage * Initiative * Responsibility

(Contd.)

	■ Encourage participation	* Leadership * Self-respect * Forgiveness * Concern for others * Self-sufficiency
Gems Collection: Participants search for superior ideas emerging during presentations and interactions.	■ Reinforcement of learning ■ Enhance capability of looking for good ideas	* Curiosity * Discrimination * Spirit of inquiry

ANNEXURE—B

Excerpts from the Participants' Reflections

(Published in *ACADEME*, a Journal of Academic Staff College, Himachal Pradesh University, Shimla)

1. "… I have definitely come back refreshed with new ideas, thoughts and feelings and have also reconstructed my opinion about my colleagues as well. The persons associated with the Academic Staff College were simple, humble, sincere, hardworking, knowledgeable, kind and concentrate. They were kind enough to let me speak and express myself freely and we did interact freely. The resource persons were good and enlightened. Yesterday Kamini suggested that we should begin the classes with a prayer and end with the National Anthem as it was done at the ASC Shimla, for which you have agreed graciously. I would also suggest two minutes silence. Initially the silence should be guided and later on it can be withdrawn though our students are adults …… I would also want you to introduce yoga in a very serious manner… Yoga will make a person physically fit, mentally stable and spiritually strong, it will definitely go a long way in improving society…. We have to do something, Madam, whatever we can. Again I am reminded of our Director of the ASC when he said a day before we left, when we were discussing the thought for the day, 'even a dog cleans the place, when it is about to sit, why can't we do it?' I think we should also do a little cleaning up, do our part to make this world a better place to live in."

   Veera M. Bharda, K.L.E. Society's College of Education, Hubli (A Participant's Open Letter to Principal of Her College, *Academe*, Shimla, ASC HP University), Vol. VIII, 2001, p.55.

2. "Hallmark of the day used to be the hotly debated discussion on 'Thought for the day' which used to be in relation to environment. Another feature was interaction among the participants and with resource persons. Almost every participant presented useful talk on the topic of their choice which enriched our knowledge on different science subjects. We enjoyed two field visits to Darlaghat and Kufri and Chail. Celebrations of Environment Day—5th June were more than practical in approach rather than traditional lectures. We

participated actively in spreading the message of 'Be Eco friendly' and perhaps this was the reflection of what we learned in the auditorium of ASC.

Mr. K.V. Vaidya, Sr. Lecturer,
Department of Zoology, MCM DAV College, Kangra, H.P.
(An Opportunity to Develop All Round Personality,
Academe, Shimla, ASC, HP University), Vol. VII, 1997, p. 48.

3. "Last, but not the least is the utility of this programme. Apart from it being a professional compulsion for a higher scale, it helps us to be a good teacher, a patient listener and a wise acceptor. We can easily induct techniques like brain-storming, debates, think tank, symposia, presentation, quiz, reporting, group discussions and tests in our daily teaching routine, which makes lecturing less boring and a class room a more lively place. Through the application of the above we are able to inculcate values of education and infuse enthusiasm for learning amongst the student community."

Dr. Charu Sharma, Lecturer in English
Govt. College, Kullu, H.P.
(ASC: A Rainbow,
Academe, Shimla, ASC, HP University), Vol. VII, 1997, p. 49.

4. "But the one month of exposure to new and seemingly simple sounding ideas that teaching is a creative act, a teacher must be innovative, modest, friendly and human, created an inner turbulence that made me realize I had so much to learn as a teacher, so much to give as a person and so much remained locked within me. The programme had tremendous impact on my mind. Yes! I said to myself, a teacher is a human being not a dictator or a high pontiff to hand down dictums of lectures to a passive audience with a stupid and stiff expression on his/her face. Slowly, the grime and dust of years of rigid attitudes started getting washed away by the avalanche of ideas and information during the course. It was a fascinating process of my inner transformation and renewal. The programme provided me with an excellent opportunity to understand myself better, reassess my attitudes towards my work, my students and myself. It helped me get out of the cocoon of outdated and obscure notions."

Ms. Atiya Singh, Govt. College Hamirpur, H.P.
(From Text-Book to Self-Realization,
Academe, Shimla, ASC HP University)
Vol. IV, No.1, 1994, p. 29.

5. "At the completion of the course I found myself a totally changed, reformed and enthusiastic teacher, full of confidence and determination, looking forward to implement the newly acquired skills and techniques into action. The course also afforded me the opportunity for introspection whereby I could realize my shortcomings and made all efforts of overcome them, by acquiring new skills and techniques."

Dr. Devika Chandel, Lecturer in Pol. Science,
Govt. Degree College Solan.
(Orientation Programme: A Stimulating Experience,
Academe, Shimla, ASC HP University)
Vol. IV, No.1, 1994, p. 37.

6. "The programme opened my eyes and I took a pledge there and then to adopt and implement at least some of the things learnt there as part of my classroom instruction. Back to my college, I have started work on my plans and am convinced that the dividends are fairly fast...The first thing I have started is to know my students. Detailed information is collected on the very first day. It is analyzed and the abnormal, shy and uncared for students are identified. I give them individual attention and then, through counselling motivate them to adopt a positive and progressive attitude towards life."

Mr. J.L. Aggarwal, D.A.V. College Abohar, Punjab,
(Impact of an Orientation Programme on my Teaching,
Academe, Shimla, ASC HP University)
Vol. III, No.1, 1992, p. 31.

7. "The Orientation Programme of ASC under HPU pinpointed my deficiencies in the field of teaching, interaction with my students, personality, psychological aspects of learning, teaching and various other hidden factors, which are necessary for a teaching professional. The programme also clearly gave the participants ways to improve upon those deficiencies. These deficiencies may slightly vary from one

participant to the other but the fact remains that they do exist. My point of view to be a good participant and hence draw the maximum benefit is that ONE MUST HAVE A GOOD DEAL OF PATIENCE as a prerequisite with a sanctified conscience. He/she should try to gain something new and not the Certificate only."

Shri. Ng. Pradeepkumar Singh,
D.M. College of Science, Imphal,
(A Touch of Illumination,
Academe, Shimla ASC, HP University)
Vol. VIII, No.1, 2001, p. 59.

PART–V
VALUES IN ACTION

25

Teaching of Human Values in Professional Courses

K. Aiyadurai

Introduction

Professional education all over the world provides the knowledge of high standard, principles, latest inventions and their applications. The students undergoing such courses apply these in their institutional training and project works. Constant working on the acquired knowledge, make them specialists in their respective fields. Their experience and effort on the technology application enable them to be innovative and creative. Postgraduate and research studies strengthen the base of theory and technology for further use to the welfare of mankind.

Value Crisis

Most of the professionals have become money minded. They have the only target of minting more and more money overlooking their accountability toward society. They hardly feel grateful to the society for their success.

In countries like India, the contribution of the family members, towards the education of the younger generation is significant. Huge amount of money and efforts are spent on imparting professional education. In addition to this, the contribution of the Government by way of subsidizing the education from primary level to the professional level is also very much considerable. Such huge amount of money spent on subsidy, is the contribution of the society as a whole, by way of taxes and tariffs.

Of late, the tendency of a larger number of youths, after qualifying their examination and entering into profession is that they forget their own family members. They leave their family members and parents to their destiny. The money mindedness and selfishness lead such youth to many vices, which ultimately make their lives miserable.

To the society also, they fail to do their duty. The money dominated attitude makes them blind towards the poor and sufferers. Doctors, surgeons, scientists, engineers, teachers and such other professionals are thus going against the social expectations.

Moreover, too much of professional involvement, for earning more and more, alienates the individual from his/her own unit family. This leads to their non-attention to their own children. Even though such people are able to meet the material needs of their children and spouse, by means of not involving much time with family members, they are unable to meet the psychological needs and expectations of the people around them. This affects the family life in general and the growth of the children in particular. When both the parents are involved in profession like this, the fate of the children in the unitary family is still worse. They feel themselves as 'orphans', ships with radars.

The students should be made to be guided by their conscientious. This realisation can come only be self-realisation. His responsibility towards society must be realized by himself. Teaching ethics and social issues would serve as basic eye opener to the students on this line. With this basic knowledge, he will be able to realize the values in life and may practice it along with his profession.

A start in this direction, at the earliest, is the basic need of the hour.

Recently, it is accepted worldwide, that technical and scientific knowledge must be enriched by inculcating basic human values among professionals. This will lead to a high level thinking of ethical and social issues criteria in academic accreditation. For the implementation of this concept, inclusion of ethics and social issues throughout engineering, scientific and technical curricula, would serve as a powerful means.

Ethics and Value education must from the part of the curricula in technical education.

Ethics is a scientific study of morals, which deals with basic principles, that guide human conduct and also how these principles can be applied to concrete situations. Principles of ethics have to be understood correctly and applied to concrete situations in life. This governs both private and social spheres of life.

Value Education is the other side of the coin. Technical graduates coming out of professional institutions must learn certain values also, which are set of principles of standards of behaviour, regarded desirable and important and held in high esteem by the society in which the person lives. As the fruit of the services of the technologists are going to reach the society at the ultimate level, concern for the humanity must be inculcated in the minds of the technical students.

The Proposed Programme

A subject on Ethics and Value Education must form part of the professional curricula. The title of the subject may be, 'Ethics and value for professionals.

Objectives of the Subject

1. To understand ethics as basis for human development in various dimensions viz., physical, intellectual, emotional, moral and social development.
2. To promote social consciousness among the professionals to achieve unity and fellowship.
3. To facilitate critical thinking.
4. To spell out accepted norms and counter values and their implications.
5. To achieve a humanistic attitude by having concern for others.

These objectives are to be specific in framing the curriculum for the subject. The awareness to the society and human needs makes the knowledge, built up in a more perfect manner. This will develop work ethics in the career of the young professionals, and make them to true servants of the society.

Duration of the Course

The duration of the course may be for one year of 100 hours. This may be imparted in the final year of the degree programme as a common subject to all specialties and branches of professional education. On completion of the course, when the candidates came out to show their talents, they must realize that their professional skills must be utilized for the good of others.

Contents

(i) *Ethics:* Meaning, principles of ethics, ethics in Private life and in social life.

(ii) *Institutional Influence:* Home, politics, society, government, environment, media and religion.

(iii) *Meaning of 'values' in life:* Values at different levels, viz., personal, social, moral and spiritual and behavioural. Understanding the rights and duties of individuals in a society.

(iv) *Personality development:* Dimensions of human development understanding of self and family as the basic social unit. Character building and morality building at various levels.

(v) The contents proposed are not conclusive. They can be extended to any level according to the requirement under various situations.

Methodology of Inculcating Values

Teaching method for this subject must be on the participatory basis, with more involvement by the students in the learning process. It is proposed as input session by the teacher. 50 per cent of the contents may be based on problem-solving exercises on certain practical issues in the groups, 25 per cent through case study and 25 per cent by self-preparation by students.

Students are able to understand and learn better, when the teachers use appropriate methods. Some of the interesting methods that could be attempted are as follows:

(i) Teacher-Student discussion in the classroom on specific topics.

(ii) Discussion among students in-groups, on specific topics, with teacher as moderator.

(iii) Case studies.

(iv) Slide shows followed by discussion.

(v) Students to give commentaries on the themes of some important films/media exhibit/short stories.

(vi) Question-answer session.

(vii) Sharing of student's experience followed by brain storming session.

This methodology would be beneficial in making the students to involve themselves in a better way than the regular lecturing method.

Evaluation of Performance

Evaluation of the level of achievement of the students in this subject must be two-folded.

The course teacher may evaluate the performance of the student up to 50 per cent through the continuous assessment. This may be done by observing the student's involvement in the classroom, in the discussions and problem-solving sessions throughout the year/semester as the case may be.

The remaining 50 per cent of the marks may be for summative assessment at the end of the year/semester, based on question papers with questions of objective, descriptive and problem-solving nature.

Thus, the students are to be evaluated in full taking into consideration the knowledge acquired in the subject and the application of the same relevantly in appropriate situations.

The author would like to make note that many of the educational institutions, run by religious machineries in India are offering courses on Moral education, Ethics education, Value education and Social Analysis, at different levels, right from school to undergraduate level in arts and science colleges. But such courses are not imparted in other educational institutions and professional institutions so far. The attempt of including ethics and social issues in all the professional courses would be of immense benefit to the society as a whole.

26

Role of Physical Education in the Development of Values

Y.P. Sharma

Due to progressive mechanization and industrialization physical comforts are increasing. Despite every comfort of life, hazards are increasing rapidly leading to mental unrest among the people. There is need at global level for the revival of human values.

An individual is influenced by his family, friends, playmates, neighbours, institutions, etc. He acts according to the group and environment to which he belongs and shares norms with others whose social roles are closely interlinked. Sports are a dynamic social force in every culture. Sports have become an important part of the nation's culture throughout the world. Sports are important to society as it affects the behaviour of human beings. It helps in behaviour modification of students (Borse, 1998). Sports and other physical education programmes can affect the social prowess and human values. According to NPE, 1992 the importance of physical education in helping man to come out from various self-created problems arising out of modernization of society cannot be undermined. Comprehensive and diverse physical education programmes can help a great way to overcome the present crises (Singh, 2000). It is an education of and through human movement where many of educational objectives are achieved by means of big muscle activities involving sports, games, gymnastics, dance and exercises (Barrow, 1983).

Process of Socialisation

The process of socialization starts from the birth of a child. But at the time of birth he lacks the necessary elements of social life. With the passage of time he changes and moulds himself according to the standards and needs of society. This process of change and development is nothing but socialization. As a result of this process, man accepts socialization as a part of social behaviour and tries to make adjustments with his fellow men. It is a process of mutual influence among themselves, which leads to accepted patterns of social behaviour. Process of socialization involves the following contents:

Sympathy

Sympathy influences the social development of a child. In childhood, a child needs help. Parents provide him love and sympathy. Through these he acquires self-confidence and develops an attitude of identifying himself with family and society.

Co-operation

As a result of co-operation, social qualities get developed in a child. When he sees others co-operating, he learns to reciprocate.

Social Techniques

In childhood parents impart knowledge to a child about behaviour and other accepted patterns of society. This teaching and training helps an individual to develop beliefs and moral values.

Imitation

An individual living in a particular family and society acquires traits of other individuals. He imitates them and tries to act accordingly. This act helps him to develop social qualities of life.

Situation Perceiving

No one can behave in a similar manner in all the circumstances. One has to change his behaviour according to the situation. This process of perceiving the situation is very helpful in acquiring social ideals.

Identification

After identifying himself with his parents, neighbours and the members of the society an individual develops different patterns of behaviour.

The process of socialization is very important for the development of the individual and society. When a child is born, he does not have the social qualities. Through the process of socialization child is encouraged to act in accordance with the accepted values and ideals of society. It is through the process of socialization that one learns what one is expected to do. With the help of interaction through different agencies one learns to adjust and re-adjust his behaviour and acquires social qualities to become an integral member of society.

Socialisation Through Physical Education

Physical education can play a significant role in the socialization of individuals. Physical education through the activities establishes the social sense. It is based on the accepted social and democratic principles. A balanced physical education programme, offering wholesome activities, produces persons possessing desirable qualities of sense of fairness, co-operation, control of emotions, forgiveness, unselfishness, etc. The playground is a laboratory for developing these social characteristics (Uppal, 2000). A teacher of physical education tries to sublimate the energy, enthusiasm and emotion of the pupils towards the socially desirable qualities and prevents the students from being diverted to an unwholesome community life. Games and wholesome form of recreation and amusement provide opportunities to develop close association among individuals. A physical education activity not only educates boys and girls to become healthy individuals but also teaches them to become responsible members of a social group. Through physical education activities one learns much about working together with others towards a common goal. Sports form a socially integrating factor, with common interests and enthusiasm. Co-operation and competition needed for the development of a well-adjusted personality are present in games and sports. In a playfield all are equal, whether they are rich or poor. Regardless of education or the status, the victorious is given prominence and due recognition. Every one enjoys equal opportunity of exhibiting his skill and worth.

Physical education and sports play very significant role in a modern society. They are important to an individual, group, a nation and world. Olympic games are successful in attracting many countries for participation. Throughout the world physical education activities have popular appeal among people of all ages and sex. Physical education and sports programme help in socializing in the following ways:

Helpful in Inculcating Discipline

While playing the participants have to strictly adhere to rules and obey the decisions of the judges. In case they commit any mistake they are penalized for that act. In addition they have also to follow the routine rituals before, during and after the match.

Helpful in Developing the Sports Ethics

Physical education programmes play important role in developing the qualities of sportsmanship, fair play, obedience or rules and sacrificing self-interest for the sake of the interest of the team and the institution. One is taught to respect the sport concerned and obey the rules and regulations of the sport. All these qualities go a long way in developing sports ethics.

Worthy Use of Leisure Time

Physical education activities have enabled people to utilize their free time through meaningful participation in sports and games thus preventing the youth from indulging in unsocial and delinquent acts.

Helpful in Adjustment

Each sports person is different from the other and faces problems of adjustment within the team or group. Physical education programme equips individual sports person to get adjusted and follow group norms.

Contributes to Group Cohesion and Harmony

Physical education programme helps different players of a team to play as a group and excel during competition. The members of a team develop oneness and sacrifice self-interest for the sake of common goal.

Positive Attitude Toward Sports Activities

Benefits of sports participation help people to look at physical education positively. Physical education programmes have gone a long way in changing the outlook of the people. Various organizations have realized the importance of games and sports participation. Thus people of all ages have changed their outlook and the participation in such activities has increased.

Helpful in Developing Leadership Qualities

Physical education programmes provide social interaction among players of a team and between different teams, which goes a long way in developing essential qualities to be a good leader. Players participating in games and sports develop all essential qualities, which are important for a person to function as a good leader.

Role of Physical Education in Promoting Social Values

In sports and physical education activities the participants take part together regardless of caste, creed, race or any other consideration. The performance of every participant is appreciated for his achievement without considering his background and team affiliation.

Physical education programme helps in developing traits such as initiative, trustworthiness, loyalty, unity, patience, tolerance, helpfulness, sympathetic attitude, social consciousness, dependability, etc., which are essential to develop democratic outlook in a citizen.

Physical education programmes teach us the art of handling victory and defeat with pride. These programmes enable participants to be fair to others. Physical education programmes provide a social laboratory for students to learn how to work with others in a co-operative manner, develop an understanding of rights and feelings of others, and to contribute towards the common purpose of the group to promote a feeling of social consciousness.

Participation in physical education programmes contribute to the development of following social values:

Followership

Physical education develops traits of successful followership, respect for authority, abiding by rules, recognition of rights of others and a sense of fairness and co-operation with those in command. Through physical education, students may also learn to accept defeat without a feeling of hostility or resentment.

Sympathetic Attitude

Participation in sports activities inculcates sympathetic attitude among the participants. Injuries in physical activities are very common. As and when a participant gets injured, his own teammates and even opponents develop sympathetic feeling towards the injured person. This type of feeling comes to every sports person spontaneously. On such occasions even the players of the opposite team forget any bad feeling and ill will. This type of behaviour can be frequently seen during physical education activities, matches and competitions.

Broader Outlook

Physical education programmes prepare the sportsmen to accept healthy criticism and he is always willing to accept the viewpoint of others. Good sportsmen do not have mean mentality.

Helpfulness

The quality of helpfulness is another important social value developed through physical education among the participants during training and competitions. There are several situations when players of opponent teams collide during a competition and one player falls down and sportsperson of opponent team helps the sportsperson lying on the ground.

Self-discipline

Physical education programme helps the participants to be more disciplined. Abilities of self-discipline and determination are developed for achieving their success through rigorous training. Winning is not only based on physical skills and other qualities but also on the will and desire to achieve success.

Patience

Physical education activities develop patience among the sportspersons. Several situations arise during competition when sportspersons exhibit patience. Players are called upon to show patience when referees and umpires unknowingly give a wrong decision during a match. Through physical education players are taught to be patient and show utmost respect to the officials. If a player loses patience that may in turn result in loss of concentration and a defeat.

Group Cohesion

A sense of group cohesion also develops through physical education programmes. In team games, group cohesion is very important. Nobody can think about winning if there is no group cohesion in a team. Group cohesion comes automatically in a team because every player of the team wants to win the match. All the members of a team make a combined effort to perform well and win during a competition. Harmony is necessary for group cohesion. This act of group cohesion also plays a vital role in actual life.

Tolerance

Tolerance is a very important social value. If a sports person does not have patience, he cannot tolerate the wrong decisions of the officials or misbehaviour or provoking gestures of an opponent. In physical education activities every player faces such situations and tries to tolerate such situations. In this way sports persons get practical training of patience.

Social Consciousness and Sense of Values

Through physical education activities, sports persons feel and develop a concern for their mates and opponents. These programmes instill goodwill for others, a way of life that fosters morality, ethical behaviour and individual dignity. Values and judgements such as what is wrong and what is right are developed and adherence to democratic principles and a respect for others is cultivated.

Harmony

In physical education programmes like sports, participants of a team belong to different casts, creeds and religions but they gel together when they become the members of one team. They live together. They understand and adjust with each other. When a team plays a match with another team, this harmony can be observed easily. Sports are a common denominator for all. They all play as members of the same team and play for the attainment of common goal.

The attainment of these social values to a great extent depends upon the sports environment. If there is a healthy and positive environment, participants are sure to develop social values. No doubt programme of physical education can inculcate social values if physical education teacher and coaches play positive role and emphasis is laid on qualities like, fair play, honesty, tolerance and patience.

REFERENCES

1. Borse, Shook, S. *et al.* "Behaviour Modification. Through Sports: A Pilot Study on Tribal Students." Paper Presented in XI National

Conference of Sports Psychology at Hydrabad. Osmania University, 6-8 March, 1998.

2. Barrow, Harold M. "Man and Movements: Principles of Physical Education", 3rd Ed., Lea IC. Febiger, Philadelphia, 1983.

3. Singh, Ajmer, *et al., Modern Text Book of Physical Education Health and Sports.* New Delhi: Kalyani Publishers, 2000.

4. Krupat, Edward. "Reading and Conversation in Social Psychology". *Psychology is Social Brington England*: Scott, Foresman and Company, 1975.

5. "National Policy on Education—1986" (With Modification Undertaken in 1992), published by Human Resource Development, Department of Education, New Delhi.

6. Uppal, A.K. Sc. G.P. Gautam. *Physical Education and Health.* Delhi: Friends Publications, 2000.

27

Education in Human Values: A Case Study of Sri Sathya Sai Baba's System of Education

Neeta Khanna

We are facing today some multidimensional hazards which were never visualized before. In spite of the ever growing wonders of science and technology, we are living in a turbulent and worried world under the dark shadow of war and annihilation. Our growing progress in controlling our material world has not been matched by corresponding advances in human character and virtues. Value crisis is a global phenomenon of our times. Rapid scientific growth and technological advancements resulting in industrialization has threatened our age old moral standards. Many of the philosophers and educationists feel that human values are disintegrating in all walks of life, both public and personal. Education can play a vital role in the inculcation of values in the society. The present system of education is taking very little care in this regard. There is an immediate and urgent need to over haul the present system of education. It is easy to bring such changes in the system if we can find a model which can be followed to achieve the goal. India has a very rich cultural heritage. It is a land of great saints and philosophers who have given their own philosophy and ideas about what education should be. It was in this context that the present study on Sri Sathya Sai Baba's system of Education in Human Values was conducted. The title of the study was Sri Sathya Sai Baba's Concept of Education in Human Values: An Analytical Study.

Sri Sathya Sai Baba incarnated on 23rd November 1926, in a quiet little village, Puttaparti in Andhra Pradesh, which has now become a world famous Spiritual and Educational Centre. Baba revealed his mission clearly through a letter to His brother on 25th May 1947, in which He writes that He has a task to foster to all man kind and ensure for all of them lives full of *ananda* and to lead all who strayed away from the straight path into goodness and to save them. He re-affirmed his Vow to remove sufferings of the poor and granting them what they lacked. He further stated that he will accomplish His Mission by the re-establishment of Vedas, establishment of *Dharma*, revitalization of the system of education, transformation of humanity and also through unity of faith.

The purpose of the study was to analyse thoroughly Sri Sathya Sai System of Education in order to draw meaningful inferences for implementing the systems of education else where also. An intensive study of literature/discourses of Sri Sathya Sai Baba, and the literature written by various authors about Baba was made. It was considered important in order to review the life and mission of Sri Sathya Sai Baba and also draw out definite meaning of five human values. A direct study of the educational system of Sri Sathya Sai Baba was of great help in identifying techniques for the development of human values. Besides drawing methodological implications for inculcating and developing human values in students studying in secondary schools, an extensive study was also made of the activities being carried out in the hostel as well as in the classroom, in order to understand how these were helpful in developing a strong system of values.

The data for the study was collected through intensive interviews with students and teachers of these educational institutions. Besides this, the technique of observation was made use of, to collect information which was not otherwise available. Further, perception of eminent scholars available in the shape of their articles and speeches was also analysed.

The tools were also developed to study the level of interaction between faculty members and students, between Sri Sathya Sai Baba and students, among students and among the faculty members. Perception of teachers and students about the educational system was also obtained.

For the purpose of conceptualization and instruction, five basic Human Values were identified. These have been termed as human values, as they relate to five domains of human personality. A brief discussion of all these four values is given below:

Truth

Truth is considered to be the highest human value and is connected with the intellectual domain of our personality. It is considered to be highest due to our firm faith in its infallibility. As Sri Sathya Sai Baba puts it, "Truth is neither the description of thing as one has seen, without exaggeration or understatement, nor is the narration of the incident as one had heard it. Truth is that which elevates and holds forth ideals. It is the light that illumines man's path to God." Truth has been considered as a hierarchical concept as the reality is understood at different levels of perceptions. The truth as perceived by senses is called as 'Perceptual Truth' and is at lowest level of hierarchy. This truth is limited to the perceptual abilities of the individual. It therefore, can vary from person to person and is not permanent or absolute. That is why it has been placed at the lowest level. There is another from of truth which is considered at a higher level and is arrived at through reasoning which is not wholly based on experimental science. This is called the 'Truth of Inference'. The highest form of the truth, has been termed as 'Absolute Truth', which is beyond the reach of time and space. It is always and ever existent and does not have a beginning or an end. It is real *SAT*, or *SATHYA* and is fundamental and self-revealing. As explained by Sri Sathya Sai Baba it is something that is not, modified by the time or space or 'guna' and should stay the same forever, unaffected and unchanged. This truth can only be revealed by intuition.

Righteous Conduct

"*Dharma* or Righteous Conduct for Sri Sathya Sai Baba is that which sustains, saves and sanctifies." It is adherence to the universal moral law—"Do unto others what you wish others to do unto you." *Dharma* is the Divine Law that is inherent in the very structure of the Universe. It is the foundation for the functioning of all living organisms and the very basis of the welfare of the humanity. *Dharma* is the Divine Justice that upholds truth and order in the universe.

Sri Sathya Sai Baba (1981) has given five types of *Dharma*. First type of *dharma* has been termed as 'Atma Dharma'. This includes actions directed towards the individual himself, in search of inherent great motive force which is behind his knowing, willing and acting powers. 'Vriti Dharma', or the moral code which regulates and sublimates man's passion. 'Varna Dharma' is the code that prescribes restrictions and regulations to channelise man's impulse and instincts in fields that are special to his place in society. It is the law of division of labour in the society. Fourth type of *Dharma* as stated by Baba is 'Ashrama Dharma' which lays down prescriptions of discipline for the blossoming of the spiritual consciousness during the four stages of life namely. *Brahmacharya* (studentship), *Grithastha* (householdership), *Vanaprastha* (an anchorite) and *Sanyasa* (recluse). 'Samanaya Dharma' is the code of conduct of man as a man towards other men. Last *Dharma*, as given by Baba is *Stri Dharma* which includes code of conduct exclusively for woman. According to Baba, *dharma* is the moral path. Moral path is light, the light is *Ananda*.

Peace

Peace is related to the emotional aspect of human personality. It is the state of bliss (*ananda*), mental equipoise, tensionlessness, it is the state of *Sthitaprajna* (a condition of unwavering mind) as explained by Lord Krishna in Bhagawad Gita. It is the state of stillness of thought, a controlled state of all the fluctuations of the mind (*Chitta Vritti Nirodha)*. Peace connotes the negation of desires, anger, greed and hatred. It is the awareness of the beauty, majesty and omnipresence of God that opens up the springs of '*Shanti* in man's heart'. It is the calm contentment arising from the right attitude towards action.

Love

Love manifests itself in various forms like sympathy, compassion, mercy, kindness, charity, fellow-feeling, friendliness, respect, reverence, social service, nationalism or patriotism, love for the whole world as *Vasudhaive Kutumbhakam.* Lastly, as devotion to God, love is to be equated with universal love, knowing no barriers. It has to attract all hearts. Its manifestation should be compassion for suffering man, and grace for the needy. Service to human beings is the real manifestation of love.

Development of Human Values in Sri Sathya Sai Educational Institutions

Three approaches for teaching human values are being successfully tried in these institutions. These are: *(i)* Direct Approach, *(ii)* Indirect or Incidental Approach and *(iii)* Integrated Approach.

Direct approach consists of five major techniques which are practiced in a special class of education in human values for which there is a period for 40 minutes everyday in each class in Sri Sathya's Sai Educational Institutions. The five techniques are Silent Sitting (Tuning-in), Prayers, Group Singing, Story-Telling and Group Activities.

Silent Sitting (Tuning-in)

The techniques used for silent sitting are simple. All it requires is asking the students to sit in a good steady posture, close eyes and think and feel good. The teacher has an option of leading a 'Conducted Tour' of thoughts of students while making them think, by painting a verbal picture, or the beauties of nature. For younger students, stimulation of some kind is required. This can be achieved by making students imagine all such things that they love and admire including a beauty of a flower, a beautiful scene like dawn, sunrise, moonrise, dusk, floating clouds etc. However, this kind of stimulation is not required for older students. It has been empirically proved that silent sitting considerably improves the memory of the children. It has also been found effective in gradually getting rid of certain negative emotion like anger, greed, lust and envy. Flashes of understanding and knowledge from within were also experienced by the student leading to the awakening of the intuition. It has been found that a regular practice of silent sitting improves the quality of fitness of work. The method is very useful in instilling the value of truth and peace.

Prayers

In common parlance, prayer means asking god for some favour, protection, help guidance etc., but this is not the real meaning of the prayer. It is undertaken more for the love of being in communion with the Lord, with feeling of complete surrender to His merciful will. Prayer can be in the form of *Stuti* of *Stotras* chanted in praise of the Lord, *Prarthana* or supplication, *Subhashitani* i.e., expression of noble thoughts or feelings. This technique has been found very useful in promoting the values of Truth, Peace, Love and Non-violence. Prayer is able to achieve this multifold goal because of its components of melody, meaning and memory.

Group Singing

Group Singing is singing in chorus with either one or more persons leading and the others following each line or the song or even all singing together. The most important factor in group singing is that the devotional feelings should be the undercurrent of the song. Group Singing should be conducted either in the prayer hall or in the open. Song should be easy containing values of love for God, motherland, nature, some ideal, etc. Meaning of value words used in the song must be explained to the students. Group Singing has proved very useful in inculcating the value of love, patriotism, devotion, love for nature, co-operation and peace.

Story-Telling

Story-telling is both an art as well as a science. The aim of story-telling is to elevate man's spirit and to cultivate an inner vision which makes man finally realize his real self and to inculcate certain values in life. If used effectively, this technique has great potential of inculcating all values. The teacher should be a store house of interesting stories and should be able to make selection of the story judiciously, keeping in view the values which are to be inculcated.

Group Activities

Group activities entail participation of a group of students and in effect the whole class. Group activities can be organized in the assembly hall, on the playfield, in the classroom or even outside school campus. These activities include cultural activities, literary activities, games both indoor and outdoor. Activities outside the school campus include, seva activities like; feeding the poor; collecting clothes and other articles and money to help the needy people; visit to educationally important places, organizing cultural programme in the community and nature study etc. Group activity, as a technique of inculcating value has been found very useful in promoting co-operation, self-confidence, self-inquiry, creativity, concentration, etc. All human values can be promoted through group activities in the garb and guise of game and other events. All these direct methods of inculcating values can be tried out in the schools. However, before trying these methods, it is important that required inputs are provided to the teachers whom we entrust this crucial task.

In the incidental approach, the teacher takes the advantage of a chance incident as it arises in the classroom, in the school campus, or on the playfield to teach a value by correcting, praising or discouraging certain behaviour. The chance incident can be used to develop any of the basic values. Sometimes, the situation can even be created by the teacher to see the reactions of the students to assess their values.

The third approach for inculcating values is to integrate values with curricular and co-curricular activities, whenever and wherever one may get opportunity do to so. This method has been found to be very useful as it does not require extra time for imparting values.

Strategies for the Implementation of the Model

An intensive study of Sri Sathya Sai Baba's system of education in human values leads us to the conclusion that it is possible to inculcate values in the student by adopting a system of education having 'Education in Human Values' as a prominent component. Such a system will greatly help in producing individuals with a value system which can ensure happiness of the individual and harmony in the society.

For implementing the strategies, the teacher training programmes need overhauling. A component related to values should be introduced in the curriculum of teacher training programmes, but it should be ensured that this component is not taught like ordinary theory courses.

Activities should be organised in such a manner that values are automatically imbibed and desired change in the attitude takes place. Reward and punishment both, if used judiciously, can be very effective in value inculcation. Punishment, not in the form of physical torture, but in some other refined manner like, temporarily depriving the child of teacher's love and care or his closeness, works well.

If we are really interested in inculcating values among children in all its seriousness, it is important that the head of the teachers training institutions be selected after thorough screening. Only revising the curricula will not serve the purpose unless we have right person to implement it effectively. For the development of values there is a need to have cordial student teacher relations devising special co-curricular activities and improving school climate.

The study also presents model of free education which aims at development of character and wholesome development of personality. It amply reveals the need for taking out education from commercial arena and making it spiritual oriented, in addition to the secular and material education. The study of Sri Sathya Sai Educational Institution reveals that it is within the realm of possibility and practicality for society to have a system of free education.

This study also throws light on positive and wholesome influence of teachers when they relate themselves to each other and to their students in a spirit of love, care and exemplary behaviour.

Head of schools and the teacher, teaching in the school should be the person having a good value system of their own. This also needs a commitment and strong will on the part of those responsible for managing the affairs of education in the country.

School-community interaction is an important instrument which can be effectively used to enable students to relate themselves to the needs of the society and also in the comprehension of social realities. Involvement of students in service activities outside the four walls of the institution helps the students to develop love and concern for the poor, weak and helpless. It motivates them for selfless service. Such activities can be made a regular feature of schools in the state.

To conclude such an improved system of education will greatly help in producing individuals with the value systems, which can insure happiness of the individuals and harmony in the society, despite the prevailing diversity.

REFERENCES

Bashiruddin, Z. (1982), *Significance of Prayer*: In S.R. Rohidekar, Shanta A. Diwakar, K.B. Prabhu Prasad. *Education in Human Values Handbook* for *Teacher Part II*. Sri Sathya Sai Bal-Vikas Education Trust, Prasanthi Nilayam (A.P.).

Burrow, L. (1987), " Group-Singing—The Power of Music". *In Sathya Sai Education in Human Values Handbook for Teachers Part II*. Sri Sathya Sai Bal-Vikas Education Trust, Prasanthi Nilayam (A.P.), pp.105-106, 140.

Chaudhary, S. (1985), *Silent-Sitting: In Report on the Orientation Course–cum Workshop on Human Values*. Department of Eeducation, Government of Himchal Pradesh, Shimla. p. 48.

Diwakar, A.S. (1982), *Technique of Teaching Prayers*: *In S.R. Rohidekar*, Shanta A. Diwakar, K.B. Prabhu Prasad. *Education in Human Values Handbook for*

Teachers Part II. Sri Sathya Sai Bal-Vikas Education Trust, Prasanthi Nilayam (A.P.), pp. 18-19.

Gokak, V.K. (1973), *A Value Orientation to our System of Education*. M.M. Gulab and Sons, Gulab Bhawan, New Delhi.

Gokak, V.K. (1981), *The Syllabus for the Education in Human Values Course*. In V.K. Gokak and S.R. Rohidekar (Eds.) *Teachers' Handbook for the Course in Human Values*. Sri Sathya Sai Bal- Vikas Education Trust, Parsanthi Nilayam (A.P.). pp. 52-53.

Gokak, V.K. (1985), *Human Values, Higher Education and the Six Aspects of Reality*. In Seminar on Education in Values. Sri Sathya Sai Education in Human Values Trust in Co-operation with Govt. of A.P., pp.18-19.

Jagadeesan, J. (1981), *Symposium and Exhibition on Human Values for the Far East*. Sri Sathya Central Council of Malaysia, Malaysia.

Jumsai, A.O.(1991), *Prayers: In Sathya Sai Education in Human Values*. Handbook for Teachers. Sathya Sai Foundation of Thailand, Bangkok. P. 98.

Kapani, M. (1990), *A Study of Education in Human Values—Concept and Methodological Implications*. Unpublished Ph.D. Thesis submitted to Sri Sathya Sai Institute of Higher Learning (Deemed University), Prasanthi Nilayam.

Kasturi, N. (1982), *Loving God*. Sri Sathya Sai Books and Publication Trust, Prasanthi Nilayam (A.P).

Khanna, N. (1995), *Story-telling: In S.Saraf (Ed.)*. Education in Human Values: Programme Implementation. Apeejay Education Foundation, New Delhi.

Maslow, A.H. (1959), *New Knowledge in Human Values*. Harper and Brothers, New York.

Palkhivala, N.A. (1982), *Convocation Address: Sai Sathya Sai Institute of Higher Learning*, Prasanthi Nilayam. In Sanathan Sarathi, Sai Sathya Books and Publications Trust, Prasanthi Nilayam.

Pandya, R.C. (1959), *Measurement of Modern Educational Values from Different Viewpoints*. In M.B. Buch (Ed.), First Survey of Research in Education (1974).

Saraf, S. (1993), *Bhagavan Sri Sathya Sai Baba: The Eternal Educator*. M.D. Rajan, Typographic, Wadala, Bombay.

Seshadri,C.(1992), *Education in Value: A Source Book*. Sri Aurobindo Marg, NCERT, New Delhi.

Shyam Sunder (1991), *Divine Whispers: Sri Sathya Seva Orgnisation*, Himachal Pradesh, Shimla.

Sri Sathya Sai Baba (1987), *Convocation Address: University News*. Association of Indian Universities, New Delhi.

Sulochna, T. (1982), *Character Development. (Through Group –Activities).* In S.R. Rohidekar, Shanta A. Diwakar, K.B. Prabhu Prasad, *Education in Human Values Handbook for Teachers-Part II.* Sri Sathya Sai Bal-Vikas Education Trust, Prasanthi Nilayam.

Venkataraman, R.(1990), *Convocation Address: Sri Sathya Sai Institute of Higher Learning,* Prasanthi Nilayam. In Santhan Sarathi, Sri Sathya Sai Books and Publications Trust, Prasanthi Nilayam.

28

Human Values, Quality in Education, Judiciary and Professional Development: A Critical Review

Mehraj Uddin

The Perspective

Education plays a vital role in improving standard of living of the people. It is a fundamental pillar of human rights, democracy, sustainable development human values and peace. Education is a dynamic process by which knowledge, character and behaviour of a person are moulded in a positive direction. Education is a preparation for social life and to help an individual to acquire knowledge and skills as would enable him to meet social demands of day-to-day life. Education is the single most important factor, which assists in improving practical skills, which, in turn, raises productivity and production.[1] It liberates an individual from ignorance, oppression and exploitation. It leads a person to the highest moral conduct and deepest spiritual insight.

Education inculcates in human beings, the basic values of being a human and to behave in a humane way. Education at what so ever level it may be, can't achieve its basic purpose, unless it addresses itself to the humanity and human values.

Quality and Value Education

Education in general and higher education in particular is in a flux. The basic reason for this is the changing and increasing paradoxical, nature of relationship between the society, state and higher education system.[2] The values in education along with quality and market demand have over the years suffered a setback. There is an on-going concern that higher education is not able to respond sufficiently to changing needs of the economic and social challenges.

In the present era of knowledge explosion and technological revolution, the most under-current of thought is that higher education depends too heavily on public funds and it needs to be more cost conscious. The rapid expansion of higher education, the fast escalating cost of educational apparatus, and the apparent inability of the government to provide adequate financial support to the institutions of higher learning and the tax-payers question why to bear the burden, when the values have suffered a set-back and the beneficiaries are from the affluent class of the society.[3] It also raises issues regarding the quality in higher education and importance of education in human values.

On the other hand, the response of academicians, to all this is one of bewilderment and a sense of injustice, underlying the reaction is the assumption that investment in higher education is an investment in future for pushing forward the frontiers of knowledge, the preservation and development of culture and producing competent citizenship. The quality has become the touchstone of higher education in the last two decades of 20th century. In the education sector much of the discussion and debate, which was hither to focus on standards, has now shifted to quality and values. The main reason for this is not because of the concern of people working within the sector, but mainly because of the increasing pressure, from the students, would be employer and funding agencies to demonstrate that institutions of higher education have to play a dynamic role in the socio-economic development of the country.

However, despite all these tall claims and counter claims, the beneficiaries of higher education, student's parents, employers, would be employers, funding agencies and society in general, have serious concern and doubts, about what is happening in higher education. The fact remains that the higher education system has come under clouds and it is here the question of quality along with values in education come to the forefront and the entire brunt is on the teacher. The value oriented education, which has been an integral part of the educational system in every human civilization, has under gone a tremendous change and by and large has been replaced by the modern materialistic considerations.

Objectives and Values

The basic objectives of education, if analyzed in letter and spirit do provide for promoting cause of humanity and development of human values and value education in every respect. Some of the basic objectives of education are identified in the following terminology:

1. Education is a continuous process for human development;
2. Education is an injecting process of the following values:
   - Concepts of rights and duties;
   - Concepts of humanity and human rights;
   - Concepts of equality and equal rights;
   - Concepts of nature and natural rights;
   - Concepts of environment and environmental protection;
   - Concepts of reason and reasonability; and
   - Concepts of tolerance and patience.
3. Education is a moulding process of one's character and personality in a very positive direction;
4. Education is helping process to seek truth and to avoid error;
5. Education is a leading process to attain highest moral conduct and to gain deepest spiritual insight;
6. Education is a inculcating process of citizenship and a sense of responsibility; and
7. Education is a vital process for Human Resource Development, Nation Building and National Development.

Pt. Jawaharlal Nehru as early as 1947, while inaugurating Convocation at Allahabad University observed: "A University stands for humanism, reason, tolerance, adventure of ideas and search for truth."

He further pointed out that it stands for the onward march of human race towards even higher objectives. In nutshell, it can be said that the basic objectives of higher education are generation of knowledge, transmission of knowledge and application of knowledge. The International Human Rights Commission in its report, identified the following as the basic objectives of higher education:

(a) Learn to learn;

(b) Learn to do;

(c) Learn to learn; and

(d) Learn to live together.

Teachers and the Society

The teacher is an important figure in the entire social set-up. The teacher has a pivotal role in moulding the moral fibres, character and aptitude for educational excellence among the students. The teacher has a very important role in shaping the career of the youth. The Supreme Court of India in a case[4] pointed out that though teaching is the last profession in the job market, but the role of a teacher is central to all the process of formal education. The teacher alone could bring out the skills and intellectual capabilities of the students. He is the 'engine' of the educational system.

Status of the teacher reflects socio-cultural ethos of a society. It is said that no people can rise above the level of its teachers. Teachers in the past used to command respect in every society. The teachers were committed to their profession and dedicated to noble mission. The goals were set and there was no scope for the teachers being affiliated to any party or with the tendency to earn more and more by opening teaching shops. The commercial interests were unknown to the teaching community. The doer's category of teachers was omnipresent and doubter's or dreamer's category of teacher was in small number. The entire scenario has now changed and the values have been replaced by the materialistic considerations.

The fact remains that majority of the teachers at present are not in a position to command respect in the society. They don't enjoy the freedom to devise the curriculum for their students. It is very difficult for the teacher to engage in the creative and innovative work, consequently performance of a vast majority of the teacher is beyond one's satisfaction. This of course affects the entire educational set-up.

The question arises that who is responsible for all this? Is it the society or the teacher concerned? Where are the values? What percolates down to the young generation? It is difficult to respond to all these issues, but the fact remains that almost all the segments of the society work under the influence of corruption. The corruption has penetrated very deep in the social set-up and the educational system is no exception. The teacher being a part of the society can't be expected to be different than that of other members of the society.

The society has a lot of expectations with the teachers, but at the same time education is not a priority sector for the Government. The facilities for professional development are not in accordance with the changing scenario, despite the fact that training in the educational sector is being increasingly recognized as a major input in improving job performance of the personnel engaged in the delivery of educational services.[5] Consequently, the teachers are not in a position to keep pace with the knowledge explosion. A number of studies[6] have revealed that facilities for professional development in higher education are limited and have been availed only by a small proportion of the college/university teachers. Further, unplanned integration of the technology into teacher education has been considered to be the most common barrier to wider use of information technologies by teachers. Moreover, it is also found that most of the teachers are not prepared to use new technologies.[7]

The teachers themselves have contributed to their present plight and are not in a position to make their place in the society. The teachers like others working in the public and private sectors, have fallen in the corrupt network and consequently have lost their respect and status in the society. The following observation of a public school student[8] speaks in volumes about image of the teachers and value system in the present day education:

> "I feel ashamed in laminating the very fact that today's teachers are also not so worthy. There is no difference between a street hawker and a teacher today. Teachers have become business-minded and professionals. They weigh everything in terms of money... Today taking tuition has become a fashion as well as a need. Fashion in the sense, that everyone has become dependent on the tutors and need in the sense that teachers themselves motivate rather induce the students to take tuition's."

The observation of the student is a reflection on the present educational system in general and a teacher in particular. It is true that by and large some teachers are found of material and short-term gains and are usually found very busy on their teaching shops in promoting their business concern. They prefer tuition's for material considerations rather than teaching and research in their educational institutions. They are committed to their self-interest rather than to their profession. The teachers because of this tendency have lost their creditability and don't command respect. The teachers are here, teacher are there, but good teachers are rare.

The performance and status of the teachers are linked with a number of variable factors. The important factors are service conditions, work culture and avenues for professional development of the teachers. The out-put in any system cannot be better than that of the input. The input component is very important for bringing out any change in any system. Further, knowledge grows from more to more and the quality and refinement of culture are limitless. Knowledge is created as well as borrowed from others and culture and values are fed and maintained by indigenous resources, creative urges and heritage of the past. The University and other Educational Institutions of higher learning can make direct and vital contributions in this aspect of social change of education and therefore, have the greatest responsibility.[9]

The teacher stands on a very pivotal position and is charged to realize the basic objectives of the education. A brief review of the educational system of any human civilization in its historical perspective, makes it obvious that the basic purpose of the education has been value oriented and the teacher used to command highest respect in the society irrespective of his or her economic status. It is a part of the total system and what is going on in the other segments of the society has a direct impact on the overall functioning of the educational institutions. The values in the entire social set-up including educational set-up have changed; the quest for education has given its way to the need for degrees. Values of the students, parents, employer, employees and that of the society have changed.

Quality Education and the Judiciary

The quality control in higher education has not been the concern of the Commissions and Committees only, but various other segments of the society have also shown their concern and suggested measures thereof. The issues pertaining to higher education are being discussed at various forums. In fact a number of forums has come into being for the purpose.

The judiciary has also shown its concern for the quality control in higher education and in a number of cases has highlighted the importance of professional development of the teachers for the overall improvement in the system. The Supreme Court in Andhra Kesari Education Society case[10] emphasized importance of value education and professional development of the teachers in the following words:

> "The teachers need to be endowed and energized with needed potential to deliver enlightened service expected of him. His quality should be such as would inspire and motivate into action the benefited. He must keep himself abreast of ever changing conditions. He is not to perform in a wooden and unimaginative way. He must eliminate fissiparous tendencies and attitudes and infuse nobler and national ideas in younger minds."

The apex court maintained that the teachers should be subjected to rigorous training with rigid scrutiny of efficiency, as it has a greater relevance to the present situation. The ill trained or sub-standard teachers would be detrimental to our educational system, if not a punishment to our children. The Government and the University must, therefore, take care to see that inadequacy in training of the teachers is not compounded by any extraneous consideration.

The Supreme Court in yet another case[11] highlighted the importance of the teacher-training in the following words:

> "...the teachers must keep abreast with ever changing techniques, the needs of the society and to cope up with the psychological approach to the aptitudes of the children to perform their vital role..."

The Court further observed that the teacher-education programme has to be redesigned to bring in a system of education which can prepare the student-teacher shoulder the responsibility of imparting education with living dynamism and human values. Education being closely interrelated to life, the well trained teacher can instill an aesthetic excellence in the life of his students. The traditional stereotyped, lifeless and dull pattern of chalk, talk and teaching method has to be replaced by a more vibrant system with improved methods of teaching, to achieve qualitative excellence in teacher education. The education in human values should be given top priority at every level of education.

Conclusions and Suggestions

Education is a complex concept and refers both to a process as well as to product. Education as a product is viewed as the sum total of what is received through learning, that is, acquisition of knowledge, skills, attitudes and values, transmission of culture development of personality and liberation or self-actualization. As a process, education involves the act of developing these products in someone else or in oneself. One of the important activities of the educational process is teaching, which includes training, instruction and development of cognitive processes and abilities.[12]

Change is inherent in the process of living and this applies both to individuals and their societies. The pace and motivation of change vary from times of comparative stability to rapid change. Conscious direction and unconscious direction phenomena partake in the process of change which is always complex and interrelated in its various components. The urges and compulsions arise from the diverse realities of man's local, national and international life and the systems of communications and culture operating at these levels.[13]

The respect in which the society held a teacher and provided him freedom has been betrayed. While there are bright spots here and there, majority call for self-introspection. Many Commission/ Committees were set-up to improve methods and to improve accountability of teachers. Nothing concrete has materialized so far. Efforts to improve quality of education will bear no fruit unless teachers are made accountable and their work performance improved.[14]

The teacher no doubt is holding a very vital position so far as the overall development of the society is concerned, but there are various other variable factors which influence functioning of the educational institutions in general and that of a teacher in particular. Higher education, being a terminal component of the system has a special significance in the education system. The pace of development of any country to a great extent depends upon the quality of its higher education. Higher education system is an index of scientific, academic and intellectual potentials of a country. The young men and women coming out of the terminal component should be highly sensitive and receptive to the environment. Importance of human values should be given a top priority in the curriculum. Quality education should include education in human values for achieving excellence in every sphere.

The inputs and contents of education have always been governed by the concepts of 'value' but the notion of 'value' has shifted from the conventional philosophical and transcendent sense and come to rest in the market place.[15] The teachers in any case should also be equipped with an evaluative and critical faculty which can be helpful to them to face the socio-economic challenges of the country in an intelligent manner.

It is therefore, essential that the government and the community should endeavour to create conditions which help, motivate teachers on constructive and creative line. In order to ensure the quality control in higher education, it is essential to gear up the available resources and to utilize all the resources in a proper perspective.

REFERENCES

1. Ansari, M.M., *Education and Economic Development*, A.I.U. Publication (1987).
2. See NAAC publication ,"The Quest for Quality in Higher Education".
3. *Ibid.*
4. *Andhra Kesari Education Society V. Director of School Education,* A.I.R., 1989, SC 183.
5. Mohd. Aslam, *"Teachers Training Institutions:"*—A Perspective.
6. Sharma, G.D., 'Staff Development Programme in Higher Education", See Mehraj Uddin (ed) *Higher Education: Problems & Prospects* (1998), 12.
7. *Ibid.*
8. Shahla Shakir Rafiqi, Student, Jammu Public School, Talab Khatikan, Jammu, *The Kashmir Times* (Oct. 31, 99), 14.
9. Prem Kirpal, "Role of Universities as Agents of Change" Raghavan; J. Veera (ed.), *Higher Education in the Eighties: Opportunities and Objectives,* (1985), 21.
10. *Supra note,* 04.
11. *State of Maharashtra V. Vikas Sahebrao Roundale,* 1992, A.I.R. SCW, 2182.
12. Vedanayagam, E.G., *Teaching Technology for College Teachers* (1989), 1.
13. Prem Kirpal, "Role of Universities as Agents of Change", Raghavan; J. Veera (ed), *Higher Education in the Eighties: Opportunities and Objectives,* (1985), 21.
14. Koul, A.K., *Higher Education: Quality Control See Mehraj Uddin* (ed), *Higher Education*: Problems and Prospects (1988), 31.
15. Anil Wilson, *Education and Market: Making the Tail Wage the Dog,* Times of India (09.10.99), 10.

29

Science and Technology and Value Inculcation

J. Shashidhara Prasad

In the past, the knowledge of the world as a whole was simply referred to as philosophy without any distinction. The Vedas and Upanishads are the store-houses of knowledge which encompass everything connected with the world as a whole. Great thinkers of the Vedic period and great masters of the West like Plato, Aristotle and Socrates are good representatives of holistic approach of thinking. In the beginning, knowledge was imparted in the name of theology.

Break up of Holistic Approach

As the boundaries of knowledge expanded and extended, the traditional metaphysical approach of considering the "World as a whole" was rejected. It was then thought that the physical world was separate. By focussing on particular problem domains and constructing grossly simplified idealised models, there was the possibility of mathematical conceptualisation from which one could predict the limited aspects of the system under consideration. Through the construction of such interlocking paradigmatic structures, physical science purports to account for all aspects of nature and even claims to account for mysteries such as consciousness and dismisses as non-existent the transcendence of normal space time causality linked with paranormal phenomenon. Thus, the physical world was separated from the moral world with which it had been united for a long time. The knowledge of the world as a whole was thus divided into natural philosophy and moral philosophy.

Physical World and Development of Science

A further implication of the vastness of our physical universe and the separation of natural from moral philosophy is the movement known in modern times as scientific specialisation. Science, that is natural philosophy, proceeds as the information given by the senses. The line of its attack is thus limited and we cannot hope that anything but limited objectives can be achieved. Science does not profess to solve ultimate problems. On the other hand, it seeks to solve limited problems with a known degree of accuracy and a known margin of error. The desire for exact expression and for the translation of observation into terms of measurement has penetrated every branch of science including biological sciences. Further, science, true to its principle of limited attacks and limited objectives has its own working rules of causality. Normally we discuss only certain particular types of sequences and treat them as related and the relation being regarded as cause and effect. Thus, the physicist will deal only with physical, the chemist only with chemical and the biologist with only biological sequences. In the course of this process new relationships may be discerned or become more apparent, as for instance, in the physical state of the heavenly bodies or of the relative constitution of parents and offsprings. Thus will arise new sciences—astrophysics and genetics—which will limit their scope to the relations in these particular fields. In doing so, we tend to end up compartmentalising science into various branches with rigid boundaries. This is highly artificial and results in abhorring the holistic view of the world. Then the appearance of our world would depend on how we look at it—that is on our "mood". We may be in a scientific, artistic, emotional or social mood. The resultant of all the ways that we have of looking will determine the conception of our world. This is similar to the description of an elephant by a set of blind persons who will describe it as they perceive individually by their sense of touch. Therefore, it is imperative that to get a clear unified picture a holistic approach/view is absolutely essential.

The Present Trend in Science

We can make out from the above discussions that in the initial stages of the development of science, there was no compartmentalisation. But as more and more discoveries and inventions were made, the spirit of specialisation evolved and scientific discoveries were classified under one or the other of basic sciences viz., physics, chemistry, biology, astronomy, genetics etc. In due course, the progress and proliferation made in science became so vast and fast, that almost ninety per cent of everything we know in the sciences has been generated in the last fifty years. With this information explosion, different basic sciences have lost their boundaries. Consider the list of disciplines—mathematics, physics, chemistry, biology, anthropology, the arts and humanities and theology. This list is not in random order. It represents roughly the sequence of prerequisites. Theology requires the knowledge of arts and humanities; arts and humanities benefit by a knowledge of anthropology; for a proper understanding of anthropology a knowledge of biology will be helpful; a biologist must know some chemistry; a chemist must have a working knowledge of physics, as a physicist is lost without mathematics. The concepts of atomic weight, specific heat, valency, the drawing of periodic table and the constant use of physical methods by chemists indicate that chemistry is really a subset or a branch of physics. One of the most decisive discoveries in biology, viz., the double helix structure of DNA and the recent advances in protein crystallography suggest that biology is a huge branch of chemistry.

The laws of the world can be represented by a gigantic pyramid with a triangular base, with mathematics as the bottom layer, physics, chemistry and biology occupying the subsequent layers and the arts and theology at the top. To understand any layer profoundly, it is necessary to plunge into the discipline beneath it. The identical stability of the pyramid on any one of its faces indicates that each discipline is as important as the other in the present-day context, and is complementary for a proper understanding and appreciation of nature. The problems that we face now are becoming more and more multidisciplinary. At each point in this development, we notice new magnitudes of complexity and integrated organisation. The pyramid of knowledge is neither static nor fixed. It is continuously growing and its growth is at all levels, the low as well as the high, the high as well as the low. What has been implied by Shakespeare through his creation Prospero—the unity of science, art, echnology, moral choice, magic craft and delightful stage illumination—has been realised. One of the best and earliest examples is of Newton, who unified mechanics, astronomy, algebra, geometry and optics. We see that this is substantiated more eloquently in Grand Unification.

Development of Technology

A study of the historical development of technology indicates that it owes its ancestry to one or more of pure sciences. Useful technology has emerged in the wake of fundamental scientific advances. The contributions of physicists like James Clerk Maxwell, H Hertz for communication systems, William Shockley, John Bardeen and Walter Brattain for solid state electronics are some of the examples of relationships between science and technology. Oersted's discovery of magnetic field associated with a current electricity, discovery of galvanic action and electrolytic cells by Volta and Faraday are technology driven scientific discoveries. The latest in the run, the high temperature super-conductor is also an example of reverse process. The modern science of mechanics which involves the geometry of space, time and motion began when instruments became available to accurately measure the intervals. There are innumerable number of examples of the interplay between basic science and technology in the fields of space, computer, nuclear and medical sciences, all of which are modern by any reckoning. Thus, we can see that technology is driving science as fast as it is being driven by science.

Interplay of Science and Other Disciplines

Sir C. V. Raman has rightly put that Science is a fusion of man's aesthetic and intellectual function devoted to the representation of nature. It is therefore, the highest form of creative art. So science has the same driving force as music, art and literature and nourished by the same source of longing. One can also perceive that there are parallels between developments in modern art and science. The shift from naturalistic to increasingly abstract art in the late nineteenth and early twentieth centuries coincided with the development of more abstract models in science. It may be tempting to dismiss this as a mere coincidence. But it is not a mere chance that while modern abstract art was being developed, physicists moved from a servile borrowing of visual imagery, abstracted from the world of sensory perceptions, to the construction of physical theories that generated their own imagery. The strong case for a deep cultural relation between artistic creation and scientific creativity has been brought out by Arthur Miller in his book "Insights of Genius: Imagery in Science and Art." The cultural interrelation between art and science can be appreciated in the emphatic statement of Richard Feynmann in his reaction to the theory he had just developed with Murray Gellmann—There was a moment when I knew how nature worked... It had elegance and beauty. The Goddamn thing was gleaming. The underlying unity that unifies science and art—art including aesthetics, poetry, architecture, and music can be appreciated in terms of symmetry and repetition of patterns that encompass all that is beautiful,—be it a simple molecule or the most beautiful structure—Taj Mahal, Gol Gumbuz, Cathedrals or Brihadeshwara temple or other creations of art and architecture are magnifying monuments not because they are just beautiful. They are paradigms of nature; a microcosm of nature's symmetry. Many surmises of scientific fiction have been realised. Scientific ideas have their seeds in social phenomenon and likewise the behavioural pattern could be very well appreciated in terms of scientific ideas.

A crystal is though by definition an ideally perfect one is never totally perfect in reality. It will have many defects and impurities. Bhagavadgita speaks of contradictory qualities co-existing. In crystallography the phase of the structure factor is always governed by the phase of the heavy atom in a crystal. This exemplifies the statement that One man with confidence makes a majority. The soft mode behaviour of a crystalline system governs the phase transitions of the system. So also, the very delicate structure of the sensitive social structure determines the state of affairs of the society. The quantitative techniques of physical and mathematical sciences including statistics such as modeling, non-linear and stochastic equations and self-organisation could be applied to complex social, economic, political and biological systems indicating the interplay of diverse disciplines. Science is also intimately related to the science of mind. The para-psychological predictions of the basic structure of matter by Leadbeater and Annie Besant and the universal truths enunciated by our ancient sages are being appreciated by the recent discoveries. The power of the prayer and meditation is a good example.

Impact of Science and Technology on Society

The holistic approach of the past for the understanding of the world without and within us was destroyed by the scientific thought evolved as a result of the works of Galileo Galilei, Francis Bacon, Ren´e Descartes and Isaac Newton. Descartes' statement *Cognito ergo sum* (I exist because I think) resulted in the fragmentation of the human personality with 'mind' separated from 'body'. The method of breaking up thoughts and problems and arranging them in their logical sequence was extended to living organisms as well considering them as machines. Descartes said, I do not recognise any difference between machines made by the craftsmen and the various bodies which the nature alone composes. I consider human body as a machine. The mechanistic view and the reductionist approach was extended to social sciences also. No doubt, the compartmentalised view amongst the science subjects is getting shattered gradually by the advances made. But the world view based on "Cartesian divide" or "Cartesian partition" between matter and spirit or body and mind continues to dominate.

The scientific discoveries and technological inventions have accelerated the process of social change reducing the world to a global village. Science and Technology promise a better way of life and material satisfaction and gives hope of genuine optimism and excitement. But they also give rise to anxiety to a gnawing apprehension of man's alleged loss of personal freedom, of certitude, of psychological sincerity and of identity. Further, they pose threats to humanity like the terror and error of the nuclear bombs, bio-weapons and laboratory mistakes which are relatively pedestrian in contrast to earth threatening asteroid and human (or non-human) caused climate change and particle physics experiments with the potential to rip apart the space time fabric of our universe. Each of these phenomena has the potential to threaten human civilisation on earth. This is like the choice between the red pill and blue pill in the movie 'The Matrix.' "You take the blue pill and the story ends. You wake in your bed and believe whatever you want to believe. You take the red pill and you stay in wonderland and get to know how deep the rabbit hole goes." Morpheus offers a choice to Neo.). Science can be considered as natural or amoral whereas technology can affect the domains of intellectual, aesthetic and moral values. Should we therefore say 'no' to science and technology and forgo many wonderful positive contributions society receives from them? Instead there should be a rethinking to humanise education by cultivating values through a new order based on scientific and technological training with essential components of scientific humanism and necessary discrimination to use the scientific or technological advances properly.

Science and Technology and Values

Today, education is mistaken to be just science and technology. Science and technology have become mechanistic and dehumanised. But as Sri Sathya Sai puts it, "It is the dynamic action which is more powerful than the knowledge of science. Knowledge without wisdom, action without prudence, music minus melody, speech not based on truth, friendship bereft of loyalty, society not marked by discipline and education without humility do not earn the admiration of men." "Education must be brightened by means of discrimination and spiritualization" and a proper value system has to be evolved for proper use of scientific and technological advances. Great scientists of the century, W. Heissenberg, P.A.M. Dirac, Louis de Broglie, E. Schrodinger, Max Planck and Wolfgang Pauli were influenced by the Indian ethos engrained in the Upanishads and Vedas/Vedanta and maintained that there was an essential synthesis and hence harmony between science and spirituality. Man has lost peace of mind and sense of security. There is no sign of growth in 'divine vision' along with the scientific gadgets. Daily life is becoming more precarious. Morality and justice have declined. Avariciousness and unhealthy competition to acquire gadgets has lead to corruption and bribery. Exhibitionism has overtaken humility. There is a decline in human character.

Value Inculcation

The first step in relating science and technology is to enable students to learn to regard science as one of the several and parallel and equally valid areas of human experience. This will equip them in understanding the interrelationship of human knowledge represented by a pyramid as discussed earlier. A necessary second step in relating science and technology to values is to encourage students to consider value questions which arise when scientific content of the curriculum has an impact on their immediate experience. Teaching science with a focus on values provides the students with a means to interpret what they have learnt within their own experience. Such learning helps the student to become self adaptive as science related to social conditions change. Consideration of the relationship of science to personal decisions and major social problems is imperative. They should develop value sensitivity by examining real life problems in the context of science, technology, society and the need to be placed in a framework of a more explicit study of the interaction between science and the value component of social structure. The interrelationships between human experience and the broad themes in our society are not at all taught. Some broad objectives have to be explicitly incorporated:

- To see the similarities and differences between the various subjects studied and have an open minded respect for all of them (holistic view).
- To be aware of particular way in which science affects arts and humanities.
- To appreciate the fact that science attempts and unravels the simplicity and unity of nature and that man cannot play the role of Creator.
- To be aware of the moral consequences and dilemmas that will be the offshoot of scientific knowledge viz., arms race, over population, environmental pollution, abortions on sex determination, extensive use of calculators and computers for small problems and brain being relegated to second place, overheating of earth, ozone hole, etc.
- To practice honesty in word and deed.
- To develop spirit of co-operation and team work.
- To be open to others' view points and opinions.
- To develop patience and perseverance.
- To develop an attitude to apply scientific methods and technological achievements to private and public ethical decisions.
- To learn to 'Care for others' as Sai Baba often reminds 'Love all. Serve all'.

Also special focus may be made on the following:

- To provide opportunities for students to think about an identify their own values in relation to those of others.
- To respect the value system of the society and recognise that individuals will not respond to problems in the same way but at the same time to recognise the need for enough commonality to preserve society.

- To appreciate that there are aesthetic solutions to human problems in addition to scientific answers.
- To go beyond the description of scientific facts and consider as to how they can be best used to serve society.
- To recognise human action as something more than statistical expectation.

In order to achieve these ends, science teaching should invoke the values that undergrids the scientific endeavours and reflect the values such as truth, freedom, originality, scepticism and dissent, order, communication, integrity, open-mindedness, curiosity, objectivity, commitment and persistence and creativity. Values can be inculcated either by direct or indirect and curricular or non-curricular approaches. These goals can be achieved if and only if the teacher who moulds the student is aware of the facts and has wide vision and perspective. The teacher should be inspiring with personal integrity. It is also very essential to drive home the fact that science and technology blend with spiritualism by the examples of the developments in this direction. The para psychological evidences revealed by Edgar Cayce, the proof of the five bodies of man (see "Thought form", by Annie Besant and Leadbeater), and astral aura associated with different moods through Kirlian photography by Frank Baranowski, the records of near death experiences, the prediction of the existence of quarks and isotopes by clairvoyance by Charles Leadbeater and Annie Besant have been scientifically established. The recent scientific study on behavioural changes (Moghal *et al.*) at the level of genes in response to environmental conditions/experiences is evidence to the karma philosophy. By proper blending, fragmentation of mind, soul and body may be prevented and by which man may live in harmony with nature. Such attempts are being made in some Universities in U.S.A. But the most important contribution to vibrant value inculcation is by Sri Sathya Sai Baba who has laid a firm foundation in this direction with His infinite love to elevate man to super man by making him to understand his own divinity. The holistic blend of Science, Technology and Spiritualism is exemplified by the Upanisadvakya:

Purnasya purnamadaya purnamevavasisyate.

30

Value Orientation in Science Teaching

K. Anil Kumar

Introduction

Man stands on cross-roads, as he helplessly witnesses the strange paradox that has engulfed the whole world. On one hand, are the amazing marvels of Science and Technology and on the other the sighs of discontent and confusion? One side is replete with signposts of man's conquest of ever-new vistas of matter and space and the other, with directionless echoes of man's elusive quest for peace. Logic fails to throw any light on this inconsistency that while the domain of comforts is expanding endlessly, the one for whom they are intended, is becoming unhappy.

Education has played a very important and vital role in the development and evolution of humanity. But yet, we are experiencing a crisis of identity because we have not been able to train and discipline our minds. The world around us offers many good things; it also attracts and nurtures our beliefs, desires and ambitions. However, the growth of our personality at present is directed outwards and in this process we tend to lose touch with our inner nature.

The human mind has the capacity to develop and utilize the wisdom, knowledge and understanding, which we gain in life through our interactions in society. At the same time, there is also the possibility of finding the source of peace and discovering the nature of the human spirit. These are the concepts, which have guided different philosophies. One must learn to educate the human mind. But what is education? What is learnt today in schools through academic studies are intellectual concepts. Intellect is only one aspect of the human mind. There are other aspects of the mind, which do not deal with or reflect the law of the written word, but are more intuitive in nature.

We need to adopt a whole new change of perspective in teaching any subject. We have to give equal attention to the 'within' of every subject. We are used to imparting knowledge of the external changing form and structure, while we rarely pay any serious attention to the 'within' of every subject. By within, we mean an *unchanging eternal reality* of every entity. Iilya Prigogine, winner of Noble Prize in Chemistry laments, "Classical science has forgotten Nature's interiority." Lincoln Barnett in his study of Einstein's contribution to modern thought, says, "In the evolution of scientific thought, one fact has become impressively clear; there is no mystery of the physical world which does not point to a mystery beyond itself. All high roads of the intellect, all byways of theory and conjecture, lead ultimately to an abyss that human ingenuity can never span. The further he extends his horizons, the more vividly he recognizes the fact that as the physicist Niels Bohr puts it, "we are both spectators and actors in the great drama of existence." Man is thus his own greatest mystery. He does not understand the vast veiled universe into which he has been cast for the reason that he does not understand himself."

It is here that the values, the five cardinal values, *Sathya, Dharma, Shanti, Prema and Ahimsa* as enunciated by Bhagawan Sri Sathya Sai Baba, are of immense use. The practice and precept of these Values 'link us' to the core of our being, 'the within', 'the unseen eternal aspect.'

The Importance of Human Values

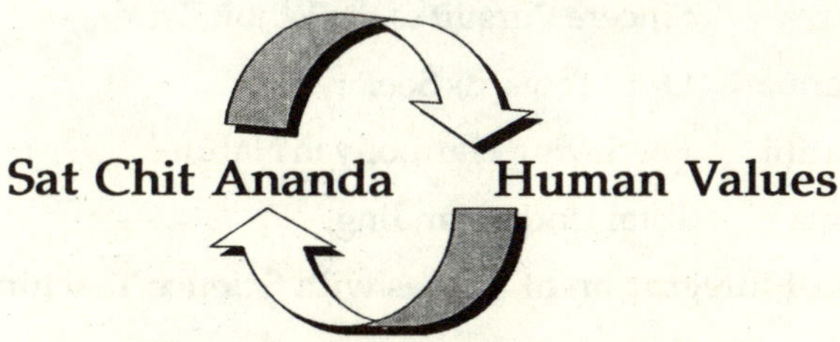

The Unseen–vs–The Seen

To remind ourselves of this inner core and to draw strength from that conviction is Education in Human Values—Educare. To contact this underlying truth we need to focus our attention constantly on these values.

Correlation of Human Values in Science Teaching

Since, the origin of the whole creation is from the primordial single undivided energy (The Big Bang Theory) all the various branches of Sciences, for that matter whether it be Science or Spirituality both deal with the same subject. One attempts to look *within* and perceive the *cause-Spirituality*, while the other looks *without* and perceives the *effect-Science.* By definition Science is the pursuit of TRUTH, the Whole Truth, therefore, unless the student of Science develops an ability to discern the within along with his ability to discover, measure and analyze the tangible, his training is not complete. We cannot isolate something and turn it into a science and say that our study stops there; truly, Science is a perspective of Reality and all aspects of it have to be taken into account. Science explains and glorifies the external, without as much giving a fleeting mention of the substratum, the foundation, and the cause. Therefore, actual pursuit of Science should give adequate attention to the basis of existence and thus build a stable super structure. Hence, we only need to change our perspective of reality and accept a more Holistic approach. As mentioned earlier, values form the bridge for man to reach within and contact this eternal source of Bliss.

We have Five Values; *Sathya, Dharma, Shanthi, Prema* and *Ahimsa;* these are the five aspects of Inner Reality. Among the various courses we teach we can see the reality through them. We will now attempt to see their relevance and connotation in pursuit of Science:

Values	*Connotation in Subject Teaching*
Sathya	Sincere Pursuit of the Whole Truth.
Dharma	Duty Towards Society.
Shanthi	Percieving Harmony in Nature.
Prema	Total Understanding.

Process of Integration of Values with Science Teaching

Love

It is love that unveils the Reality. Why did Newton see that fall of the apple and not someone else? There are millions of other human beings who might have seen an apple fall from a tree a number of times... innumerable people on innumerable occasions. But why Newton only...why suddenly did it strike him when he was sitting there in a chair in his garden, looking at this apple coming down? Because of all the thinking that he had done, all the experience he had of this perspective...of things in motion, of matter behaving in a particular way. He had spent his life on that question; he was geared up to that. That is why this came to him and was revealed to him. It is because he had loved thinking along those lines. It is this love that drives you to a desperate pitch "voyaging through strange seas of thought, alone..", as Wordsworth said, and enables you to see new things, discover new forms, and gives you the peculiar delight that comes to one who has seen Reality. Love is the fundamental requirement for the pursuit of any endeavour. Love is the undercurrent of all the other Human Values.

Sathya

Sathya or Truth could be understood as fearless sincere pursuit of Knowledge inclusive of Self-knowledge.

Implication of VALUE in the SUBJECT

Develop a sense of AWE

Underlining UNITY

SATHYA
SELF–KNOWLEDGE
(Perceive the Unseen)

Derive Lessons from Nature

Perceive a Design in NATURE

This sincere pursuit of Reality has four connotations in the subject teaching, namely:

- To Perceive the underlying Unity.
- To develop a sense of Awe and Reverence towards Nature and Natural Processes.
- To perceive a Design and Harmony in Nature.
- To Derive Lessons from Nature.

When we address these four aspects of any topic, we are in effect practicing Sathya in Teaching; also we impart this Value to the students. This is applicable to all subjects; any subject can be analyzed from this angle, since that subject is only another perspective of the same Reality. I shall substantiate this approach taking examples from Chemistry.

SATHYA—Underlying UNITY

WETHER IT IS BREAD,
TEXTILE, CELLULOSE (PAPER),
WOOD, SUGAR etc.,
All are made up of
same Elements, namely,
CARBON,
HYDROGEN and
OXYGEN.

Whether it is Carbon soot or Diamond or Graphite (Allotropes).

Biochemically all living beings are ONE

- When we teach the Allotropes of Carbon, we need to draw their attention to the underlying unity, that whether it is invaluable diamond or the worthless (so-called) soot, both are made of Carbon. Similarly, when we teach polymers and Industrial Chemistry, we can draw their attention to the fact that whether it is sugar, starch, paper, textile or bread, all are made of the same three atoms, namely, Carbon, Hydrogen and Oxygen. The difference is only in the external form, at the atomic level there is an underlying identity. As it is said in Upanishads, *Mruth pindam ekam bahu bhanda rupam*—that is, in all the different variety of pots and plates the clay is the same. This also tells us not to give excessive importance to the exterior shape and structure. Thus, the value of "avoidance of greed" is effectively taught.
- The biochemical reactions, Glycolysis or Kreb's cycle, are common to all the living cells. So is the case with a number

of other reactions within the cell. Thus, at the cellular level or the biomolecular level, there is an underlying unity. Similarly in all the myriad variety of life forms there is the same single life force. Bhagawan Sri Sathya Sai Baba says, "All men are cells in the same Divine Organism, Divine body. That should be your faith, your fortune, your fort, your fullness." *Ekam Paratma Bahu Deha Varti.* "The ONE Primordial energy lives in many bodies."

We will now consider the other aspects of Sathya, namely,

- To develop a sense of Awe and Reverence towards Nature.
- To perceive a Design and Harmony in Nature.

The Major Elements of Value Oriented Teaching

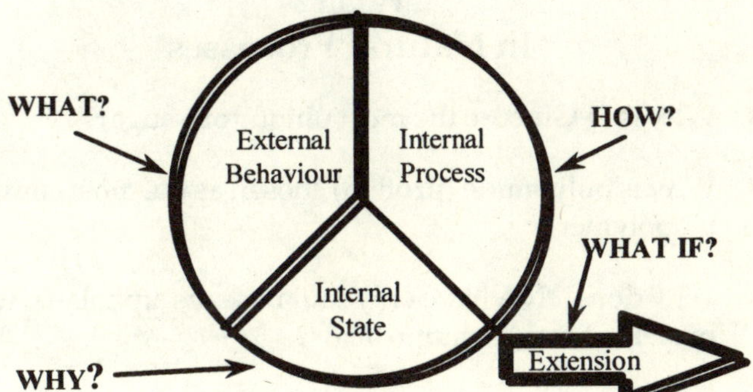

Sincere pursuit and incisive thinking form the brick and mortar for the super structure of Science. Questioning what we perceive, posing questions, such as, What, Why, How and What if, is essential to the deepen appreciation of the subject. Unfortunately, most of the school level, graduate level and to some extent even the postgraduate level teaching focusses on the *What* and *How* aspects of all that we perceive. In other words, they are content explaining the *External Behaviour (What?)* and *Internal Process (How?)*, neglecting the *Internal State (Why?)* and the *day-to-day application (What if?)*. We shall take an example to substantiate the discussion:

- When we teach the biochemical processes, we tend to ask what are cells, tissues, what are the biomolecules, etc., in effect we describe the external state, we also address the questions with regards to how these biochemical processes function, in effect explaining the Internal processes. However, we very rarely dwell on the aspect of why a particular processe is going on? Why is it the molecule being used for a particular function? Why is the cell organized as it is? These questions tend to make us understand the Internal State. Many a times we do not pose these questions more because these do not form a part of our syllabus. In our experience we observed that posing these questions and attempting to answer them is very rewarding. It makes us gain a greater appreciation of the subject, along with a substantial value input. I will highlight a few such examples, in Chemistry teaching.

WHY?
In Natural Processes

- Why is D-Glucose the most ubiquitous sugar?
- Why is polyamide (protein) chosen as the most common biopolymer?
- Why does DNA have only four bases as alphabets, while proteins have 21 amino acids?

- Taking up one such question—why a polyamide? Let us travel along and analyze the requirements of the biomolecule, which could replace the protein. These biomolecules act as, structural components, hormones, anti-bodies and biocatalysts. Of these the action of biocatalyst/anti-body is vital and involves a whole gamut of non-covalent interactions with the substrate molecules. In fact, it would not be an understatement if we say that life is sustained by the enzymes, since all the transformations in the biosystems occur at low temperature and in aqueous media, catalysts are essential for smooth or rapid energy release and transfer. These catalysts have to be highly efficient and highly specific if precise patterns are to be followed. If bond-breaking and bond-forming reactions are to be performed on a specific starting material, then a suitable specific catalyst capable of recognizing the substrate must be constructed around that substrate. In other words, a substrate molecule and the specific reaction it must undergo must be translated into another molecule/structure of much higher order, whose information content perfectly matches the specifically planned chemical transformation. Only large macromolecules can carry enough molecular information both from the point of view of the substrate recognition and thermodynamic efficiency of the transformation. Hence, these macromolecule essentially has two important functions:

- Molecular recognition and
- Transformation/reaction/chemical transformation.

Hence, the macromolecule for the purpose of molecular recognition has to be a rigid structure, or so to say "frozen", while for the purpose of reaction dynamics it should be "breathing". Also, since no biological system can be non-degradable (otherwise the planet by now would not have any space left), the macromolecule should be degradable with a minimum expense of energy. Now, with the apparently conflicting requirements of "rigidity", "flexibility" and "facile degradability", when we analyze all the common polymeric units (from their IR stretching frequencies) it becomes fairly apparent that only *a polyamide bond, with its partial double bond character gives the necessary rigidity and flexibility and its single bond (that too an acid derivative) makes cleavage a minimum energy process.* Thus, of all the common polymeric units, such as, amide, ester, urethane and thioamide, only polyamide comes out as a winner.

- Similarly, we see that of all the sixteen (16) isomers that are possible for a aldohexose, only D-Glucose has all the bulky hydroxyl groups equatorially positioned in the ring form making it the most stable molecule. We can go on in this strain, all these prove beyond an iota of doubt that, *From Microcosm to Macrocosm the entire Creation is singly ordered to Perfection.*

This approach leads to a sense of adoration and awe at the Natural processes, it also makes us feel humble. Hence, a core value of Humility and Reverence develops in us.

Coming to the fourth aspect of *Sathya*, viz., "To derive Lessons", this deals mainly with drawing of suitable analogies. In Science we tend to unravel the mysteries of Nature, we also know that Nature is Best Teacher; therefore it becomes obvious that Science itself should be full of Lessons applicable for our day-to-day living. To illustrate this, couples of examples from school Chemistry course are cited:

- The periodic table gives a powerful message. We see that it is mainly divided into elements that readily give electrons—we call them Metals and elements that take electrons—we call them Non-metals. Metals are known to be lustrous, strong, malleable and ductile, while Non-metals do not have luster, they are brittle (weak). We clearly see that *Giving leads to strength and luster while taking (greed) removes our luster and makes us weak*. Therefore, greed has to be avoided.
- In the study of biomolecules, we observe a clear difference in properties of monomers vis-à-vis their corresponding polymers. For example, Glucose is so very sweet that we cannot consume large amounts of it, while the polymer of same glucose (that when glucose is linked up to another glucose molecule as a chain) is bland and is the source of energy for us all. Similarly amino acids are bitter, but when the same amino acids are joined in a polymeric manner we have proteins, which are very tasty. The analogies that can be drawn here are the following:
- United our individual limitations get nullified.
- United we become more useful to society.

Implication of VALUE in the SUBJECT

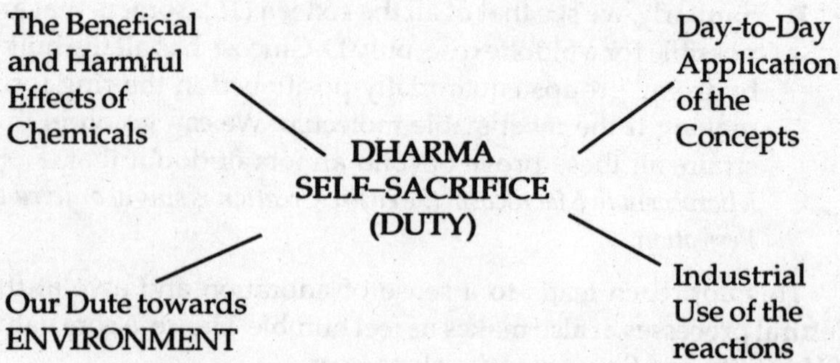

Dharma

Dharma has four connotations in Science teaching, namely, teaching of:

- Day-to-day application of the concepts.
- Industrial uses of the reactions/products.
- The beneficial and harmful effects of chemicals.
- Our duty towards Environment.

When we address these four aspects of any topic, we are in effect practicing *Dharma* in Teaching; also we impart this Value to the students.

When we teach the concepts it is necessary that we extend this knowledge to explain common occurrences, such as, for example, why does milk boil? (water does not), how does an automobile run? What is cement? Why does it become so strong? etc. This kindles keen interest for the finer aspects of the subject, at the same time making the student aware that; all that he studies is of practical relevance. This will equip the students with adequate knowledge and ability to apply his knowledge. But this will not suffice, as we have seen what havoc has been caused by indiscriminate usage of this knowledge. As Albert Einstein says, " What we have done thus far creates problems that we cannot solve at the same level as we created them." The problem facing us is that living in a building we forget the very land over which the building has been built. Hence, it becomes imperative, our *Dharma*, to bring to the notice of the students the beneficial and harmful effects of Chemicals. While teaching this subject we need to draw their attention once in a while to the environmental issues and ones duty towards fellow beings and towards Mother Earth. Equipped with knowledge of the beneficial and harmful effects of chemicals, the student should be motivated to constructively contribute to the society. Bhagawan Sri Sathya Sai Baba says, *Unless the desire to do service is earnest and the skill to do it is cultivated, students will remain a burden to the community.*

Shanthi

Peace or mental equipoise, are terms used to explain Shanthi. A person in harmony with himself and the society around is peaceful.

Shanthi (Peace) has two connotations in Science teaching, namely:

- Perceiving a Design and Harmony in Nature.
- Study of Symbiosis and Synergy.

When we address these two aspects of any topic, we are in fact practicing Shanthi in Teaching; also we impart this Value to the students. Science deals with understanding Natural processes. There is an element of aesthetic value even in the rational scientific approach. Be it in the cascading electron transfer reactions of the photosynthesis or the stunning patterns (fractals) of colours on the butterfly wings, a student of science at some point in his study stumbles on amazing beauty inherent in Nature. Teaching of the routine syllabi should be infused with this aesthetic value and the focus should be on the interrelatedness of all the life forms. This would sensitize the teacher and the taught and will provide the aesthetic satisfaction. Perceiving the Harmony in Natural processes can develop this value. We have to constantly focus our attention on this inherent harmony in Nature around.

Conclusion

The aim of all education must be to study a piece of Reality so completely as to realize and experience all the aspects of it. In the normal secular mode of education we do not experience much at all. We read about a subject, we study it, at the most we discover a few underlying and hidden laws and principles, but we have not experienced the joy of it. We have not experienced the totality of this reality and realized that all this complexity of subjects and fields of study relate to only that ONE reality. But once we make the proper kind of study, seeing them all as perspectives, it will take us to this principle of Delight, and give us the total experience of Reality. And once we have that, life will change all its colours and education will not only have made men of us, but it will have enriched our sensibility. It will have made us know life, as it ought to be known and studied. We see that what we call, in the cold, dead language of our educational system, academic subjects, are in truth, in the living language of Spirit, perspectives in which you see the Reality revealed. As shown before, we can study these various subjects through these four features of Reality (Human Values). In each case the Reality will be revealed, although through different perspectives. In other words many new insights will be generated. Education itself will be raised to a new height and a new freshness, and what is more it will no longer be dead learning. We'll have experienced this joy ourselves in teaching of it, and once we do that we have really fulfilled ourselves and ignited a number of these young students that sit in front of us. By this approach, we will have taught them something really worthwhile and given them some work to do for a whole lifetime.

31

Managerial Excellence and Human Values

Shashi Verma

Transnational processes and emergence of new patterns of behaviour dominate modern management. The research (Inglehart, 1997) shows that the societies around the world are experiencing the process of 'Post-modernization'. There is a paradigm shift from economic efficiency, bureaucratic authority, and scientific rationality, toward greater human touch, individual self-expression and equally empowered diversity. The emphasis of post-modernization is on transcending the dualities that deem science and technology as superior to religion and spirituality; economic growth and monetary power as superior to aesthetic and human considerations; and present and future as advancement superior to the past. It seeks to incorporate metaphysical, cultural and historical forces as the integrated elements of a new context. In the new context, the forces of change are being propelled by globalization, liberalization, information technology and falling walls of geographical boundaries and privatization. This has thrown new challenges, to the modern management, of managing the whole world as one market. This global market is characterized by the complexities caused by emerging diversities at different levels. Some of the contemporary developments, which are dominating the working of modern organisations, can be identified as under:

- Information Technology has provided qualitatively better and quantitatively huge information for decision-making.
- Automation has simplified the processes, increased the

production efficiency, created requirement for skilled manpower and 'knowledge worker.'

- Diversity in the aspirations of manpower serving in the modern organization has multiplied with the entry of women, disadvantaged sections of the society, etc.
- Cross-cultural influences have created a new type of requirements for effective interpersonal relations.
- Competition at different levels is increasing with the intricacies in the market forces.
- Management is becoming more like a one village. This extends both opportunities and threats to the working of organizations.
- Genuine concern for realizing total quality calls for value-based management functions

Changes have both positive and negative effects on the management of modern organization. While they are paradise for the innovative and progressive organizations, stale and bureaucratic organizations look at them as stumbling blocks in performing even their routine functions. It has been observed that in all transitions and turmoil in the socio-economic systems, sense of commitment and responsibility is disappearing. This has resulted into deterioration in work culture and work ethos. Organisations have become sick both economically and socially. This sickness is the reflection of mental and moral sickness of the society itself. It is being realized that solution lies in incessant harmonizing between science and religion, technology and spirituality, economy and people and culture and history.

Management Job

Management is basically concerned with the accomplishment of organizational goals through the judicious utilization of human energies besides other resources. Many times, the process of goal realization may exploit the human resources. It has costs, which may apparently appear to be non-significant and intangible. But in long run organizations fall without much of rattle. At the time of joining an organization, the individual enters into two types of contracts with the organization. While one is formal contract to provide services in lieu of certain economic package, the other one is psychological for fulfilling non-economic aspirations which many times remain unattended. People do form sub-coalitions with the objective of pursuing their individual interests, which may go sometimes against the organizational interests. This affects the overall working and satisfaction level of people. The manager has to develop an environment where the individual aspirations and values are truly matched with the organizational culture.

In the emerging scenario, management, to me, is getting work done with others by the influence of executing certain responsibilities suffused with human values. Hierarchy is in fact a structure of responsibilities not the power or influence. Real power lies in the human values. When management conducts itself in terms of human values, it only provides a new strength to its command of technical know-how, which is vital for the administration of an organization. In absence of moral atmosphere all plans for production, modernization and profit may fail. Human values help management by fostering amongst the members of the institution virtues that encourage the self-management.

Ethical principles apply equally to business enterprise, as a business enterprise is a corporate citizen and it has obligations to society. Its existence is determined by the acceptance by the society. Therefore, the stress has changed from attending to the aspirations of the stockholders to the needs and welfare of stakeholders.

Secret of Excellence in Organisations

Based on the empirical evidences, the fact that values play important role in making of 'excellent organization' is well accepted. Organisations stressing on techniques rather than values may lead to efficiency in operations but certainly not to the making up of an effective organization. A number of research studies demonstrate that the excellence has much contribution of people who cherished certain human values. It is the sound philosophy based on the core values and work ethics that are the bases of good business. James Collins and Jerry Porras in their book entitled *Built to last* conclude, " Companies that enjoy enduring success have core values and core purpose that remain focused, while their business strategies or practices endlessly adapt to the changing world. Core values are the essential and enduring central tenet: Core purpose is company's reason for being."

Effective management is ethical in its behaviour. Ethics deals with the principles and standards that a person uses in determining what is morally good or bad conduct in interpersonal and social dealings. It is therefore, a process of valuation; and ethical insight may be described as intelligence in evaluation. The gist of all theories of ethic that when one is confronted with the problem of deciding what is right, or wrong conduct, ask yourself whether the behaviour is in the best interest of society? If yes, the behaviour is good, otherwise, undesirable.

To some the relevance of human values in business may seem to be contrary to its objectives, as business is regarded as the playground for unrestricted self-interest, greed and avarice. But the situation is different in the present times due to the increased competition in the market. Perhaps without genuine caring and service to the customers, the future of any business is gloomy. For providing right type of service, values have to be imbibed into the daily business life.

Modem management processes emphasizing on time management, effective interpersonal skills, self-management, total quality management, organizational development, innovations and creativity, transformational leadership and cross-cultural management require the active participation of employees, suppliers, creditors, customers and intermediaries. Managers are trained to apply different techniques of management but in the absence of values in their conduct, many times they are deficient in creating mutual trust, commitment and motivation.

Values—the Real Strength of Human Resource

Human resource is different from other factors of production in the sense that this factor is not an object but a person. Most of the times, it is observed that so-called modern man has transformed himself to be a commodity. He invests his energies for achieving economically profitable exchanges. This has resulted into widespread corruption, inefficiency, wastages, greed, non-working culture, and mistrust in the organizations. Research shows that rational and scientific approach of management, based on logic and calculations has not been very successful. Many times, it has led to more exploitation and tendency to manipulate human behaviour to work harder even at the cost of their peace of mind and health.

'Economic man' of Adam Smith and FW Taylor could not sustain his motivation on the slippery ground of the assumption that the man lives for bread alone. Elton Mayo's 'Social Man' could stand his social aspirations to certain level but ultimately he looked for something different. Abraham Maslow provided a solace when he opined that man strives to self-actualize and is motivated at the higher level of his need hierarchy. 'Self-Actualized Man' remains nearer to himself and his fellow men.

There are certain basic beliefs that determine the way we think, feel and act. They are observable in the form of preferences or biases. It is observed that the values are formed and shaped in the family and by the social environment. Values are the real wealth of human beings. The man of values always believes that work itself is worship and the whole process is a communion between the two. It also reconciles work ethic and ethics-in-work. Quality of internal human environment is reflected in the external quality of work.

Spiritualists believe that the body, mind, and the *Atma* together constitute the human being. The body concern action. The mind relates to cognition. The spirit relates to Being. Action, Cognition, and Being together make up humanness. Unified expression of body, mind, and spirit is called *Sath-chith-Ananda*. Body and mind change but *Atma* remains divine, indivisible and unaffected by worldly affairs. Human values get fertile land in the realization that he is divine. Values originate from this realization. According to Sri Sathya Sai Baba, human values are born with human beings and are covered by the door of heart. Through the key of love the safe vault of heart is opened and there emerge the human values. Love is the basic value from where flow whole life and other values. Thought prompted by love is truth. Truth put into action is right conduct. Right conduct always leads to peace and peace to non-violence. If thought is purified, words will be truthful and sweet and will fructify into right actions.

Regarding the development of human values, the *Gita* provides enough insight into theory of self-development that is useful for holistic living and social improvement. The *Gita's* sprituology is not only relevant for psycho-spiritual environment at the work place but also developing the fundamental human values. According to *Gita,* a person with a set of certain qualities is described to be a divine person or a person with full of higher universal human qualities. He is fearless with purity of heart and steadfast in knowledge; straightforward, austere, inner voice of self and the divine types knowledge; non-injury, truth, absence of anger and absence of crookedness; vigour, forgiveness, fortitude and absence of hate. Stress on self-knowledge helps a person to know the working of human psyche. It is said that there is no better purifier than the self-knowledge. Through the raft of self-knowledge one becomes a winner.

An effective manager is a true *yogi* who has even mindedness in success or failure, moderation in his habits, passion for excellence, and skills for perfection in action. The greatest strength of human personality lies in the value of *nishkam karma,* that is, action without attachment to the fruits of action. *Karamayoga* is the theory of positive action as well as a theory of detached action. Its correlate *karmavada,* suggests that intentionality of action is crucial to the moral result of actions. Perform *karma* without longing for the fruit. Such advice may look to be incongruent with the practices where, people believe that wealth cannot be acquired through fair means. Prosperous people are looked upon with mistrust and doubt. It is because of lack of faith, integrity and trust. Corruption has become all-pervasive. The tendencies for bargaining and haggling demonstrate that the business is not fair and it may loot a person who truthfully believes the businessmen. The past has contributed in the development of this type of thinking, particularly when the toiling masses had the impression that the feudal classes did not share the surpluses among them.

Deceitful and corrupt management cannot lead and inspire people. It is the value-based behaviour of a manager that inspires the subordinates and lead to more satisfying and productive relationship. A man enters organization to seek the satisfaction of his expectations. These expectations emanate from this identity itself. At the physical level, he would like to do a work, which is of his liking. Appreciation and acceptance of his creative and analytical thinking will motivate him more at mental level. Feelings need to be harnessed by way of selfless compassion, sympathy, and empathy. At the super conscious level, it is perhaps the realization that all are one and united. Any harm caused to the organization is harmful to not only the people serving in that organization but to the whole humanity.

Stephen Covey writes, "The character ethic is based on the fundamental idea that there are principles that govern human effectiveness—natural laws in the human dimensions that are just as real, just as unchanging and unarguable 'there' as laws such gravity are in the physical dimension. Principles are like lighthouses. They are like lighthouses that can't be broken." These natural principles outflow out of human consciousness and are part of human conscience, such as integrity, honesty, human dignity, service, quality or excellence, patience and encouragement. They are universal in nature.

Indian insight probes deep into human identity, through different levels of its awareness of existence—physical to mental, intellectual, psychic and intuitive. The probe transcends all these levels and discovers human identity in its absoluteness as Existence-Knowledge–Bliss. India had identified the goal of life to reach this end state of Being and had attributed the highest value to it. All human action is regarded as instrumental in achieving this objective, and is not valued as an end in itself. This value drive is unique in man and it is called *maanava dharama*. This is eternally inherent in man and so it is also *sanathana*. Work is of instrumental value towards achieving this terminal value. According to Indian psychology, such work strategies may be different in pattern, but the motive is to cleanse the mind stuff and cleanse it absolutely. The appropriate work strategies adopted to cleanse the mind are considered ethical.

According to Indian psycho-philosophy, all work done by us is subjective and is done for our own benefit. Work always enlightens and liberates, hence quality work, according to the Indian view is itself a spiritual discipline. When a man works with a clear conscience he develops a wisdom that accommodates quality variations as duty and morality, ruled by the higher plane of mental existence to which that person belongs. The highest Ideal of work-life is non-resistance.

There are the fundamental principles that could resolve conflicts between personal values and organizational values. If a man honours his commitment and works efficiently, a high quality of work life will be maintained even if that commitment is honoured at the cost of other personal desires.

The value of selflessness is the key to resolve a number of conflicts. Quality of work life is the refection of moral value in action. The highest leadership can be found in one who is totally ego less; who has been able to merge his narrow individual will into the Cosmic Will. Without integrated personality composed of intelligence and integrity one can hardly develop as leader. Team building process is more efficient and successful if members share similar values and concerns. It is said; he leads best who serves best.

To conclude, Modern Organization is faced with the cruel challenge of market competition and degeneration of overall moral atmosphere. If it works with the human values in its operations, which can be understood as the spring of energy, it will rise to achieve and will be able to sustain organizational effectiveness. Human values give life to the organization without which organizations are concrete structures of rules and regulations, hierarchies, positions, technology and selfish. It is human values, which convert work into worship and 'work of art'. All functions of management, say leadership, team building, communication, interpersonal relations, controlling, and motivation become simpler and effective, if manager adopts human values in his behaviour while dealing with people of diverse backgrounds and personality patterns.

32

Values and Environment

Kiran Rekha

Environmental ethics is the environmental competence which should be developed through education. The word 'ethic' is derived from 'ethos' or way of life which is a philosophical discipline for human beings. Environmental education, formal and non-formal, is the means to establish environmental ethics as a competence in individuals and societies through imparting awareness, knowledge, skills, attitudes, commitments for actions and ethical responsibilities for understanding, respecting and taking actions for the protection and improvement of the environment for the present and future generations. The contributions of the major religious traditions can be considered as basic concepts used for environmental ethics in education. There is a need of educating the masses to develop a holistic attitude towards various issues of environment. Man is confronting with numerous problems regarding the environment i.e., pollution, depletion and deterioration of natural resources. The reasons of environmental crisis are multiple including over exploitation of resources, misuse of technology to pollute, population explosion, and ignorance of causal relationship in nature. The root causes of all these disturbançes are mistaken human values and attitudes. These degenerative changes can be corrected with the help of serious ethical approach. This can bring basic change in man's attitude towards nature, population growth, use of technology, and main's own place in nature. The self-regulatory mechanism of ecological homeostasis can be restored with development of ecological attitude in human beings.

In order to bring about a change in our attitude towards the environment we need an ethical basis for it. The source of the ethical principles needed to solve environmental crisis could be metaphysical, rooted in religion. This could be done by considering: (1) Nature to be a creation of God, (2) God as immanent in Nature and (3) Nature as the house of God. Ancient Indian religion and culture have respectful attitude towards the nature and all God's creations including living and non-living ones. The theological aspect of environment as dealt in ancient Indian religion and culture is presented as follows:

(a) Ecological protection in ancient Indian culture.

(b) Need for environmental ethics.

(c) Values and protection of environment.

(a) Ecological Protection in Ancient Indian Culture

Indians accept nature as divinity. Various rivers, trees, sun, moon, animals, mountains, oceans, etc., are part of religious ceremonies. These are considered so sacred that it is said that particular God and Goddess have made their abode in them. This theory of nature is enormously affected by the theory of creation which recognizes that every element, object and living being in the universe is created by the same Supreme Being, and so human beings have no special dominion over nature. The Hindu religion has respect for nature in three basic elements, faith in God, non-dualistic view of Purusha and Prakrity and a set of rules for duties and worship. The concept of "Sacred forest" is needed very ancient. The sacred trees and forest are especially significant in the Hindu, Jain and Buddhist cultures. Anand Coomaraswami has identified the 'Kalpavriksha'—the tree that fulfills all wishes—as the banyan tree, whose roots could be traced to as far back as the ancient vedic culture. Trees symbolized life that always regenerates itself and is immortal. As early as eight centuries before Christ, Jainism upheld the philosophy of 'ahimsa' and propounded a world view built on respect for a religious veneration of the natural world. The Indian psyche has grounded itself on intimate links with all nature. Ecology is a recent science but the poetic roots of a collective eco-consciousness go as far deep as the earliest Rig Vedic hymns. A strong feeling of man's participation in the universal order pervades the Veda; man is inseparable from his cosmic environment, he is not distinct from it but imbued in it. The ancient traditional Indian way of life was objectively correct, rationally sound and ecologically valid. It is perhaps the excess pressure exerted on the earth by one single species, Homo sapiens that has led to an erosion of this bio-centric view of life.

Vedas, Upanishads, Puranas and other scriptures of our religion give a detailed description of trees, plants and wildlife and their importance to the community. Trees have been considered as an essential part of dwellings and they were planted, protected and considered as sons, as told in *Mahabharata*. Among various plants Tulsi has special place, besides its medicinal properties as described in *Ayurveda*, it is worshipped daily by Hindu ladies. Almost all the sixteen *sanskaras* from birth to death are performed with the help of different types of plants and their produce. *Tulsi* and *Peepal*, *Bilva*, Mango and Banana leaves, Mangowood, *Kusha* grass, etc., are essential to perform *yajans* in the families. Various trees and plants are not only worshipped but cutting of green trees has also been prohibited. In Charak Samhita destruction of forests was treated to be the cause of ruining the nation and human beings. People were definitely aware that their existence depended on the welfare of flora and fauna of the country. In Durga *saptasati* it has been clearly said that so long as the earth has mountains, forests, trees, plants etc., human race will continue to survive. Relationship of man with the nature and animals was not that of ruler and ruled but rather a relationship of mutual respect and kindness. Killing of birds and animals was strictly prohibited in ancient scriptures. Among all animals, the worship of cow has been given special place. Several animals have been named as vehicles of God/Goddesses, such an animal receives religious protection.

The ancient tradition followed by such great religions as Buddhism, Christianity, Sikhism and Jainism, directed to follow the wise advice of sages. Buddhism believes that nature will yield to man for more than just the material requisites without which life is impossible. Precious medicinal herbs, along with all kinds of other animals and mineral substances were considered as gift of Lord Buddha to mankind. Any needless injury caused to any living organism including trees was described as 'sinful'. Buddha was very critical of animal sacrifices and the pleasure of hunting. Human inhabitants under the doctrine of Lord Buddha had compassion towards all creatures. This was realized by a wise old monk saying:

"Love all God's creation, the whole and every grain of sand in it. Love every leaf, every ray of God's light. Love the animals, love the plants, love everything. If you love everything you will perceive the divine mystery in things." Christian thinkers believe that each living organism is a unique individual, a mysterious other, and a fellow subject having an intrinsic value. Guru Nanak in Sikhism indicated that the whole universe is interrelated as whatever relation is in the universe the same relation obtains in the microcosm. In the traditional sherpa culture of Himalayas there is a positive and intimate relationship between the people and the mountain (means the mother of long, good life). Jains have respectful gestures for even the invisible organisms of the nature.

Religious philosophers were strict to a person who caused pollution and civic sanitation was the main consideration in those days. The sacred books are full of examples which tell us about people alertness against the pollution and environmental crisis. Prohibitions were announced by kings also e.g., the King Ashoka prescribed various financial punishments for killing of animals. Thus as discussed above, protection of the environment has been an important facet of ancient way of life. In order to restore ecological stability and homeostasis, appeal to scientific, philosophical and religious principles can bring the desired results.

(b) Need for Environmental Ethics

According to Indian culture, abuse and exploitation of the nature for immediate gain is unjust and irreligious. Religion can be considered as simplification of philosophy and science for the use of the common man. Man is the trustee of the universe and is authorized to use natural resources, but has no divine power to control and dominate over the nature and its elements. Environmental ethics as propounded by ancient scriptures and the seers continued to exist in society and were practiced by not only common man but even by rulers and kings. It was a network of moral guidelines towards environmental preservation and conservation which became part of their way of life. Every minor environmental problems were dealt with giving proper solution. Man must abide by the natural laws or face dire consequences.

Keeping the water pure was considered very essential. Ancient thinkers were very much aware of the reasons which cause pollution in water. They advised: One should not cause urine, stool and cough in water and also blood and poison should not be thrown into water. Foul smelling, discoloured, muddy, spoiled by birds—such water creates diseases and is called polluted water according to Charak Samhita. Manu warns the people not to take a rotten food which may cause diseases. People have been very careful to observe such bindings and morals for the welfare of the society as a whole. Even the rulers and kings followed these conditions and tried to create an example for others. This was ancient Indian value system and way of life which assisted in developing a stable eco-ethics. However, during recent fifty years, greed and chauvinism have overtaken all religious principles—Need of today is that environmental ethics based on various religions of the world should be developed. Such environmental ethics can be defined as a system of moral guidelines which governs man's attitude, behaviour and actions towards the natural environment and entire universe. These guidelines suggest how man, either as an individual or as a group, should interact with his surroundings. *Dharma* is the realization of the rhythmic unity of all beings; it calls for an ethical relationship with all and everything.

(c) Values and Protection of Environment

To rectify the environment is a challenge before us to accept. The present ecological crisis is based on the modern man's overpowering ego of having enslaved the nature with the help of modern technological and scientific devices. But as these activities are also destroying the environment, we face anxiety and to clear this, there is need of moral guidelines, an ethical framework, of environmental ethics. Hindu religious norms and values are already strong enough to provide us with appropriate moral guidelines. Love and respect for all nature is at the root of Vedic metaphysics that is conceived in an environmental ethic. Similarly norms and values enunciated in religions, like – Christianity, Buddhism, Jainism, Sikhism and Islam etc., may also be drawn and an International Environmental ethics should be developed to save the humanity as a whole from the present environmental crisis. Human values and norms drawn from various religions can lead to achievement of complete environmental harmony. Self-realization is necessary so as to become less ego-centric. Self-realized person will identify more with others as well as with nature beings as well as in the ecosphere. Religious approach can provide a justification for unity in diversity of nature. Once it is realized, man no longer exploits nature, he rather respects it as a 'House of the Lord'. All the scientific, philosophical and religious perspective collectively can provide us guidelines for taking action in the direction which would protect and conserve the environment for generations.

The points extracted from the inter-religious environmental ethics and ecology are as given below:

(a) The well being and flourishing of human and non-human life on earth have intrinsic and inherent values.

(b) Richness and diversity of life forms contribute to a realization of these values and are also values in themselves.

(c) Humans have no right to reduce this richness and diversity except to satisfy vital needs.

(d) The flourishing of human life and culture is compatible with a substantial decrease of the human population.

(e) Present human interference with the non-human world is excessive and the situation is rapidly worsening.

(f) Policies must be changed and these policies affect our basic economic, technological and ideological structures.

(g) The change in air attitude will bring an appreciation of the quality of life rather than adhering to an increasingly higher standard of living.

Our future is in our hands. How we take care of present will determine the future. If we are fair with the nature, it will be fair with us. Our living patterns will be in commensurate with the inherent values of nature. These values are sacrifice, patience, co-operation, non-violence and co-existence. Man has to develop such values in relationship with the nature.

33

Effective Administration of Educational Institutions: Lessons from the Indian Heritage

N. Sivakumar and U.S. Rao

Introduction

Higher education in India is at a cross-roads. This may sound like an overused cliché but is true because our higher education system is facing greater challenges in the twenty-first century. This scenario has emerged because of certain developments over the past few years: For the first time, India is recognised internationally as a nation, which is providing value-added trained human power at a premier level. Indian experts are now persons who generate wealth and also are the backbone in many global science and technology revolutions. Indians have made their presence felt in the field of information technology (both in software and hardware), electronics, biotechnology, pure sciences and economics; in financial management and in fields related to humanities and social sciences (University Grants Commission, 2005).

In spite of this silver lining in the globalised scenario, there are several concerns regarding the education scenario and its administration in India. As Dubey (2001) remarks, "ever since independence, education for all has been one of the major concerns of the Indian Government. Even though the education scenario in India in the past few decades has been characterized by massive quantitative expansion at all levels, it is still faced with a staggering backlog of high illiteracy rate." Another concern is that of accreditation and recognition. While the UGC has constituted the NAAC and the Supreme Court in the process has derecognized several private universities, there is still a cry for "liberalizing higher education and doing away with the Education Raj" (Jalote, 2005). Similarly Sharma and Sharma (2002) have analyzed several problems of Indian education from diverse angles such as explosion of knowledge, educational methodology, education of the scheduled castes and scheduled tribes, women education, population education, adult education, wastage and stagnation in primary education, diversification of secondary education courses, multi-purpose schools, curriculum construction, textbook nationalization, standardization in education, vocationalization, religious and moral education, evaluation and examination, student unrest and indiscipline and so on.

Value-Based Education Administration Framework

India has a distinguished heritage in education administration. It had some of the most well-known universities like Nalanda and Takshashila and several Gurukulas, which imparted education, based on human values. Not only the education was value-based, but these institutions were also administered in an ideal fashion based on the highest ethics and morals. In this paper this historical heritage of value-based administration of educational institutions has been analysed.

Administration based on values firstly needs an organization philosophy, which is clearly defined. Leadership for the organization should be in consonance with and based on the organizational philosophy. An organization culture, which defines the values that are supposed to guide behaviour of the members of the organization and promotes ethical behaviour, is a necessity. Additionally, value based administration includes inculcating socially responsible behaviour in all the members of the institution (Sivakumar and Rao, 1996). This paper thus uses the following framework of value-based administration:

- Organization philosophy.
- Value-based leadership.
- Organization culture promoting ethical behaviour.
- Inculcating socially responsible behaviour.

These aspects have been studied through an analysis of several Indian scriptures, which expound on education administration such as the Vedas, the Upanishads, the *Dharmashastras* and other scriptures. Also the descriptions of historians and scholars have been used to explicate several issues.

Organization Philosophy

Organizational philosophy refers to the basic purpose of the existence of the organization (Gupta, 1992). According to Peters and Waterman (1982), the organization philosophy defines the values of the organization. Indian scriptures describe the philosophy of educational institutions in terms of the social goals, which the educational institutions had to achieve through the imparting of education. The following observations regarding ancient Indian education explains this aspect:

- One of the important prayers of students and teachers of ancient schools included the words *Saha Nau Bhunaktu* taken from the Upanishads. According to Sarmah (1978), "The aim of education was to bring about efficiency signified by the motto *Saha Nau Bhunaktu* and the elimination of distress and poverty from the society leading to social justice and the welfare in the state."
- Mookherjee (1989) observes on the philosophy of ancient Indian educational institutions as follows: "The making of the nation or the country was in charge of these schools. Their aim was to produce whole men who would perfect the society and the country."
- According to (Sarmah, 1978) education in ancient India had the important purpose of inculcation of the spirit of social obligation in the students. Thus education was not regarded as a mere process of transmission of information but as a means to make the human mind broader, richer, more compassionate and more society oriented. When the graduates of ancient Indian educational institutions left the portals of the universities and faced the question mark of life, they were told to remember that as a citizen of the country, as members of a community it was their duty to assist in the process of social progress and social development."
- Venkateshwara, (1980), describes the philosophy of educational institutions in ancient India through the methods of teaching adopted by the teacher. According to him "the methods adopted in ancient Indian educational

institutions were according to the needs of the society by the most intelligent and unselfish brains with no other object in view than social welfare and social progress. The Indian educator went a step ahead and his task was to prepare his students not only for organised social life in the world, but also for spiritual evolution in progress through eternity. Hence in all faculties of the ancient scheme of the arts and science the dominating force was ethical, social and spiritual."

Thus, scholars describe the philosophy of educational institutions in terms of promoting social progress and welfare.

Value-Based Leadership

The Indian heritage allots primacy to the teacher and venerates him as the leader of educational institutions. In established ancient Indian educational institutions like Nalanda and Takshashila universities the leaders were the administrative heads and Professors. On the other hand, in the individual Gurukulas the *Acharya* or teacher was the leader. The second component of value-based administration is value-based leadership, which can be studied under:

- Leadership values.
- Relationship between teachers and students.
- Management by example.
- Importance of values for administrators.
- Establishment of moral behaviour in administrators.

Leadership Values

Leaders of Indian educational institutions were men of character. According to historians, the Chancellor of Nalanda University was Shilabhadra during the time of visit of Ywan Chwang to India. His travel records (Watters, 1973) state that Shilabhadra was unique in learning and character. His eminent virtue and advanced age caused him to be regarded as the chief member of the community. Ywan Chwang also describes another professor—Jnanachandra by name who had a model character.

Fahien another Chinese traveller describes a professor named Radhaswamin (Mookherjee, 1989) and states this professor was of clear discernment and much wisdom, who understood everything and who was living by himself in spotless purity. I-Tsing a third Chinese traveller states that "the great professors were reknowned as much for their character as for their learning."

As regards *Acharyas*, Indian scriptures state the following:

- Apastamba *Dharmasutra* (i,1,1,12) states that teachers should possess sacred learning and must be devout in following law.
- Panini's Asthadhyayi (the first book of sanskrit grammar) (i,I,I,7) states that a teacher should be diligent and should teach with care.
- Susrutha Samhita (the ancient Indian treatise on medicine) (Chapter iii) declares that "the teacher physician should be devoted to *Sathya* and *Dharma* (truth and righteousness)."
- Mahavagga lists the following qualities of the Acharya (i, 36): (1) well up in moral practices, (2) self control, (3) wisdom (4) helping tendency, (5) modesty, (6) fear of sin, (7) not transgressing moral codes, (8) perseverance and (9) ability to train pupils in proper conduct and *Dharma*.

Thus, literature on educational institutions in ancient India describe the qualities the teachers and professors should possess for the effective value-based administration, which include: Truthfulness, Righteousness, Kindness, Cheerfulness, Humility, Wisdom, Self-control, Equanimity, Fortitude, Forgiveness, Perseverance Patience, Simplicity, Purity, Contentment, Honesty, Forbearance, Modesty, Charitability and Punctuality.

Relationship Between Teachers and Students

Indian scriptures describe the close relationship that should exist between the teacher and the student. This relationship is described below:

- The Paraskara *Grihyasutra* (1.8.8) states that the teacher will speak the following words while accepting a student: "thou heart should dwell in my heart, my mind should follow with thy mind; in my world thou shalt rejoice with all thy heart, thou shall love me and in me thy thoughts shall dwell."
- The Apastamba *Dharmasutra* (1.2.8.24) declares that "the

teacher, loving the pupil like his own son, shall teach him the sacred science with full attention."

- The Mahavagga (1.32.1) asserts that 'the *Acharya* has to consider the *Antevasika* (student) as his son, and the Antevasika ought to consider the *Acharya* as a father. Thus these two, united by mutual reverence, confidence and communion of life, will progress, advance and reach a high stage the sacred discipline."
- Finally, I-Tsing the Chinese traveller reveals what he had noticed during his travels in India: "In case of a pupil's illness, the teacher himself nurses him, supplies all the medicines he needs and pays attention to him as if he were his own child."

Management by Example

The professors and teachers in Ancient India were examples for others in conduct and behaviour. The term 'Acharya' itself describes the aspect of being an example to others. *Acharya* is rooted in the term 'Acharana'—one who leads by his own practice or behaviour. Thus Sarmah (1979) states that the teacher was called *Acharya* because he showed the students the right path to follow, the moral virtues to be cultivated and the social obligation will be performed in the future. According to Ywan Chwang (Watters, 1973), "teachers at Kashi were an active influence on the students due to their pure conduct and perfect virtue." He further states, "the teachers at Nalanda were very strict in observing the precepts and regulation of their order and so were looked up to a models by all India."

Importance of Values for Administrators

A teacher who practices virtues attains spiritual merit. Thus, the Manusmriti (2.160), declares that a teacher whose speech and thoughts are pure and perfectly guarded gains the full rewards of a spiritual life. Further, a person who passes all his life with his teacher and serves him reaches the highest goal of life (i.e.) spiritual beatitude (2.249).

I-Tsing a Chinese traveller talks of titles the teachers could get due to the cultivation of values. Thus, a teacher could get the title of 'Bahushruta' the highest title a teacher can get, only when he is well-known for his virtuous conduct.

The Indian scriptures also mention the reciprocal obligation of a student towards his teacher. This is described below:

- Apastamba *Dharmasutra* (1.1.2.2) declares that a student should always do what is serviceable to his teacher. It also states that (1.4.25) in case a teacher unknowingly breaches a rule; a student may point out to teacher about it privately or should either perform the neglected duty himself.
- Charaka Samhita (8.4) a treatise on medicine states that a pupil should always serve his teacher with steady devotion being grateful to all that the teacher has done for him.
- Finally, Apastamba *Dharmasutra* points out to the ill effects of pride to teachers in the following words (1.4.13.4), "A teacher elated with successes becomes proud, a proud man transgresses the law and through the transgression of law he is ruined."

Establishment of Moral Behaviour in Administrators

The teacher of ancient times, who was the leader of educational institutions, was a person of very high character. He had devoted his life to simplicity and pursuit of knowledge. Material gains were not his pursuit. Thus to establish a teacher constantly in righteousness, the scriptures appealed to his urge for pursuit of the highest truth. Thus Manusmriti in this context states (2.160-161):

- The teacher, whose speech and thoughts are pure and ever perfectly guarded, gains the whole reward, which is conferred by Vedanta.
- Let the teacher, even though in pain, not speak words which cut others; let him not injure others in thought or deed; let him not utter speeches which make others afraid of him; since these will prevent him from gaining the realisation of the highest truth.

Therefore, value-based administration according to the Indian heritage begins with teachers of character who manage by example. Teachers should maintain close relations with students to guide them on the correct path. Thus leaders of education institutions take charge of the proper administration of these institutions.

Organization Culture Promoting Ethical Behaviour

Organization culture is defined as the commonly used and relatively stable beliefs, attitudes and values that exist within an organization (Williams *et al.*, 1989). Establishing a value based organization culture in an educational institution is based on:

- Defining the core values to be inculcated in students.
- Selection of students.
- Promoting ethical behaviour.

Defining the Core Values to be Inculcated in Students

Literature on educational institutions in ancient India point out the values the students of these institutions should possess. These are indicated in the following statements:

- The Baudhayana *Dharmashastra* states (1.2.3.20)—"A student shall be truthful, modest and devoid of pride."
- The Gauthama *Dharmashastra* declares (2.17)—"The student shall avoid bad habits like stealing and injuring others."
- The Manusmriti points out (2.177-180)—"A student should avoid ostentation, anger, covetousness, idle disputing, back biting and lying."
- The Apastamba Dhamrasutra put forth that (1.1.3.13)—"The student showed be forgiving, must have sense control, must be untiring in fulfilling his duties, be modest, energetic, free from anger and envy and avoid sloth."
- The Mahavagga commands a student that he should abstain always from: *(a)* injury to others, *(b)* stealing, *(c)* Impure practices and *(d)* Telling lies. (i. 12, 3-4).

Selection of Students

Scriptures dealing with education in ancient India lay down strict criteria for admission of student members into an educational institution. Thus, the Yagnavalkya Smriti (1.28) gives the following qualities of students who are worthy of receiving education: "Gratitude purity, intelligence, humility, service orientation, good health and trust worthiness." Manusmriti (2. 115) declares that education has to be delivered only to a person who is pure, of subdued senses, chaste and attentive. Similarly Yaska's Nirukta (an ancient Indian law book) (ii, 3,4) quoted in Mookerji (1989) states that "learning should not be given to a person who is jealous, who is wanting in simplicity and straight forwardness, or one who is devoid of self control."

Susrutha Samhita (Chapter ii) prescribes the selection criteria for a student into the science of medicine or Ayurveda as follows: "Good manners and morals, courage, humility, intelligence, patience, purity of body, mind and speech and forbearance."

Ywan Chwang describes the difficulty of admission into the Great Nalanda University—"Of those students who wished to enter the university the majority are rejected and only two or three out of ten succeeded in getting admission (Watters, 1973). In the Vikramshila University there were great scholars who minutely tested the skills, ability and moral aptitude of students before admitting them into the university. These scholars were called *Dwarapalas* (i.e.) those who guarded the entrance of the university to select appropriate candidates (Mookerji, 1989)."

Finally, one can know from the Chandogya Upanishad (4.4.1 to 5), regarding the way Satyakama Jabala who was uncertain of his parentage went to sage Gauthama for joining his education institution and was admitted purely on the count that the spoke truth.Thus admission into ancient Indian educational institutions was based on the moral character of the candidates.

Promoting Ethical Behaviour

In the ancient Indian institutions of education, the students were advised to behave ethically as this would spiritually elevate them. Thus the Apastambasutra declares that "The student whose acts are in consonance with moral rules attains spiritual perfection" (I.25.9 and 11). This advice to the student ensured that they always adhered to ethics. Similarly teachers were promoted to higher administrative posts based on their character. Thus the Chancellor of Nalanda University, Shilabhadra by name was promoted to the post because of his eminent virtue and advanced age and maturity (Ywan Chwang quoted in Mookerji, 1989).

In ancient Indian universities the teachers were reknowned and honoured by all. I-Tsing the Chinese traveller to India (quoted in Mookerji, 1985) states that the teachers of Nalanda were renowned as much for their characters as for their learning, in both of which they aspired after the highest ideal. Similarly the Jataka Tales (Vol. 3, p.158) declare that teachers and professors of the Takshashila University were world renowned, being authorities, specialists and experts in the subjects they professed. Based on their character teachers and professors could get titles like "Bahushruta" or "Jagad Guru". Teachers with these titles were held in universal esteem (Venkateshwara, 1980). The Manusmriti divides teachers into three categories—Guru, Acharya and Upadhyaya-based on their knowledge and moral excellence (2.140-143). Each of these were more honoured than the others, on the basis of their status and righteousness (2.145).

Similarly, in ancient Indian universities any immoral behaviour by the teachers or the students was punishable (Manusmriti 8.300 and Narada Smriti 5.16). The punishments were meted out in the form of fines (Yagnavalkya Smriti 2.18) and in extreme cases even through the expulsion from the educational institution (Mahavagga 1.57). Thus universities in ancient India had an ideal culture. The students were rigorously selected on the basis of their character and imparted education, which would promote value-based behaviour. Similarly, teachers were promoted on the basis of their moral behaviour. Thus, the two watch words for culture building in education institutions in ancient India were *character* and *competence.*

Inculcating Socially Responsible Behaviour

Apart from inculcating character, it is also important to encourage social responsibility among the students and teachers. Scriptures of India show that the students were educated in their social responsibilities, so that they may perform them in the future, when they take up leadership positions in the society. The basic lesson taught to them was *loka samastha sukhino bhavanthu*—meaning 'let the whole world be happy'. The students were encouraged to work for social welfare keeping this principle in mind. The Taitiriya Upanishad advises the student who is on the threshold of making a career in the society as follows: *Satyam vada. Dharmam chara. Mathru devo bhava. Pithru devo bhava. Acharya devo bhava. Athithi devo bhava.* The meaning of this advice is "speak the truth. Perform always the righteous action. Worship your father, mother, preceptor and guest as god." The students and teachers in ancient India were also urged to perform only those acts which satisfy their conscience (Apastamba *Dharmasutra* II.29.11), thus leading to value based decision-making.

Lessons for Value Based Administration

The present-day educational institutions have several lessons to learn from the Indian heritage. These include:

- To promote ethical behaviour, the institution must have a basic goal or philosophy of promoting social and national welfare. Unfortunately we find that educational institutions today have become centers of business and therefore have lost their original focus. This leads to deterioration in ethical behaviour, which must be urgently rectified.
- Teachers and administrators who are the leaders of educational institutions are the must first set an example to others by their conduct. This is clearly evident from educational institutions of ancient India. However, this is missing in today's educational system. Teachers have lost their authority as models of character. This needs to be changed to improve the system.
- It is necessary to modify admission procedures to clearly emphasise on character of students. But current day educational institutions focus more on competence of the students at the time of admissions. The entrance examinations to several prestigious institutions emphasise mastery of subject knowledge. In this process, an even more important facet namely character of the students gets ignored. The level of unrest and indiscipline in the campuses bear testimony to this.
- According to the Indian heritage, the most important criteria for promotions was the character of the teachers. In several educational institutions today, promotions of teachers and administrators are based on experience and patronage. The Indian education system can reach lofty heights, when it pays attention to this important facet of rewarding teachers and administrators based on their character.
- Teachers must treat their students lovingly as their own children. They must work for the betterment of students. This close bondage was reflected in the ancient Gurukulas.

However, today this relationship has been desecrated into a commercial relationship, with no scope for love, reverence or concern. Teachers must change their attitudes towards students to create this sacred bond.

- Students were inculcated into socially responsible behaviour in ancient India. They were taught that *Service to Society is Service to God*. However, it is unfortunate to note that no emphasis is placed on social responsibility today. This leads to highly individualistic behaviour with no concern for the society.
- The undercurrent of education as per the Indian heritage was spiritual transformation. Today the emphasis has shifted to secular education with spirituality playing no role in education. This needs to be rectified to inculcate value based administration in educational institutions.

Conclusion

In this chapter the value-based administration of educational institutions according to Indian ethos and heritage was analysed. The lessons to be learnt for today's institutions were also highlighted. It is necessary to take adequate action in this regard, so that the education system of India will regain its original glory.

Dedication

The authors humbly dedicate the paper to Bhagawan Sri Sathya Sai Baba, the Revered Chancellor of Sri Sathya Sai Institute of Higher Learning, Prasanthinilayam, Andhra Pradesh.

REFERENCES

Dubey, Surendra Nath: 2001, *Education Scenario in India-2001*, New Delhi, Authors press.

Gupta, C.B: 1992, *Contemporary Management*, New Delhi, Ashish Publishing Company.

Jalote Pankaj: 2005, 'Education in India: Past, Present and the Future. Ideas, Policies and Initiatives', *Economic Times*, April 18, 2005.

Mookerji, Radha Kumud: 1985, *Local Government in Ancient India*, New Delhi, Daya Publishing House.

Mookerji, Radha Kumud: 1989, *Ancient Indian Education—Brahmnical and Buddhist*, New Delhi, Motilal Banarsidass.

Peters, Tom and Robert, A Watermann: 1982, In *Search of Excellence*, New York, Warner Books.

Sarmah, J: 1978, *The Philosophy of Education in the Upanishads*, New Delhi, Oriental Publishers.

Sharma, Ram Nath and Rajendra K. Sharma: 2002, *Problems of Education in India*, New Delhi, Atlantic Publishers.

Sivakumar, N. and U.S. Rao: 1996, *Guidelines for Value Based Management In Kautilya's Arthashastra, Journal of Business Ethics*, Vol. 15, pp. 415 to 423.

Ventakeshwara, S.V: 1980, *Indian Culture through the Ages: Education and Propagation of Culture*, New Delhi, Cosmo Publications.

University Grants Commission: 2005, 'UGC's Vision and Strategy for Xth Plan', www.ugc.ac.in

Watters: 1973, *On Yuan Chwang's Travels in India*, New Delhi, Munshiram Manoharlal.

Williams Allan, Paul Dobson And Mike Walters: 1989, Changing Culture, London, Institute of Personnel Management.

Index